Arapaho Women's Quillwork

Arapaho Women's Quillwork

Motion, Life, and Creativity

Jeffrey D. Anderson

University of Oklahoma Press | Norman

Library of Congress Cataloging-in-Publication Data

Anderson, Jeffrey D., 1958–
Arapaho women's quillwork : motion, life, and creativity / Jeffrey D. Anderson.
p. cm.
Includes bibliographical references and index.
ISBN 978-0-8061-5583-8 (paper) 1. Arapaho women—Social life and customs. 2. Arapaho women—Religion. 3. Arapaho art. 4. Quillwork—Great Plains. 5. Indian beadwork—Great Plains. I. Title.
E99.A7A48 2013
978.004'97354—dc23
2012017571

The paper in this book meets the guidelines for permanence and durability of the Committee on Production Guidelines for Book Longevity of the Council on Library Resources, Inc. ∞

Interior layout and composition: Alcorn Publication Design

Contents

Illustrations

Plates

Figures

Diagrams

Acknowledgments

I am grateful to the Social Sciences Division of Colby College for grant funds to support the research phase of this project. My thanks also extend to Hobart and William Smith Colleges for aid to defray some publication costs. Also, I recognize the wonderful assistance provided by staffs at the American Museum of Natural History, National Museum of the American Indian, National Museum of Natural History, Field Museum of Natural History, Carnegie Museum of Natural History, and Denver Art Museum. As for all my research and publications over the past twenty-two years, I am truly fortunate to have the support of the Spoonhunter family and the Northern Arapaho Nation. Some other people who helped out with this project and deserve thanks are Marsha Bol, Dee Cuch, Ray DeMallie, Candace Greene, Vanessa Hernandez, Agnes Logan, Melissa Rinehart, Marge St. Clair, Kristen Welsh, and Ken Williams.

Abbreviations

AMNH	American Museum of Natural History, New York
BMNHC	Burke Museum of Natural History and Culture, University of Washington, Seattle
CMNH	Carnegie Museum of Natural History, Pittsburgh, Pennsylvania
DAM	Denver Art Museum, Denver, Colorado
FMNH	Field Museum of Natural History, Chicago, Illinois
NAA	National Anthropological Archives, Smithsonian Institution, Washington, D.C.
NMAI	National Museum of the American Indian, Smithsonian Institution, Washington, D.C.
NMNH	National Museum of Natural History, Smithsonian Institution, Washington, D.C.
PIM	Plains Indian Museum, Buffalo Bill Historical Center, Cody, Wyoming
PMAE	Peabody Museum of Archaeology and Ethnology, Harvard University, Cambridge, Massachusetts
RMM	Riverside Metropolitan Museum, Riverside, California
SDMM	San Diego Museum of Man, San Diego, California
UNSM	University of Nebraska State Museum, Lincoln

Arapaho Women's Quillwork

Introduction

While conducting fieldwork for the Field Museum in 1901–1906, Cleaver Warden, a boarding school–educated Southern Arapaho, had an unusual experience while observing the Northern Arapaho quillwork artist Firewood embroider a tipi ornament: "If I am not mistake[n] she was making a day tipi which has more yellow quills. Whether by constantly eyeing the design or disc and glancing at her suddenly caused the strange vision I could not say, but even viewing other objects seemed to picture out alike;—that is there were rays of those colored discs on everything in the tipi, for the sun was shining brightly then. Since then I have had trouble with indigestion" (Warden-Dorsey 1903–1906: Box 2, Folder 46: 11). Warden saw and documented this and many other kinds of motion in Arapaho women's quillwork, but these have not been seen in full, let alone understood well by academic perspectives for over a century.

One immediate reaction of first-time viewers to various circular quillwork designs is that they are similar to the wheels used for inducing hypnosis and have a somewhat dizzying effect in that way, but a softness, pathos, quietness, and deepened sense of color can be seen as well. I experienced a different aftereffect during my research for this book. After studying hundreds of items of quillwork at the American Museum of Natural History, I walked out of the collections rolling my suitcase behind me to the subway for the commute to the airport and my flight home to Maine. I felt very alone and missed a lot of people, especially my daughter, whom I had taken to the airport the day before so that she could return to her life in far-off Australia. I was emotionally exhausted and had just been viewing quilled disks with a magnifying glass to identify the minute details of the stitching for quill application. The subtle luster and diffuse glow of the white, red, black, and yellow geometric designs had overwhelmed me with quietude during the last hour of the day. Beneath speckles of dirt that had accumulated over time, the radiance of the original material showed through, including the soft natural ivory pallor of the undyed quills, the unique deep tones of Arapaho red and yellow, and the contrast provided by the matte black of the fibers used as dividers. Color mixed with the biaxial symmetry of form and the visual movement generated by the disks and lines. My feelings of beauty and sadness intermingled with the realization that all of the kinds of movement once associated with quillwork had come to an end. The artifacts had been returned to the still darkness of the storage spaces where most have resided for over a century. To speak to some critiques emerging in some readers' minds, this was not a romanticized feeling of remorse for lost Arapaho culture, for Arapaho people and

I know that they have kept other ways and found new ways to keep life moving "in a good way" and are thus by no means at the end of the trail, as many imagine they are.

These and other realizations turned my thoughts to the relationship between quillwork and seeing movement in so many forms. For example, I recalled a story called "Big Owl, Owner-of-Bag" (Dorsey and Kroeber 1903: 239–46), to which Warden often refers, in which an evil being's pursuit of the human family is slowed down by a series of quilled items the mother leaves behind on the path. Big Owl's eyes become fixed on each item, forcing him to count all of the rows of quillwork on each before moving on. While the designs are beautiful to humans and generate life direction, they thus have the opposite effect on life-threatening beings and forces that cannot seem to see beyond the details to the grasp the whole. Like the dizzying effect on humans of encountering the tornados of Whirlwind Woman (Neyóoóxetusei), who originated the spiraling motion on disks, quillwork can alter one's normal perception of the world for positive or negative life purposes.

I have to say that this project has made me dizzy many times. This is largely the effect of my efforts to understand commentary, reviews, or prevailing discourse from academic voices, both in anthropology and in Native studies, about issues pertaining to indigenous material culture and art. Those who spoke from familiarity with Arapaho cultural and historical context made sense to me, but sweeping exclusionary, precautionary, binary, and ruthless critical viewpoints along the way only seemed to be voiced from some place at a great distance from the evidence. At times, whirling buzzwords seemed to be a morass on the path to seeing quillwork rather than tools for enhancing ways of seeing more clearly, which, ironically, is their intended function for human observers.

My thoughts turned to the fact that, despite the wealth of evidence I had examined, Arapaho quillwork has not been the subject of an enduring research history in anthropology, has never entered modern appropriations of indigenous art forms as so-called primitive art in any significant way, and has not been widely represented as a significant tradition in Plains or Native American art history, let alone world art history. Most of the recognized published surveys of Native American art either ignore it completely or provide just a brief, encyclopedic entry. Hanging out at the few museum displays of quillwork during my research, I noticed that quillwork does not draw viewers' gazes today as much as the more stereotypical forms of Plains Indian material culture.

Arapaho quillwork also does not connect to contemporary pan-Indian forms and ways of seeing associated with them. Objects adorned with quillwork offer a visually understated tone much like the plaintive, low timbre of old Arapaho songs, which were once quite popular among many tribes but are now overshadowed and being replaced by the sharper, faster modern-style powwow songs. Quillwork is thus a cultural layer overlain by the sequins, beads, abundant feathers, and sharp chemically based hues of the flashier styles of modern pan-Indian creativity. There is a slowness to quillwork that is perhaps being lost with the acceleration of culture in so many ways described by Arapaho elders to me many times (see Anderson 2011). One can also see in quillwork's motion a modality still alive among Arapaho people, saturating moments of shared pathos, pity, and beauty mixed together. Because these quillwork objects were originally studied or collected over a century ago, very few eyes have appreciated the vitality, meaning, and motion in these creative forms.

There are many shapes of movement and types of meaning in Arapaho quillwork; this book tries to bring them back into our fields of vision.

If I may raise a caveat at the outset, my aesthetic appreciation of quillwork is not simply the immediate reaction to which critical perspectives often reduce the researcher's gaze but, rather, is informed by a career of research on Arapaho culture and engaged anthropological work in the Northern Arapaho community. Alfred Kroeber's work on the Arapahos' artistic symbolism (1983) first sparked my interest in Arapaho culture over twenty-five years ago, at about my life's midpoint and a time, incidentally, when I had no direction. During my field research and work in several jobs and capacities in the Northern Arapaho community for over five years (1988–94) and many summer visits since that time, art has been ever present, including collaborative efforts to bring knowledge of old art forms into current cultural education curricula, replicating and improvising with old forms for contemporary creativity, and local, intensive study of all publications, major collections, and archives pertaining to Arapaho art. In our efforts, the material collected by early ethnographers was far more useful and relevant than current generalizing critical discourse in anthropology or Native American studies. The concerted research phase of this project has been ongoing for over six years, including examination of hundreds of objects in the anthropological collections mainly compiled by George Dorsey, Cleaver Warden, and Alfred L. Kroeber; hundreds more added to collections from private sources that had not been studied before; intensive reading of a vast amount of unpublished archival materials; and applying and revising theoretical understandings I have put forth in many previously published works (Anderson 2001a).

The trajectory of the chapters is sequenced to permit readers to see and understand motion and meaning in multiple contexts and on a number of levels of quillwork: (1) chapters 1, 2, and 3 survey the multiple types of meaning interconnected and mobilized in quillwork forms, colors, numbers, and configurations; (2) in chapter 4, quillwork is contextualized in Arapaho mythical space-time, values, meanings, and connections; (3) as a continuation of my earlier studies, chapter 5 examines the role of quillwork in generating movement in the life trajectory in the lives of both Arapaho women and their relatives; (4) investigated in the same chapter is the entire creative process of making quillwork, from the collection of raw materials to ceremonial production to symbolic exchange; and (5) in chapter 6, the changing meanings and values of quillwork are traced from their original contexts to those that evolved through the history of cultural contact involving researching, commoditizing, and preserving quillwork for various aims.

Quillwork art was neither just decorative nor merely complementary to men's art forms and ceremonies. From an indeterminate time in the past until the early twentieth century, Arapaho women maintained a ceremonial order for porcupine quillwork artistry that was at the very heart of religious practices, an ultimate concern for life, a sense of beauty, and identity as human beings. In short, it was more than "art," as art is framed by Western traditions, and cannot be reduced to that label alone. Before relocation on reservations in the 1870s, Arapaho people moved on the vast and diverse landscape of the west-central plains of North America. Their culture was not pristine and untouched, for many influences of Euro-American contact changed Arapaho life in profound ways, including the introduction of the horse, more extensive trade, and contact with other peoples pushed out onto the plains.

By the early nineteenth century, they traveled on lands that extended over what are now mapped as the eastern parts of Colorado and Wyoming and western sections of Kansas, Nebraska, and South Dakota. Valuable objects embroidered with quillwork traveled with them and were used in everyday life. As camps were set up, women raised the unique tall, white Arapaho lodges in the three-pole style and then attached the various quilled tipi ornaments. Inside lodges, quillwork embroidery with very similar colors and designs adorned pillows, bed covers, and various storage bags. Cradles, moccasins, and robes carried or worn by relatives of the makers also moved about the camp bearing the similar red, yellow, black, and white porcupine quillwork designs that were unique to Arapaho peoples.

Arapaho women's quillwork art and its study are unique in many ways. First of all, researchers have been unable to establish exactly when or where Arapaho women began doing quillwork, when or where it became a sacred tradition, or how it changed in history. Connecting the record of Plains prehistory to Arapaho people has not been possible through archaeological or ethnohistorical research. Despite constructed and now-accepted views of Arapaho origins in the Great Lakes region, there is no archaeological or documentary evidence that permits an exact determination of how and when the bands that came to be known as Arapaho entered the plains region. This gap has generally predisposed the accepted historical narrative to presume that all Plains peoples are recent arrivals and all their traditions are relatively new. In this gap, there is admittedly a lot we do not and cannot know about the history of quillwork. Offering a chronological or comparative history is also difficult. Accession records for quilled artifacts in museum collections generally indicate only dates of acquisition, which do not necessarily reflect dates of production, because many items were kept, perhaps for long periods of time, as family or personal heirlooms. In addition, there are some curious unique sides of Arapaho quillwork history. In chapter 6, I advance the argument, using indirect evidence, that Arapahos were in the plains–Rocky Mountain region prior to the introduction of the horse and that only in the Arapaho context among Plains peoples is quillwork likely as old as other core traditions, such as the Sun Dance. In other words, the notion that Arapahos adopted the ritual form of quillwork art from other groups in the historical period beginning with Euro-American contact in the mid-1700s is highly unlikely.

While quillwork was an art form throughout indigenous cultures of the northern half of the continent, it was a sacred practice only in the Plains culture area and only among Arapaho, Gros Ventre, Blackfoot, and Cheyenne peoples. With the exception of the Gros Ventres, with whom Arapahos share a common culture and similar language, among no other Plains group was quillwork so closely tied to core rituals and mythological events (as discussed in chapter 4). As Claude Lévi-Strauss recognized in his study of Arapaho mythology, "While Arapaho quill-work ranks among the best in North America, their art was imbued with mysticism up to a point which cannot be matched elsewhere. Quill-work was impregnated with ritual and women especially trained at it sought supernatural help through prayers and fasting before undertaking a task" (1973: 18). As the discussion of mythical foundations in chapter 4 establishes, quillwork was once associated with the highest Arapaho ideals of perfectibility, beauty, purity, and piety. Quillwork was instrumental or at least present in the origins of culture, human beings, and the earth itself. Though not listed among the system of sacred lodges in the *beyoowu'u* (all the lodges), quillwork was closely tied to the Sun Dance, as well as to men's age-grade lodges and the women's Buffalo Lodge. Paraphernalia for all the lodges bore quillwork designs. That tradition has been largely overlooked in anthropological studies but is taken up in chapters 3, 4, 5, and 6. Most interesting about Arapaho quillwork is that it was an entirely women's endeavor and under the exclusive ceremonial authority of senior women. The Seven Old Women quillwork bundle owners held the ultimate human authority over quillwork, were included among the most respected elders, and thus were closely linked to the Seven Old Men bundle owners responsible for directing all the ceremonial lodges. The quillwork guild passed on the exact designs and proper techniques in each new generation to young women who showed the right level of maturity as defined in the Arapaho way. When a bundle owner retired, the remaining members selected and initiated into the guild the most accomplished quillwork artist from the next generation. In a ceremony open only to senior women, the initiate received the bundle and thus took the seat to the left of the retiree. Quillwork was the highest form of strictly women's ritual agency for generating life. As I have discussed elsewhere (Anderson 2001a: 173–84), women were responsible for arranging many of the life transition rituals that took place in the home or tipi, such as the various children's ceremonies held to mark growth or achievement. Navel cord bags, first tooth, naming, first walk, and first hunt feasts to honor children were organized by mothers, aunts, and grandmothers. Quillwork itself was indispensable for supplying an infant's first home in the cradle, making objects for marital exchanges between spouses' families, and, through robe making, ensuring men's successful returns from war party expeditions. In a tradition that continues today, women were also responsible for most of the paraphernalia, gifts, and food that appear in ceremonies with men as the public actors.

Within each type of ceremonial quillwork, Arapaho women artists created a fixed number of styles and patterns. Each type of quillwork cradle, robe, tipi ornament, and leanback cover project had its own name and repeated a similar pattern of colors and shapes in all two-dimensional forms and attached ornaments. A survey for each type of quillwork of the known styles and their unique components and meanings is provided in chapters 1 and 2. Some shapes, designs, and ornaments, as well as their meanings, extended across different types and styles, as well. Each project type also had its own rank based on its comparative antiquity, value, complexity, and time commitment. These ranked projects also defined the sequence a woman followed in her quillwork apprenticeship and career. The most complex projects requiring the longest vows were completed by the oldest women.

Although once very sacred, quillwork is now regarded in the uniquely conservative Arapaho way as one among other irrecoverable traditions. While other Native communities readily revive lost traditions, that is not the Arapaho way, especially among Northern Arapahos. Winfield Coleman notes that in the 1970s both Northern and Southern Cheyenne women, for example, were reviving their comparable sewing society (Coleman 1980). Along with the Arapaho men's age-grade lodge ceremonies, the women's Buffalo Lodge, and several other ceremonies, continuity of knowledge about quillwork across generations was broken by the first decades of reservation life (1870s–1920s). For both the Northern Arapaho nation of Wyoming and the Southern Arapaho nation of Oklahoma, the loss of quillwork art and the web of gifts artists wove into social relations is one among many tragic results of the near destruction of the buffalo, forced relocation on reservations, the great deprivation those engendered, and the introduction of formal education through mission boarding schools. By the 1870s, Southern Arapahos had been forced onto the Cheyenne-Arapaho Reservation in Indian Territory and the Northern Arapahos onto the Shoshone Reservation (later called Wind River) in what is now Wyoming. By the early 1900s, materials and knowledge had grown too scarce on both reservations to keep ceremonial quillwork moving from one generation of women to another. The forces and factors involved in this loss are examined in chapter 5. Today quillwork is commonly produced in a number of Plains Indian communities, but in Arapaho ways it must be left to the past, for the line of succession for passing on the ceremonies and knowledge has been irreparably cut.

For defining boundaries between appropriate and inappropriate practices, elders have long served as the ultimate authority, and today their ceremonial leadership remains paramount (see Fowler 1982). During the period of cultural revitalization, or "neotraditionalism," at Wind River that gained momentum in 1970s and continues to the present, extinct traditions have been a source of curiosity, debate, and occasional controversy. Compared to other tribes, Northern Arapahos have long been most conservative on questions of revitalizing lost sacred practices or inventing new ones. Each time even the hint of reviving a lost tradition has been brought before Northern Arapaho ceremonial leaders, the decision has been to leave it in the past. In the Arapaho theory of practice I discuss in detail in *The Four Hills of Life* (2001a), making mistakes in ritual practices, such as trying to revive a dormant tradition, risks bringing injury, illness, or other tragedy upon one's family or even the tribe as a whole.

Researching, teaching, learning, and writing about lost traditions present curious problems and questions. One evening in 1990, early in my time working and doing research in the Northern Arapaho community on the Wind River Reservation of Wyoming, I attended a hands-on arts workshop at the largest high school in the community. Alice Blue Legs, a nationally known Lakota artist, offered a lesson on the art of tacking quills onto tanned hide surfaces or wrapping them on narrow bands of rawhide. I was there to learn from her husband, Amil, about how to make a roach, a common male dance headdress with coarse deer hair or longer porcupine quills sticking up from a woven yarn base along the top of the head. By the middle of the lesson, Amil and I were mutually frustrated with my lack of progress. On the other end of the long table, about eight women had come to learn how to do quillwork. No native-born Arapaho women were among them: all were women from other tribes married to Arapaho men or holding professional jobs at Wind River. The conversation returned repeatedly to the reasons for Arapaho women's conspicuous absence, mainly with comments about how Arapahos are just superstitious and that nothing bad can happen these days by doing quillwork.

In the twenty years since then, I have been part of many conversations with Arapaho people about quillwork in particular. Opinions range from a more progressive view that it could be done, since none of the old medicines or powers associated with it are still alive, to the most conservative view that it should not only never be practiced in any form but that it is dangerous for Arapahos to even consider owning, wearing, or touching quillwork, whether made locally or in another tribe.[1]

Most common in local knowledge is the original proscription that without proper preparation and guidance for doing quillwork one runs the risk that quills will shoot into one's eyes or other vulnerable parts of the body. Almost every elder with whom I spoke confirmed that younger Arapahos need to know about lost traditions, but questions of validity, authenticity, and proper learning venues for such knowledge arise in every discussion. Many people remember grandmothers or great-grandmothers who were quillwork artists or even keepers of the associated sacred bundles, though no one I encountered could or would say anything more than that a particular ancestor was a part of that "clan," as many folks today refer to quillwork and other old traditional societies or dances. While no one would risk doing quillwork with public knowledge, I was surprised by how many beadwork artists showed me how it is done and seemed to do it very well. On the other extreme, at a local school where I have helped out with curriculum development and planning over the past twenty years, two coffee cans full of porcupine quills have sat untouched for many years in the storage room. Language teachers mentioned to me several times that most people stayed away from them and that no one seemed to know where they came from, how to dispose of them, or why from time to time they appeared in the classrooms outside of storage. Yet quillwork bracelets made by Lakota artists were on sale as of 2008 in the gift shop of the 789 Casino run by the Northern Arapaho tribe. In our arts and crafts development initiative at the North American Indian Heritage Center (1989–94) at St. Stephens, Wyoming, we commissioned Lakota quillwork artists related to a local family to make bracelets for sale, as well as straps and loops in the traditional Arapaho style for adorning objects we made and sold. According to the elders we consulted, this was an acceptable practice. They also agreed for the most part that teaching about lost traditions was not only acceptable but also very necessary, especially among adults who are entering contemporary religious leadership roles. The big controversies I heard at the time surrounded existing publications about extant ceremonies. The question of what to do with detailed descriptions of ceremonies from which outsiders and nonparticipants are restricted raised many questions well beyond the scope of the present work.

The designs themselves are also not restricted. In the early 1980s, before I came to Wind River, a curriculum developer and Helen Cedartree, a highly respected elder and one of the strongest voices about what is appropriate in Arapaho practice, working at one of the schools made several cradles using beadwork in place of quills to replicate the old style but with some adaptations.[2] During my time (1990–94) as director of educational services at the Heritage Center we also transposed many of the old quillwork designs into other media in paint or beadwork for sale and incorporated them in curricular materials and instruction for children and youth groups as part of our efforts to revitalize traditional art forms. As what we saw as a complement to language renewal efforts, also one of our objectives, we believed that art and history should be part of K–12 and college-level cultural instruction, as well. Underlying this was the aim to clarify the difference between Arapaho and pan-Indian art forms, introduced by a larger process that has been displacing Arapaho styles in many other media and genres of cultural expression. One of the main concerns of elders and others is the struggle to maintain Arapaho creative and expressive forms against the invasion of popular pan-Indian culture. In fact, I often heard comments that "Indian culture" is even more of a threat now to Arapaho culture than is white culture. In almost all art programs in local schools, pan-Indian arts and crafts forms prevailed in the 1980s–90s; we also promoted these but believed that they should be balanced by education in traditional Arapaho forms. Generating interest in and presenting past culture to young people in the community is an ongoing challenge, though many Arapaho people take a strong interest, and that interest has grown over the past twenty years, especially among young adults taking on educational roles in the community.

Through our efforts at the Heritage Center, some old Arapaho designs, including quillwork forms, drawn both from published sources (such as Kroeber's classic *The Arapaho*, first published in three parts, in 1902, 1904, and 1907) and from local memory or family traditions, reappeared in many public spaces in the community, ranging from T-shirts and posters for various social events, powwow outfits, and artwork and crafts for sale, to permanent art forms on public buildings. We also sponsored various arts and crafts workshops for adults in the evenings. Some of the old quillwork designs also appear in the stained glass windows and murals of the renovated St. Stephen's Catholic Church on the reservation.

Another of our objectives at the Heritage Center was to gather and study evidence about Arapaho art, history, and other topics from museums, archives, and libraries around the world. This effort had been formally initiated in the early 1980s through collaboration among the linguist Zdenek Salzmann, the Wyoming Indian School system, and the Arapaho Language and Culture Commission, culminating in a published bibliography, bearing Salzmann's name as author (Salzmann 1988), of all Arapaho published, archival, and museum resources. In the late 1980s to early 1990s the task of surveying and requesting evidence about material from museums and archives was a laborious and time-consuming task, given that many repositories were only beginning documentation required in the era of the Native American Graves Protection and Repatriation Act (NAGPRA) and that online catalogue searches of holdings were still a thing of the future. Yet by 1994, when I had to leave Wind River to support my family and service my growing debts with an academic job, we had a fairly good overview and inventory of the main collections. During the era of repatriation of objects from museum collections, we turned our efforts toward repatriation and preservation of knowledge both on and off the reservation.

At that time we had planned to continue that research by visiting various major museum collections and subsequently developing local publications based on that research. Those initiatives were put on hold in my life for many years because of the sudden tragic loss of the director, who was my research partner and a well-known Northern Arapaho scholar and artist, and, with my return to academia, preoccupation with jumping through the various hoops required for professional advancement and job security. Such projects once on the top of my to-do list every day moved to the bottom, beneath teaching, bureaucratic burdens, and publishing academic works. Moreover, the size of this project was simply not doable within the short time frame allowed for tenure. Throughout all of my academic research, though, I remained attuned to local interests at Wind River and tried to make those connections in my work when and as much as possible. My second book, *One Hundred Years of Old Man Sage* (2003), for example, was compiled, after also being put off for a number of years, with the intent of bridging the gaps among academic, popular, and Arapaho readership. By 2003, I was able to return to the quillwork material and began collecting evidence from online databases and through subsequent visits to museum collections and archives.

Another related distinct dimension of quillwork is that it has never been a major commodity circulating in the larger Native American art or tourism markets. Arapaho women's quillwork art has not been part of extensive exhibits to display "primitive culture" or "Native American art." Only a handful of pieces are on display at museums around the country, usually as part of larger exhibits with broader themes. Quillwork never entered modern artists' or curators' appropriation of so-called primitive art, either. Neither the collections nor images of quillwork have been exploited in any significant way for Euro-American production of monetary or symbolic capital. No personal fortunes have been accumulated from their sale, no anthropologists' careers (including the author's) have been built on them, and no grand ideological constructions of "primitivism," whether romanticized or disparaging, have derived from them.

In the early anthropology of art, quillwork was only one among many examples cited briefly, as in Franz Boas's classic work *Primitive Art* ([1927] 1955) for a larger comparative and formalistic interpretation. As discussed in chapter 6, quillwork moved on market paths and into museum and private collections for only a very brief time and in relatively small numbers. At no point was production significantly revived or expanded for tourist or art markets, though some pieces were made at Warden's behest for the Field Museum collections and some items were refurbished for the tourist trade. This contrasts with quillwork in other tribes, such as the Lakota, Great Lakes, and northeastern peoples, for which marketing flows of quillwork are very strong today. In the local context, quillwork has also not, to my knowledge, been a major concern in repatriation for either the Northern or Southern Arapaho nation.

It has also not been in the foreground of past or present prevailing academic interests in or popular imaginings about Native American art and culture. Rather than being pushed forward to construct "authentic" art or culture by anthropology or Native American projects of identity presentation, quillwork was left sitting in the collections for over a century until we and several other researchers began to examine them again in the 1990s (Anderson 2000; Bol 1996; Greene 1992; Santina 2004). One of the reasons for this neglect is that Arapahos remain peripheral to the construction of Plains and Native American images, identity, and narratives. For example, when I passed through the National Museum of the American Indian several years ago, only two Arapaho things were on display, and they were not labeled as such. Despite much progress over the past two decades, Plains Indian women's art in general also remains understudied. Marsha Bol (1996) and Adrianne Santina (2004) contend that quillwork is among many forms of Plains Indian women's art that has been historically overshadowed by attention to male art forms. Popular and academic reifications of the male "warrior and mystic" stereotype reflect both Euro-American and now pan-Indian imaginings that "celebrate individual achievements and statuses" in history and contemporary culture (Santina 2004: 933).

Another distraction is that Arapaho women did not originally make quillwork for intentions that fit within the prevailing modern, postmodern, or postcolonial frames for defining artistic creativity or human agency. As Santina further argues, Arapaho quillwork and the women artists who made it have also been ignored because "it is likely that the prescriptions regarding the creations of ornaments and their subsequent designs also relegated them to positions of lesser importance in Euro-American art contexts, which valorize originality and creativity as vital elements of individual artistic expression" (2004: 933–34). Arapaho women's quillwork also does not fit into the prevailing oppositional models of creativity—women's creativity in particular. Women were not primarily moved to make quillwork to express their individuality against the shackles of communal conformity, to find a free space for resistance in a restrictive male-dominated structure, to create novelties that break from past artistic traditions, or with the sole intention of extending their individual agency over a wider social space of public personhood and recognition. Such misplaced frames for creativity presume a Euro-American definition of "persons" or subaltern groups that frame artists as individuals or subgroups in opposition to the status quo, instead of considering the ontologies of personhood, social relations, and creativity held by peoples themselves, which A. Irving Hallowell ([1960] 1976: 359) emphasized long ago. Where art is that tightly controlled by religion, the tendency is to reify a hierarchical model entrenched in Western history and social structure that valorizes a human-centered and individualistic ontology in opposition to a hostile natural, social, and supernatural world. Winfield W. Coleman observes about the similar Cheyenne quillwork society that outside views must not jump to oppositional conclusions: "This is the art form at once hermetic, repetitive, and charged with mysterious power: the art of a theocracy. In this sense it resembles Byzantine art; but what a world of difference lies between the egalitarian and the hierarchical societies which spawned them. The art of the Byzantium is based on the human form and is vertical in thrust, composed of harsh shapes and strident colors. It is the art of a culture striving to reconcile itself with a stern, remote Godhead, a culture trying to dissociate itself from the world, from nature" (1980: 62–63). In contrast, he continues, quillwork is the art of people living in "harmony with nature" rather than placing constrictive boundaries and imposing a sense of anxiety on people; quillwork allowed them to experience the tipi as a "microcosm of the universe" with an emotional ambience of "repose, calm, even stasis."

Through quillwork, women did assert a kind of power and control but not in the reduced sense of a Western restricted political ontology. Instead, it exhibits a pattern similar to that of Annette Weiner's groundbreaking study of Trobriand women's production of value, which adopts Hallowell's path for deconstruction, not by "operating merely within the 'politics' of social relations" but rather moving "beyond the social to concepts concerning articulation with cosmic and transcendental phenomena" (Weiner 1976: 12). The same realization has come to inform studies of women's art on the plains, as well. As Barbara Hail states in describing the Plains tipi, "At the center was the woman, the life-giver; around her the family" (2011: 119) and, I would add, beyond that the camp circle and the cosmos writ large. Women's quillwork art connected the domestic sphere to the public, and those in turn to the other-than-human realm. Quillwork, like all Arapaho religious practice, interconnected human and other-than-persons to gain blessings for life's continuation. The vast majority of studies on Plains religious practices, narratives, and artwork pay attention to forms of power only on the front stage, where men's presence appears to overshadow the often more powerful roles women played in less visible spaces—at least to Euro-American eyes—beyond the ceremonial lodge and several days of the performance itself. The misplaced concreteness reified by the domestic-public binary has a long history in anthropological studies of gender distinctions. Equally true today, the vast majority of public expressions of Arapaho sacred culture were women's productions, despite the visible fact that men are generally wearing, holding, giving, or eating them. The food, designs, clothing, and other things apparent in ceremonies were, in early ethnographers' eyes, assumed as "given" or at least not part of the ceremony itself. Such a bourgeois Euro-American male-oriented exclusion is quite evident in many early studies. Even today, in some revisionist approaches to Native American women's art there is the same tendency to segregate it from presumably "genuine" religious contexts associated with men.

Placing quillwork in wider contexts through a better understanding of symbolism and production permits us to gain some contextualized insight into heretofore understudied Arapaho women's roles and experiences in prereservation daily life, the life trajectory, ritual practice, kinship, and traditional authority. Published studies of Arapaho culture, religion, and political leadership have tended to ignore or underplay women's less publicly visible but no less active agency in maintaining continuity of Arapaho identity, life, and empowerment. Last, and of broadest concern, knowledge of Arapaho quillwork will contribute to the anthropological appreciation of art and creativity less restricted by Western-based concepts of person, time, motion, and value. Arapaho women were artists par excellence as their culture defined creativity, namely, as a life-generating ritual process.

The Western, modern assumption that the definition and purpose of creativity should be restricted to novelty or innovation (Liep 2001: 2), improvisation (see Sawyer 1998), expression of individuality, articulation of individual life histories, or breaks from the weight of tradition are culturally biased. Postmodern or postcolonial continued loyalties to this modern view often simply reify a Western and often colonizing definition of the individual, priority for teleological historicity as the primary temporality for gauging novelty, and exclusionary boundaries of what is includable in the definition of creativity or agency. Contemporary anthropological concepts of creativity and agency are themselves framed by what Walter Benjamin ([1936] 1986) recognized as a uniquely modern way of seeing that juxtaposes individual genius, breaks into novelty, extension of self into a larger space, and the aura of progress against mechanical reproduction. The temporal chronotope for framing modern (and postmodern) creativity begins with an individual's break from monotonous time that actualizes a small locus of authenticity, self-realization, and freedom in a larger oppressive space. In time, that creative moment and locus expands and is reproduced to the point of becoming a constraining replicated part of the monotony, awaiting another break into novelty. Likewise, agency is defined as the movement of individuals within constraining structures to express uniqueness as a social person. This historically specific dialectic for framing the space-time of creativity and agency did not exist in Arapaho women's quillwork. Even today, in many Native American contexts, creativity as novelty is ascribed to and aims for connections to other-than-human sources of inspiration, as through dreams, visions, and so forth.

The uniqueness or novelty activated by quillwork was not so much in the process or the product but in the social context and personal experience of the individual artist. Women created quillwork for particular relatives in unique situations of life transition. Women created quillwork not for a generic brother or niece or nephew but for a unique person they knew and cared about very much. In pledging a quillwork project, they were not likely focusing their thoughts on the thrill of making something new, becoming known for their creative genius, or feeling a sense of personal agency for its own sake. A quillwork artist's accomplishments responded to and defined the course of unique events in local, lived history and thus wove connections among particular kin and their personal histories in novel ways. As the symbolism of quillwork objects discussed in chapters 1 and 2 reveals, the meaning and value of women's quillwork was to give shape to a *future* lived time. Arapaho religion is, contrary to the common exclusion, profoundly and pervasively future-oriented but always already in a socially grounded, pragmatic sense of life movement. Both process and product were highly uniform across time, but each project was novel in the conditions it responded to, the relations it created, and the particular future it willed to happen.

Finally, contrary to contemporary anthropological tendencies to deconstruct indigenous identity and culture as simply in and of the transient surface of social action, quillwork was not simply an imagined, constructed, or invented tradition happening in the situational flow of historicity moved by economic, political, or other utilitarian aims; it was a sacred tradition that endured for a considerable length of time and preceded contact with Euro-Americans. There were cultural borrowings, such as those from the Cheyennes, and mixing of forms, but those did not remove quillwork from the domain of sacredness. A guiding concern here is to try to understand what constituted quillwork as sacred creativity in Arapaho rather than external terms, and though I am sure some will argue that this is impossible, simply on general principle, it can indeed be done here with the evidence available.

Quillwork was ritually circumscribed and set apart from other types of creativity in Arapaho culture. Kroeber (1983: 147–50) distinguished two general types of Arapaho art. One included various individualized forms in rawhide painting, beadwork, and other ornamentation. These creations required little or no ritual supervision and allowed expressive freedom in form, style, and application within less constricted parameters. Compositions could express individual imaginings, visions, dreams, or stories, and thus their symbolic meanings were more variable, though incorporating some forms similar to those used in quillwork with similar meanings. That side of Arapaho women's art conforms more to Western notions of creativity as novelty inspired by individual imagination, but it was not the most powerful form of creativity in Arapaho culture, since it was not generally associated with the sacred power to generate life. There is also less foundation for these forms in mythical tradition.

The second, or sacred, type of artistic creativity required meticulous and concerted replication of form, color, proportion, and pattern under the instructive authority of elders with the prerequisites of careful preparation, prior learning, and demonstrated conformity to Arapaho ways of living appropriate to one's life stage. One genre of this type included the body painting and paraphernalia designs required for the *beyoowu'u*, including the men's age-grade lodges, the Sun Dance, and the women's Buffalo Lodge. The designs and procedures for these were under the ultimate authority of what have come to be called the seven Water-Sprinkling Old Men, based on a literal translation of *Ciinecei Beh'iihohoho'*, related to their association with the sweat lodge (Kroeber 1983: 154). Each of the Seven Old Men, as I will call them, owned a bundle containing paints and instruments for all the ceremonies. Quillwork was another sacred art under the authority of Seven Old Women, whose roles paralleled and at times converged with those of the Seven Old Men. Each woman in the group owned a sacred bundle containing the medicines and markers needed for ceremonial instruction of younger women.

Unlike secular art forms, but like all Arapaho ritual practices, women vowed quillwork projects not for themselves but as gifts that would help relatives make the right transitions in life or overcome difficult times along the road of life through all of the four hills of life: childhood, youth, adulthood, and old age. Behind the doors of their lodges, women quillwork artists sat quietly, motionless except for their hands and eyes, for many hours each day, up to weeks at a time, precisely re-creating designs drawn out for them by the Seven Old Women, handed down from the distant past when Arapahos received them from sacred beings.

As applied to all of the many other kinds of vows in Arapaho religious life, women were motivated by the core value of *hoowouunonetiit* (translated as "pity" in English, though carrying other meanings; see Anderson 2001a: 43–63). In Arapaho, this is the most pervasive emotional modality in ritual contexts and involves a human connection to someone else facing a difficult time. It is also part of most prayers and other supplications to sacred beings, who are asked to take pity on human worshipers in turn (see Anderson 2001b, 2003, 2005, 2006). Pity is the source of movement for sacred exchanges. The literal Arapaho meaning of the term connotes making the others' movement in life "easy," as in downhill motion or not weighted down by burdens. Unlike piety or charity in Western moral contexts, Arapaho pity is regarded not as supererogatory but rather as a matter-of-fact sympathy that humans and other-than-human persons experience in social relations. Pity is more pronounced in ritual contexts. Quillwork followed the process of all Arapaho ritual practice, both past and present. A life-challenging condition affecting a relative evokes pity, which sets in motion a ritual process. At the same time, most vows also involved respect between relatives or groups, known in Arapaho as *neeteenebiit* or *bobooteenebiit,* with greater emphasis. Important for understanding how quillwork gifts were exchanged, respect was especially strong between an adult brother and sister, between a son-in-law and mother-in-law, between any younger person and an elder, and most profoundly, between anyone and anything or person with medicine. A kinsperson's vow to sponsor a ceremony is followed by a time of preparation and then the ritual itself. The entire process is guided by ceremonial elders. The ceremony involves an enclosed space, feasts, gift exchanges, prayers, songs, painting, purification, and prescribed physical movements. In the Arapaho way, shared with many Native peoples, for others to experience blessings of long and straight lives, the pledger must make a sacrifice for a specified length of time and evoke the pity of sacred beings, who then may give such blessings in return. Quillwork was such a sacrifice.

As described in chapter 5, after a woman made a vow to complete a quillwork project and prepared what was needed, a ceremony was held, for which the pledger was responsible for supplying gifts and a feast to the old women who owned the seven sacred quillwork bundles, supervised the ceremony, instructed the woman, and drew the outline for the designs to be completed. Then the artist retreated from everyday social life for a prescribed time to complete the project with a meditative, quiet, and still disposition. When finished, the gift was handed over ceremonially to the recipient, who reciprocated with a gift in turn. The true gift was the artwork's power to generate life blessings for the relatives women pitied, loved, and respected. Women embroidered quills on robes for brothers, on cradles for nieces and nephews, and on leanbacks, tipis, and other gifts for newly married relatives.

Quill-embroidered objects were considered among the highest-valued goods in the Arapaho symbolic economy. As objects moved in everyday life, women's achievements were known in a wider public space, as much as the war exploits or other achievements of men. In short, women earned respect through quillwork. As the objects they produced moved through the local economy, their personhood extended over a wider social space, which (as I have outlined elsewhere) was the main emphasis in the second and third stages of life (Anderson 2001a: 185–98). According to current anthropological concepts, this is called "agency" (Gell 1998), the movement of identity through extended relations to others in a larger space and for a longer time than the making of the object and in the social world. Underlying this agency was a unique Arapaho cultural dialectic. Namely, as individuals moved through the stages of life, they should readily make sacrifices—that is, face life-threatening situations to defend the camp, help kin in need, or assist a relative to overcome illness—and as an unintended consequence, by enduring such hardship become a widely recognized and respected person.

Quillwork as gifts moved on pathways of symbolic exchange among kin and between kin groups. As discussed in chapter 4, such exchanges narrowed the distance between kin across boundaries of respect. A woman's reputation moved outward into the camp, band, and tribe as her created gifts connected her with kin and other families outside her camp or band. When quilled things left a maker's hands, they moved with the people who wore, used, and exchanged them. What could be considered repetitive "work" became creative motion; the products of it, while adorning utilitarian objects such as cradles, tipis, or robes, imbued those objects with communal value, as Munn suggests, to negate negative values and produce positive values, in this case, life-generating motion. As such, the "community creates itself as an *agent of its own value creation*" (1986b: 100). To Munn, creativity thus aims to transvaluate dialectical values in society. In the Arapaho case, I believe, the contradiction was that between the isolation of women's productive activity in the lodge or domestic space and the requirement that women, like men, become fully engaged sacred practitioners for the general well-being of all as they moved through the four hills of life. Quillwork engaged women in communal agency to transcend that contradiction and make their own agency, generally sequestered inside the lodge, more publicly visible. The core irony in Arapaho ritual practice, as I have discussed elsewhere, is the mandate by adulthood to sacrifice one's body, work, and life for others' life movement as the ultimate concern but to be recognized collectively for enduring sacrifices nonetheless. Fasting, isolation, sponsoring feasts, providing gifts, offerings, sacrifices of flesh, quillwork, and other ritual actions were ways in which men and women affected the life movement of others by giving something basic of their own bodies and lives.

Quillwork objects publicly expressed Arapaho religious concepts associated with color, space, time, number, and shape more than perhaps any other medium. The movement of women's hands in tacking or wrapping porcupine quills into geometric forms was an iconic expression of the ultimate concern of Arapaho religion to promote life movement of long duration and with straight directionality. As elaborated in chapter 3, the straightness of the quilled lines marked the future path for a life of the same shape, and the circular rings in round disks mirrored the desire for completion of the full cycle of the four stages, or hills, of life, homologous with the four seasons and four periods in mythical history. Quillwork was thus a principal medium accessible to women for agency in generating relations not only to human persons but also to other-than-human beings and forces. It also generated metonymic connections among levels of space and time, thus constructing homology, that is, an intricate interweaving of microcosm with macrocosm, home with universe, body with world, and smaller orders of time with epochal time of long duration. Geometric forms of Sun, Moon, Whirlwind Woman, the Four Old Men, and Morning Star were among the various two-dimensional symbols women created with quills to connect the maker, wearer, and tribe to sacred beings with the powers defined by respective shapes and paths of motion to give life direction to humans, animals, and plants in the world.

There are some unique aspects of the evidence for quillwork and the research that produced it. While similar quillwork societies and ceremonies have been found among other Plains Indian peoples, such as the Blackfeet, Cheyennes, Lakotas, and Gros Ventres, there is significantly more evidence in published works, unpublished archival documents, and museum artifact collections for Arapaho women's quillwork than for any other group. Early Arapaho ethnographers left one of the largest bodies of evidence among Native American artistic traditions, but the bulk of that evidence is scattered, unpublished, and inaccessible to the public. Contemporary critical views mistakenly caricature this knowledge as "salvage anthropology" that reified culture as a closed, unchanging, and essentialized whole. In fact, Kroeber, Dorsey, and Warden never embraced an essentialist view of human creativity and never really completed the project of understanding Arapaho culture as a totality. Also, Boas and Kroeber resisted essentialism, in its original rather than currently overextended sense, by following a formalism derived from a German neo-Kantian tradition with emphases on a holistic understanding of symbolic forms and techniques and meanings in so-called primitive art.

Borrowing from a Kantian tradition of "aesthetic judgment" as formalistic rather than sensory or emotional, Boasian aesthetic anthropology posited a "twofold source of esthetic effect" in form and ideas associated with a form (Boas [1927] 1955: 13). Departing from Kant, though, Boas maintained that those ideas vary among particular cultures and are not universal in the individual human consciousness. In Kroeber's study of Arapaho art, as well as Dorsey's mission for Warden, each form as a shape, color, pattern, three-dimensional object, or total configuration was associated with a cultural "meaning," as a presumably mental construct. Inheriting a classical Greek temporality, Boas's aesthetics aims to redeem for art in all cultures a *telos* or movement toward ideal forms with the weight of tradition behind them "in the mastery of technique" on one pole and the "elevated effect upon the mind" of the viewer on the other (Boas [1927] 1955: 349). To Boas, creativity as innovation eventually settles into traditional forms of technique, which in turn become the "higher" art forms, but of course, this occurs in all cultures, not just so-called civilized ones. Here, Boas betrayed his own mission by subsuming non-Western art within a Western conception of temporalization. The meaningful movement in Arapaho quillwork is not such a telos, as we shall see.

Underlying this problem of the misplaced relationship between meaning and time is the enduring and still-unresolved opposition in anthropology that has taken many forms, such as binaries of subjective and objective, structure and practice, creativity as (re)creative and as innovation, culture as genuine continuity and as constructed in the moving present, art as collective and individual expression, and culture for itself in the American tradition and as functional for extrinsic social ends in the British functionalist tradition. To resolve this seeming contradiction, both poles must be encompassed in analysis. In this case, the inquiry looks from one angle at the sacred and enduring meanings quillwork embodied and from another at the various functions and motives it served in systems of exchange, kinship relations, women's life development, and ritual practices in general. In short, we must examine multiple functions and meanings operating in quillwork. Women did not make quillwork just for the sake of achieving sacred ideal forms: the primary aim for women was the Arapaho value of "life movement" (Anderson 2001a: 30–31), which encompasses many functions and meanings. Quillwork, along with all ritual practices, aims to generate a long, straight life for individual kin and the tribe as a whole.

Although Boasian ethnographers professed a program of understanding culture as an integrated totality, no early ethnographies of Arapaho culture came close to achieving that end. Kroeber and Dorsey (and James Mooney before them) offered many connections but rarely presented the whole. Kroeber's dissertation on Arapaho artistic symbolism, not even thirty pages in length, ironically concludes with the statement, "The great unity is the true study for the student of man" (1901: 335). While astoundingly prolific from a contemporary standpoint, early ethnographers were always on the move. After his dissertation research on Arapaho culture, Kroeber quickly moved on to the study of other cultures, mainly in California. Dorsey likewise embarked on other projects without publishing a sizable manuscript on Arapaho material culture.

Also, rather than the authoritarian, external Euro-American view that is presumed by current critics of the Boasian tradition, a significant portion of the evidence presents the voice and vision of an Arapaho researcher named Cleaver Warden. As a child, Warden attended Carlisle Indian Industrial School in Pennsylvania. After returning from boarding school to Oklahoma in 1885 he worked as an agency interpreter, a store clerk, and a tribal councilman. In Southern Arapaho cultural history, he was one of the founders of the peyote tradition. From 1900 to 1905 he worked off and on for Dorsey at the Field Museum, collecting material culture for museum collections and evidence about ceremonies, art, and mythology for ethnographic works (Dorsey 1903; Dorsey and Kroeber 1903). Indeed, I have made the point elsewhere (1997) that he should be recognized as a coauthor of some published works by Dorsey and Kroeber. Bol's close reading of Warden's manuscripts (Bol 1996) reveals that he was the main source for information about quillwork, as well as the acquirer of many of the examples remaining in museums, including the bulk of those at the Field Museum and Carnegie Museum of Natural History. As Bol recognizes, it is through Warden's collection of quillwork objects and accompanying descriptions, many of which were acquired from quillwork artists, that we know anything at all about Arapaho women's quillwork art (Bol 1996). In short, without Warden, much of the research results might indeed have conformed to modern critical caricatures of salvage anthropology.

Most of the evidence about quillwork was thus the product of a collaborative project, with at least some of the elements now prescribed for contemporary revisionist approaches to field research (see Lassiter 2005 and Clifford and Marcus 1986). Rather than a single authoritarian voice of the Western ethnographer, Warden's voice is as strong in the published works and unpublished manuscripts as that of his employers. His voice is, admittedly, often veiled in published works. Throughout this book, one aim is to let Warden's voice come through with its uniquely Arapaho poetics and visual sensitivity. This is especially my aim in chapters 1 and 2, which survey the types of quillwork Warden recorded.

Looking back on this history of research, we can see that the boundaries between anthropologists and Arapahos have been blurred since the beginning of research on women's quillwork near the turn of the twentieth century. Warden and Kroeber were probably the first males ever to be allowed to observe the quillwork ceremony and learn about the tradition, and they sat together, observed, and combined their views. Taking up a fuller argument in chapter 6, I contend that Arapahos were not, as some binary views presume, hapless victims and passive participants in such research. The existing evidence about quillwork engaged Arapaho agency and was informed by a unique Arapaho reflexivity about their own culture at the time. In short, older consultants were as concerned as anthropologists (if not more so) about the loss of their culture, including quillwork. This is particularly clear in Sister M. Inez Hilger's later ethnography (1952), based on her fieldwork in 1936 and 1940. Ironically, at a time when postmodern trends in anthropology have moved attention away from contextualizing cultural forms in totalities and history of the long duration, Native American communities are trying to revitalize culture through a return to just those frames of reference.

The boundaries of my position in this research are not so clear-cut either. I did not realize how controversial this issue had become until I left Wind River in 1994, presented a few papers at conferences (with unexpected decolonizing reactions by folks concerned with my "identity" more than the work at hand), and began catching up on some of the then-prevailing academic works on reflexivity in sociocultural anthropology (such as Clifford and Marcus 1986 and Marcus and Fisher 1986). To me those works seemed to address issues I had not really experienced concretely in fieldwork and overlooked a thousand issues that I did confront. This book is not simply my "outside" view of quillwork but is inextricably part of local Arapaho efforts that I still identify with, perhaps more strongly even than my commitment as an anthropologist to an imagined community of scholars. Negotiating this nonbinary identity is, of course, problematic in every sentence I write, every activity I undertake in the Arapaho community, and everything I do in the academy. Throughout my research, I did not have to concertedly engage "reflexivity" about my identity in the research "encounter" and context, for it was imposed on me in much more complex, concrete, and, I must say, rewarding ways than those articulated in mainstream anthropology in the 1980s and 1990s. There are local types of reflexivity for which much more is at stake than words on pages or one's position in the world. One reflects not only about being an anthropologist but also on one's family and "place" within the Arapaho tribe, the relationship of one's actions to folks from other tribes in intertribal contexts, the degree to which one's actions are appropriate or traditional, and one's identity within a larger social field. In all, my concerns here are admittedly and unapologetically Arapaho-centric, though I believe that if academic readers vested in larger issues pay close attention to the implicit as well as explicit text, there is something of theoretical value here for them.

Only when I moved away from Wind River and back into academic spaces did I realize the controversies and contradictions stirring in the then and still current dominant discourse about Native American "art" in general and art objects in museum collections. What seemed like something of local, practical value (as I relate below) and appeared as self-evidently valuable research to me at the outset began to give way to a dizzying whirl of questions. When I presented material from this research at conferences, I was met on one side with some very concerned questions about "authority," my rights as a non-Indian to do this research, imagined local controversies that were assumed to exist, and all of the other things that apparently plague researchers in other communities or that must be expressed in the perfunctory pandemic ruthless critique of everything existing in anthropology and some corners of Native American studies discourse these days. From the other, larger side, I was met with silent disinterest tacitly framed by the view, I think, that this subject matter defines me as an "old school" American or "symbolic" anthropologist out of touch with current conceptual interests. I realized, too, that I had ironically participated in the "construction," "invention," and "reinvention" of culture and identity that have engaged the critical inquiry of many anthropologists in the past few decades. Today, indigenous peoples around the world are confronted with the social scientific view that they are "constructing," "inventing," or "imagining" their culture and identities as a function of collective "agency" for political, economic, or other pragmatic ends. When combined with history, such an orientation frames all past culture in the same way, either as constructed by the observer or as constructed by the people themselves. To me, the ruthless critical discourse never moves toward anything positive for indigenous peoples. Along with other activities, I worked in and as part of the process of "agency" for defining and redefining identity for over five years and still do, albeit now in a more removed and intermittent way. Our endeavor at the Heritage Center was as academic and scientific, if with different issues at hand, as any similar pursuit in a university or museum context. All of the principal people had some anthropological training. Anthropology and fieldwork as I experienced it was and always has been a collaborative effort in and of the lived social world rather than the pursuit of the isolated individual consciousness of the Western observer. Our aim, though, was to connect the knowledge gathered locally, from published works and from distant unpublished sources, into resources that would have local applications for education and general reading. We met with resistance from many sides in this effort. Granting agencies, publishers, and academic institutions maintain criteria for review that are irrelevant to local applications and serve interests and concerns that often seem to be based on displaced and misplaced concreteness. One concern was the pervasive requirement for funding or publication that held that resources we produced must be widely disseminated in the non-Indian world as well as in the local community.

While an earlier piece on Cheyenne quillwork by Winfield W. Coleman (1980), which uses some Arapaho material, and more recent articles by Candace Greene

(1992), Marsha Bol (1996, 2001a), Jeffrey D. Anderson (2000), and Adrianne Santina (2004) have examined specific topics based on the Arapaho archival and museum evidence, the current effort moves toward an analysis based on all significant sources and collections available. I have examined all of the field notes, accession records, and unpublished manuscripts available, including the Warden-Dorsey Collection at the Field Museum, archives of the American Museum of Natural History pertaining to Kroeber's research and collections there, field notes of Kroeber and Hilger at the National Anthropological Archives, Warden's notes for objects in the Carnegie Museum of National History collections, and accession records both at the National Museum of Natural History and at the National Museum of the American Indian at the Smithsonian Institution. I examined firsthand all of the major collections of Arapaho quillwork at the American Museum of Natural History, the Field Museum of Natural History, the National Museum of Natural History, and the National Museum of the American Indian. A smaller body of images and archival documents was compiled through correspondence or online research databases from smaller museums, as well, such as the Denver Art Museum, the Carnegie Museum of Natural History, the Plains Indian Museum, and many more.

This book offers the first comprehensive and systematic study organized around concerns with movement and meaning in quillwork, including its mythical foundations; its place in Arapaho prereservation religious practice; a comparison to quillwork traditions on the plains and in North America in general; the ritual creative process of production; all types of meaning as symbolic forms; functions for enhancing utilitarian objects; aesthetic properties of rhythm, form, and motion; participation in the symbolic exchange; its function for constructing social relations; its role in women's and recipients' life development; historical changes that contributed to the extinction of quillwork; its history in Arapaho-Euro-American contact for museum collections, anthropological research, and art markets; and its position in contemporary Arapaho culture and cultural revitalization efforts.

The aim is neither to arrive at what meanings, functions, or values all Arapahos in some pristine cultural past held about quillwork nor to present a simply binary Arapaho versus Euro-American view of the history of quillwork during cultural contact. Meanings differed for the women who pledged to make quillwork, the owners of the sacred bags who supervised them, the recipients who received and used the quillwork items, the camp members who saw quillwork in their everyday world, Arapaho and Euro-American researchers who studied and collected it, purchasers who bought quillwork for sale or personal collections, museums that held and preserved it, Arapahos today who regard it as taboo, study it, or try to bring back knowledge about it, and anthropologists and other researchers today who, with various motives, have multiple views of it and their predecessors who studied it. The claim is not that one can have full access to any of these perspectives or that any one is the genuine or objective vantage point.

One aim here is to encompass many more dimensions of meaning than were originally conveyed explicitly by Kroeber's analysis and the aims Dorsey defined for Warden. Although descriptive depth and breadth are evident in these early works, most readings and uses of these works have tended to focus on one-to-one form-meaning relations. A more thorough survey and systematic analysis of the evidence provided in chapter 3 and throughout the book reveal many other dimensions of meaning than the referential function of form, such as number, color, motion, composition, spatial directionality, and mythical connections, which also function as polysemes, icons, poetic tropes, imagery, indexes, embodied knowledge, and more.

Beyond the meanings in the objects themselves, quillwork is contextualized in this book within the concrete processes of ritual production, religious sacrifice, symbolic exchange, women's formation of social relations, and the path of Arapaho life development. For the women who made them and the relatives who received them, quillwork objects were not just text-like objects displaying or expressing meanings to a public audience: there were also more and perhaps more significant types of meaning than the meanings conveyed referentially or connotatively by individual designs and styles themselves. For example, quillwork functioned as gift exchanges to nurture bonds among relatives, send prayers for a good life to sacred beings, express aesthetic ideals, preserve mythical motifs, inculcate moral values, and shape the life trajectory.

Guiding the effort to achieve some parallax of the meanings and perspectives on quillwork is a concern with motion of various types and on different levels of analysis. Quillwork activated multiple paths and shapes of motion and generated multiple interconnections among them. To overcome essentializing ways of configuring culture, it is not enough simply to exclude all efforts at interpretation or, to recover time, turn solely to Euro-American-framed historical temporality, life history, or the transiency of durée. It is also not enough to consider only products or objects set apart from creative making, social relations, and connectivities of meaning beyond the things themselves. Lest "aesthetic objects be left to float, opaque and hermetic, outside the general course of social life," they must be placed in what Clifford Geertz describes as a "feeling a people has for life." He recognizes that "[t]he talk about art that is not merely technical or a spiritualization of the technical—that is, most of it—is largely directed to placing it within the context of these other expressions of human purpose and the pattern of experience they collectively sustain" (1983: 96). The technical side, of course, should also be included, as outlined below. Following Samuel Alberti (2005: 561), I examine the "mechanics of the movement of objects from their manufacture or growth through collecting and exchange to the museum, along with the accompanying shifts in meaning and status." Thus, beyond the meanings that Geertzian models reveal in the formal sense that are generated by "transactions, attributions, and motivations," it is also necessary to follow quillwork objects, as Arjun Appadurai suggests, in their "concrete, historical circulation" (1986: 5). The book thus follows quillwork objects from their origins in the mythical context of sacred motion, to the meanings connected to sacred beings and forces, to the context of their production as sacred commodities that in turn followed unique pathways of intrasocietal exchange for defining social relationships, to forms that defined Arapaho life movement in the life trajectory, to the conditions that contributed to the loss of their production in Arapaho history, to things acquired, studied, defined, and repositioned by Euro-American researchers and private collectors, to the end of their movement in museum collections presumably to preserve their essential value and meaning against the effects of time.

Quillwork is connected here to multiple levels of movement, shape, and directionality in time and space, including the time of the vow and creation of quillwork (lasting days or weeks in women's everyday lives), seasonal changes in ecological time, symbolic exchange sequences of gifts among kin, women's agency for generating long life for the receivers of quillwork gifts and shaping their own social biographies, life cycle transitions marked and generated by quillwork for both the women who made them and their relatives, the dynamics of age-structured relations activated and changed through quillwork, types of mythically inscribed movement that quillwork symbolically interconnected, the historical movement of quillwork into museum collections in and of the relationship between Arapahos and non-Indian colonizers, and the potentialities and limitations for remobilizing quillwork in current academic, popular, and local understandings.

To start with, all human creativity is the product of controlled movement, whether of hands, vocal apparatus, feet, flow of thought, human tools, or a combination of many kinds of motion. At the basic level, quillwork was a product of ritually controlled repetitive women's movement, primarily coordinating eyes and hands for placing, proportioning, and shaping quills. As Maurice Merleau-Ponty observed, art is a synthesis of bodily motion and vision (1964). Quillwork was thus in this, as well as other ways, a form of embodied knowledge. As Marcel Mauss realized, there is more than culture transmitted by language and its oral traditions. His statements about this other side of tradition apply to many Arapaho traditions: "The use of oral symbols is but one case of the use of symbols: any traditional practice, endowed with a form and transmitted through that form, can in some measure be regarded as symbolic. When one generation hands down to the next the technical knowledge of its manual and bodily actions, as much authority and social tradition is involved as when transmission occurs through language. In this there is truly tradition, and continuity" (2006: 76).

Arapaho quillwork artists exerted considerable collective effort to maintain sacred forms as what Mauss called "techniques of the body," or "habitus," the transmission of which is often mistaken for "imitation" or mechanical replication in restricted Western-biased views of creativity as novelty, improvisation, or innovation: "The other forms of moral and material life are transmitted through direct contact, and this communication necessarily takes place in a context of authority. This applies equally as far as the emotional life is concerned. Moral and religious feelings, as well as technical or aesthetic activities, and so on, are imposed by elders on youth, by leaders on followers, by one individual on another" (2006: 76). Such knowledge transmission requires direct learning in a context of authority imposed by elders on youths or leaders on followers for inculcation of habitus and its modulation among life stages and transitions between them. This type of learning, while often accompanied by oral tradition, involves a direct communication of embodied signs. Indeed, as I have developed more fully elsewhere (2001a), this was the channel of learning that Arapaho ideas of knowledge transmission once emphasized as primary in the first stages of life. In both the flow of everyday life and ritual contexts, senior instructors taught younger people not by verbal explication alone or as the primary medium but by encouraging direct experience of practices to be mastered. One of the things I encountered in my fieldwork was the confrontation between this older type of learning and newer forms framed by Western priority on discursive pedagogies. Elders often remarked that taking notes, recording, and verbal repetition transform the direct meaning of actions and words alike. They recall that they were taught by their elders to listen and "watch on" carefully so that they would learn a task or verbal form the first time, without need of repetition, lest the speaker change the first, direct meaning and value of the knowledge conveyed.

Quillwork was thus within the realm of what is called in anthropology and many other fields today "embodied knowledge," best defined by Merleau-Ponty as "knowledge in the hands, which is forthcoming only when bodily effort is made, and cannot be formulated in detachment from that effort" (1962: 144). In the process of what I have termed "life movement" (2001a), elders shaped the motion of younger people in ways, as Mauss elaborates (2006: 76), such that "wisdom, etiquette, ability, skill" were constituted through "significant movements, and finally a series of movements the success of which is believed or known to be certain precisely because they form a chain where the first is a sign for the others to follow." Movements are indexes of other movements to follow and function also as iconic signs that connect those movements to other levels of space and time, such as ecological periodicities, the movement through the life trajectory, and movements of sacred beings established in mythical times. Consistent with all Arapaho ritual, quillwork was a controlled movement in which "physical effectiveness is confounded with religious and moral effectiveness" (Mauss 2006: 76).

Boas's concerns about art converge with those of Mauss on the emphasis on creative motion as the source of all form in graphic art such that "[t]he rhythm of time appears here translated into space" ([1927] 1955: 40). Quillwork spatializes time (see Munn 1992) but also temporalizes space, as the motion accessible to the ways of seeing a work of art, such as the movement seen by Warden in quillwork. Art thus interconnects space and time through multiple types of motion. Creativity in general, as Boas recognized, is motion in time with and within spatial forms that have become idealized in culture: "It seems certain, however, wherever a definite type of movement, a definite sequence of tones or a fixed form has developed it must become a standard by which perfection, that is its beauty, is measured" ([1927] 1955: 10). Thus, quillwork art temporalized space according to ideals extending beyond the works themselves. Paralleling Mauss, Boas sees a close association between technique and aesthetic valuation: "Since a perfect standard of form can be attained only by a highly developed and perfectly controlled technique there must be an intimate relation between technique and a feeling for beauty" ([1927] 1955: 11). While Boas's claim can be criticized as less than universal, it does apply to Arapaho quillwork.

Much of traditional Arapaho art could be described as geometrical in form, and quillwork required a geometrical precision not found in individualistic creativity. Abstraction or reduction is needed to achieve an immediacy, as Edward Sapir recognized, in which "[t]he projection of social behavior of an innate sense of form is an intuitive process and is merely a special phase of that mental functioning that finds its clearest voice in mathematics and its most nearly pure aesthetic embodiment in plastic and musical design" ([1927] 1949a: 344). The patterned regularity of actual forms in quilled objects is astonishingly exact. Combined with motion, the designs effect in art what is comparable to what Sapir calls "form-feeling" in language, an intuitive sense not located in some deep topographical layer of the human mind, such as unconscious processes, but rather in "nothing more nor less than the 'feeling' for relations" ([1924] 1949b: 155). This is what Charles Sanders Peirce calls Firstness, Alfred North Whitehead prehension, Buddhism suchness, and Henri Bergson the vital order of experience.

Quillwork thus combines abstractness with concreteness. While nonrepresentational in one sense, the meanings of forms are iconic and in a sense metonymical in that the object connoted is reduced to one or several dimensions of itself, as a geometric shape and type of motion, for example, that is, nonetheless, in and of the direct experience of it. Celestial beings and other forms are represented in quillwork by shape, type of motion, position in space, and position in temporal sequence, all of which have some empirical or at least experiential ground, as well as a syntagmatic positioning. In other words, they are not entirely arbitrary and merely constructed from the imagination. In all, there is both a connection to things in the real world and a formal "grammar" of sorts to quillwork that together define the meaning of forms and their combinations.

All art consists of a distortion or rendering in the representation of the world as experienced, which, as Boris Wiseman notes, Lévi-Strauss identifies as "reduction" (2007: 39). Artistic representations are always models of scale in which a microcosm metonymically and metaphorically represents a macrocosm or vice versa. While this may not be a universal, it does apply to Arapaho quillwork art. An entire cradle can represent the body, tipi, and cosmos at the same time. Lines can represent human or animal paths on the land, the path of the sun, and the desire for a straight road in life. The achievement of totality in the work of art as *modéle réduit* is the means by which a creation achieves connectivity. Direct representation of a basic form would not achieve the homology on multiple levels of scale. A picture of the sun could perhaps serve as a metaphorical form linking two things as analogous, but such a figure could not achieve contiguity across multiple levels of space and time. Levels are not interconnected by a metaphorical movement from concrete source to abstract target as in prevailing theories of tropes (such as Lakoff and Johnson 1980). The body, for example, is not considered necessarily more concrete than the earth in Native American cosmologies. Quillwork achieves this totalization through a spatializing of patterns paralleling Roman Jakobson's poetic function of language to project equivalence from the axis of selection (paradigmatic) onto the axis of combination (syntagmatic) (Wiseman 2007: 7). This principle holds for verbal, musical, and graphic arts alike. The spatial rhythms of shape, proportion, and color in quillwork designs project the paradigmatic meaning upon multiple levels, thus effecting homology, into multiple rhythms in motion simultaneously in the same work.

Motion within constraints is thus basic to quillwork. Carried from the Arapaho language into art, motion is one of the primary vehicles for life, meaning, and truth. As in other Algonquian languages, grammatical gender is based not on the binary of male and female, as in some European languages, but on an animate versus inanimate distinction. Animate nominal forms include humans, animals, celestial beings, and some things considered inanimate in English, such as spoon, ball, rock, tipi pole, and even raspberry. While not empirically demonstrable for all cases, the general principle is that anything or being that can move by itself—that is, has agency over movement, whether in experience or in mythical reality—is considered alive and to some extent a person or potential person. In turn, all types of animate objects or beings (whether human, animal, or other-than-human) are defined more by their distinctive shapes of motion than by traits or essences. As discussed in chapters 2 and 3, the robe designs for which we have names are all considered animate. Many creative ritual practices are about animating some objects with life or using the life-giving power of others to generate life. Quillwork had the power to generate such life and movement. All quillwork designs were thus about creating multiple kinds of motion synthesized in the same overall created object. In a single quilled disk there can be the feeling of circular motion, radiance outward from a central point, and a linear movement. All of these interconnect the motion of sacred beings, humans, and nature. First, they represent types of motion in mythical events or those made by sacred beings, including, respectively, the radiance of the sun, Whirlwind Woman's path in spiraling outward to create the earth, and the path of the sun, or Sun Road, across the east–west axis each day, itself both linear and cyclical. They are also tied to human life movement, such as the four stages of life, which are in turn associated with phases of natural change, such as the changing seasonal winds associated with the Four Old Men at the four directions. In short, quillwork is part of the wider mythico-ritual logic, which does not place humans in the center of all movement and agency in the cosmos or time. This theme is central to all of the mythical narratives surrounding quillwork, as discussed in full in chapter 4.

At the level of sacred culture, the motion embodied in quillwork was homologous with and oriented by shapes of motion at other levels of time. These defined the mythic rhythms of time and directions of space at all levels, but ones anchored in movements of celestial and other sacred beings, themselves defined more by their motion than by inherent traits or qualities. Quillwork made by women both conformed to and formed the body according to cultural ideals of life movement. In Arapaho mythical ontology, for example, walking upright defines the original humans as *3owo3neniteeno'* (for Arapaho orthography, see the appendix), a term meaning literally "getting up in the morning from a prone position people," as in rising from bed in the morning (Dorsey and Kroeber 1903: 6). One should rise with the sun each day and pray to start the day, lest, as elders related to me, one's blood become thick or, in the case of a child, the little people come to snatch one. The first cultural form an infant experienced was the cradle, which was always positioned upright and adorned in quilled designs aiming to develop a child's mind, straight body, vision, and other human capacities of an upright, straight person. Throughout the rest of one's life, quillwork was always close to the body and everyday field of perception in the form of robes, bed covers, tipi ornaments, pillows, and so forth. Furthermore, the vertical erectness of the human body is related to that of the tipi and to the straight and cyclical path of the sun each day. This connection pervades all quillwork designs. The front-facing visual orientation of the body is aligned to the path of the sun along the east–west axis, which in turn is the starting point of all time and space in the four-directionality and phasing that pervade all Arapaho ritual action.

It is thus necessary to begin with life and motion in Arapaho quillwork as primary, rather than search first for the grounding in beauty, truth, or moral/political value that frames most Western aesthetics. Quillwork designs conform to what Suzanne K. Langer, following Ernst Cassirer, calls "vital forms" in art that are borrowed from basic life processes of growth or change in the world: "The elementary pattern of feeling expressed in such world-accepted forms symbolizing 'growth' is the sense of life, the most primitive 'fulfillment'; and it is not mirrored in the physical lines, but in the created thing, the 'motion' they have. The dynamic pattern, which is actually an illusion, is what copies the form of vital feeling" (1953: 67).

Langer postulates that the power of art to break out into our immediate attention is a strangeness that is actually a "transparency," that is, the ability to be both form and feeling, or semblance and "charged with reality" at the same time (1953: 52). Art to Langer is infused primarily with life instead of meaning, value, function, or agentive purposes: "All motion is growth—not growth of something pictured, like a tree, but of lines and spaces" (1953: 67). Art connects to vital forms in experienced reality, which Langer posits as universal, but for anthropological understandings it should perhaps be framed as culturally and historically contingent, though still recognizing some level of nonarbitrariness, such as in the periodicity of day and night or the existential reality of mortality. Motion rendered in quillwork, like that constituted in myth, is tied to concrete temporalities, such as the periodicities of the sun, moon, and seasons. As "life movement," these periodicities are the stuff of life in the Arapaho sacred world for both cyclical and linear time, recognized as homologous on multiple levels. It is also thus necessary to avoid the synoptic illusion of crude spatializing binaries of motion or time, such as the dead-end linear versus cyclical quandary that has been an obsession for anthropology far too long.

The repeated motion of bending and tacking quills acquired spatial form through the rhythmic modulation of color, shape, and proportion. That motion required planning and virtuosity. Created objects retain in them vital forms of motion, travel along paths of symbolic or commodity exchange, move human eyes to look at them and within them, connect meaning and thought to other levels of time and space, and flow through many other paths for many purposes. Quillwork was created through controlled motion and generated types of idealized sacred movements in the world. Quillwork was one among many sacred ritual practices that aimed to generate what I discussed as the core topic of my first book: "life movement," the aim to generate long life, blessings, and abundance for self, others, family, and tribe (see Anderson 2001a: 31–35). On behalf of the recipient, the straightness of the quilled lines marked the future path for a straight, long life, and the circular rings in round disks expressed the desire for completion of the full cycle of the day, life, seasons, and mythical history. The motion for sewing quills in color-modulated lines, circles, and other shapes paralleled the motion of sacred beings and cosmic time established in the mythical past at the beginning of the world. In one form or project, the artist sewed the spiraling centrifugal motion of Whirlwind Woman in creating land, the cardinal directional cycle of the Four Old Men at the four directions (which is also the linear progression of the four ages of time), and the east–west road followed by Sun, Moon, and Morning Star each day.

On another level of movement, by completing quillwork projects, a woman herself moved along in the transition from the second to the third and finally the fourth hill along the Arapaho life road. Quillwork thus involved an epitomizing and explicit inculcation of appropriate adult women's habitus, to use Pierre Bourdieu's (1977: 72) concept for the structuring dispositions of practice required of women's movement relevant to their gender and to stages in the adult life trajectory. Different types of motion and agency were associated with different stages of life. As objects in lived social space, quillwork objects were also intimately related to the users' or wearers' bodies. Quillwork was ever present in sitting, sleeping, walking, and habitation of the domestic space of the tipi. As such, quillwork items were indexes and shapers of motion at the same time. They were not just art objects to be viewed and interpreted but were always already embodied in everyday motion and vision. They were immediately present in an infant's first realization of body, social motion, and local world. Quillwork also contributed to an ongoing ritualized transition for women's life movement into the third and fourth hills of life when they, like men, moved from the public, productive, useful, and active life of adulthood to the quietude of old age. Women's quillwork was present in shaping the motion of dancers or pledgers in all sacred ceremonies of the *beyoowu'u,* including the Sun Dance, men's age-grade lodges, and the women's Buffalo Lodge. Women became agents for the life movement of others while in the third stage of life but began through quillwork to withdraw into sequestered ceremonial spaces, gained access to the most sacred and powerful knowledge, and moved toward the quiet and still but more powerful form of agency over others associated with old age. In old age, both men and women spoke less, moved less, and retreated from public displays of identity and personhood but nonetheless controlled all motion in the camp. As a woman pursued a career in quillwork, she took on increasingly difficult, demanding, and sacred projects, culminating in the eagle robe and one-hundredth robe, requiring longer periods of work, quietude, and seclusion. At some point, a woman could perhaps succeed one of the owners of a sacred bag and thus achieve full transition to the fourth hill of life.

Numerous possible perspectives on quillwork are available in contemporary anthropology and Native American art history. Many of those would be critical of the efforts here. One is the question as to whether we as Western anthropological observers can translate this totalizing vitality across cultural borders without reifying our own, often "colonizing" concepts. Alfred Gell says no, because "we can never quite understand the complex relationships they embody" (1998: 80). Such surrender to complexity is convenient as a way to exclude research a priori, and such approaches have, mysteriously, become quite popular in anthropology. This book should be evidence that such absurd exclusions should be questioned. The list of banned topics or concepts has become quite long in some anthropological circles. Everything that Gell and his school claim cannot be known about indigenous art, for example, has already been recorded for Arapaho quillwork from Arapaho consultants. Of course, the next negation would be to exclude all of the evidence on the grounds that it was gathered using a flawed methodology framed by a flawed model of culture. Many researchers have looked at the Arapaho material with great suspicion because it is astoundingly large and detailed. This is fed by a general suspicion of the evidence acquired by early American anthropologists in general. The incredulity, which I have encountered in some prepublication reactions to this research, is that either the ethnographers or the Arapaho consultants overinterpreted the material in ways that go far beyond the meanings that such objects had in basic everyday experiences of them. This may indeed happen in other field contexts, but it is not consistent with Arapaho ways of knowing and speaking about tradition. Even in present times, as I have observed elsewhere, Arapaho people do not tend to overinterpret the symbolic meanings of cultural forms and practices in speculative ways that are perhaps more prevalent in other Native American cultures. Indeed, Firewood, who was Warden's main source, and other women he and Kroeber consulted probably concealed much more esoteric, sacred knowledge (and thus much more meaning) that was available to them. In fact, Arapaho women put these symbolic forms there and interpreted them for Warden and Kroeber; these patterns and rhythms are centuries old, and they are what gives quillwork its vitality. As for the anthropologists involved, they also underinterpreted the data collected: inquiries into symbolic connections are brief and spurious within the stock of ethnographic knowledge available.

I say "possible perspectives" because most of the prevailing views have not been directly applied to this subject matter. My ultimate concern here is to move the beauty, sacredness, and rich meanings of Arapaho women's quillwork art out of obscurity and stasis in unpublished manuscripts and storage cases into the public record of human and, in particular, Arapaho and women's accomplishments. If the women involved had been an undiscovered group of painters in European art history, there would be no question of why it is important to make their works known. If quillwork had been a men's tradition in Plains Indian art, more attention would have been paid to it over the past century (see Santina 2004). If it were an extant or revitalized Native American art tradition with fashionable demand in current art markets, there would be no argument about its relevance. In all, I am firmly convinced that the women who informed Kroeber, Dorsey, and Warden about quillwork intended future generations to know about a tradition that they saw disappearing in their lifetimes. In this book, I try to honor that contribution and the history that preceded it.

CHAPTER ONE

Cradles

Quillwork once appeared on many objects moving about in everyday life and most paraphernalia for almost all Arapaho ceremonies. The evidence available does not indicate whether all quillwork involved ritual preparation and performance, but clearly the apprenticeship of the Seven Old Women bag owners would have been required for all. Alfred L. Kroeber's work and the Warden-Dorsey materials at the Field Museum identify ritual practices for cradles, robes, leanback covers, tipi ornaments, tipi liners, and tipi doors, but quillwork also appears on many other things, such as awl cases, navel amulet bags, moccasins, pillows, hair ornaments, toilet bags, pouches, lodge paraphernalia, and more. Apparently there were once quilled shirt styles, too, though none survive in museums and no descriptions remain.

Cleaver Warden's field notes in the Field Museum archives (Warden-Dorsey 1903–1906: Box 2, Folder 13: 10–40) list and describe in detail almost all of the different cradle styles. Among these are two basic forms, which I refer to as the head-ornament and the lined-path types. With some variations, the former usually features a central quilled circular or rectangular (oblong) ornament on the hood, ten quilled-loop dewclaw ornaments on the peak of the hood, two twin quilled strips just above them, four pairs of loop ornaments around the hood, seven pairs of quilled straps to hold the cover to the child's lower body, and, bordering around and trailing beneath the hood, a linear banister-like array of about 80 to 110 crossbars. The second type is the lined-path cradle style, which is often a source of confusion because it overlaps with some Cheyenne and Sioux traditional designs and is not mentioned in the main early published studies of Arapaho quillwork. Three types of such lined-path cradles are listed in Warden's notes, however, and Candace Greene (1992) recognizes this as an Arapaho type in her brief survey of Plains soft-cover cradles. Arapaho lined-path cradles are generally of smoke-tanned hide, while the covers of head-ornament styles are generally of white hide or canvas. The symmetrical trapezoidal hood of each lined-path cradle has a series of up to twenty rows of color-modulated lines running parallel to the rim of the hood. Red tufts mark transitions along each line, thus following the Arapaho quillwork pattern of tufting on robe styles, moccasins, toilet bags, tipi liners, doors, and so forth. The same number of similar but shorter rows on each side of the body section of the cover run perpendicular to the line of the baby's body. Describing consistent elements in ornamentation elsewhere on these styles is difficult, though all seem to have a pair of triangular beaded fork-like pendants with bells on the peak of the hood. The bells are about the only trade good items, besides occasional beads, that appear on cradles and quillwork in general. The narrow point of each is attached to the hood. The middle portion of each has a consistent beaded rectangle with three sections, including one central color and another color for the two outer sections.

Warden identifies eighteen types of cradles, including fifteen of the head-ornament style and three of the lined-path style. From a survey of all museum collections, I have identified four other possible styles (which Warden did not classify) that in all respects conform to Arapaho cradle form and coloration. There is no evidence of any ranking of cradles, as was the case for robes. All children were given cradles, and no distinction of style between boys and girls is apparent. There is also no evidence of a requirement (present in other Plains cultures) that each cradle had to be unique. It is also unlikely in the Arapaho case that, as in the Lakota cultural practice described by Royal Hassrick (1964: 272), a child received multiple cradles as a function of a family's or child's social status in the camp. There is also no evidence for the Lakota practice through which cradles were exchanged as prestige items outside of the event of birth itself. However, Arapahos clearly received cradles as intertribal gifts from Lakota sources, such as Red Cloud's gift of a cradle to the Arapaho Chief Black Coal in 1868 following the signing of the second treaty of Fort Laramie (Greene 1992: 95). Some Lakota cradles, by the way, are occasionally misidentified in museum collections as being of Arapaho origin.

Path Cradle

The Path Cradle is the most widely represented cradle head-ornament style in existing collections. The distinctive feature is a round head disk with two vertically symmetrical red tipi triangles, a white background, and a red border, though borders vary to some extent among surviving disks. The example Kroeber describes (AMNH 50/958) contains a black fiber ring in the penultimate quilled ring position (see plate 1). He relates the meaning of the Path Cradle as follows:

> The round ornament at the top of this cradle, besides denoting the head of the child, represents also a tent-ornament, which indeed it closely resembles. The tent-ornament signifies that the child, when it has grown up, will have a tent. Above the round ornament are pendants having small hoofs and quill-wrapped loops at their ends. These represent the pendants or rattles above the door of the tent. Still higher up than these on the cradle, are two quill-wound strips lying parallel to each other. These represent man and woman, since a man and a woman own a tent together. On the ornament representing hair are several pairs of pendants having loops at their ends. These loops represent the holes in the bottom of the tent through which the tent-pegs pass. The whole cradle, owing to its shape and the fact of its being stretched on a framework of sticks, resembles a tent-door, and therefore represents it. (1983: 67–68)

Kroeber's field notes indicate that the whole cradle represents a tipi and the "long banister-like thing" the matted and greasy hair of children (1916–20: Notebook 21: 35). There are 110 crossbar "ribs" on the banister array of this cradle. Each bar has a red half on the outer rim side and a white half on the inner side, with the two sections separated by a single narrow black fiber divider line (diagram 1.1). Instead of the more

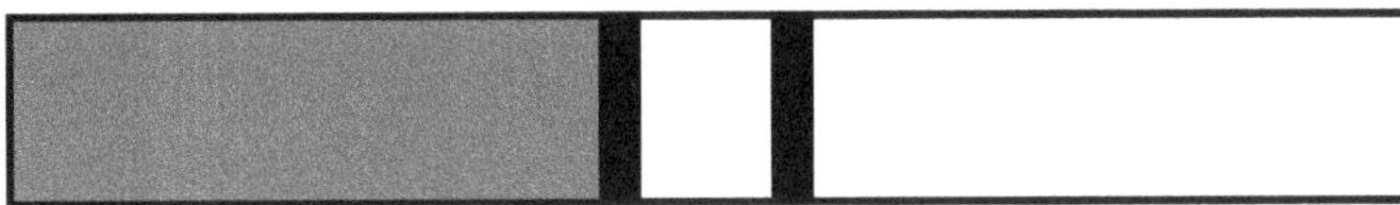

Diagram 1.1
Path Cradle Hood Lattice Bar Design

common four looped pendants, around the hood of the cradle there are four cloth medicine bags containing, according to Kroeber's notes, sweetgrass from Oklahoma (Kroeber 1916–20: Notebook 21: 35).[1]

As for other cradle ornament styles, the symbolic meanings of forms and colors are condensed symbols synthesizing iconic, metaphorical, and synecdochic connections between the body and the tipi, and in turn both of those levels of meaning connect to celestial phenomena, sacred beings, and the shapes of motion of both. The cradle was thus an infant's first social body with multiple and intersecting homologous meanings. The overall symbolic meaning of the Path Cradle head pendant is of the Sun, such that the two red triangles denote tipis oriented to the sun's path and the white background, daylight (Warden-Dorsey 1903–1906: Box 2, Folder 13: 10). In turn, the Sun was associated with a healthy and active brain function in the child.

According to Warden, the crossbar array represents the child's hair and backbone and reflects the desire for the child to have long hair and a strong, straight spine, both requisites for a long, straight life road. The symbolic supplication for extension and straightness thus applies to hair, backbone, tipi, and the child's life path itself. The line of ten looped double dewclaw pendants on the back top of the hood, Warden records, refer to the whirlwind, or whorl, of hair at the back of a person's head and also thus the "thoughts or act of the baby." Adjacent and parallel to the line of ten top pendant loops is a pair of quilled strips somewhat longer than the hood array bars but with the same pattern of red and white halves.[2] The four pairs of loop pendants on the hood rim with dewclaws aim to develop good ears and eyes for the child but also refer to the four sets of eyes of the Four Old Men who sit at the four directions watching over and protecting all humans. The seven pairs of quilled bands on the body, as on all cradles, are often referred to as "ribs" and aim to give strength and straightness to the baby's ribs and legs (Warden-Dorsey 1903–1906: Box 2, Folder 13: 11).[3]

Diagram 1.2
Red Path Cradle Head Disk Design

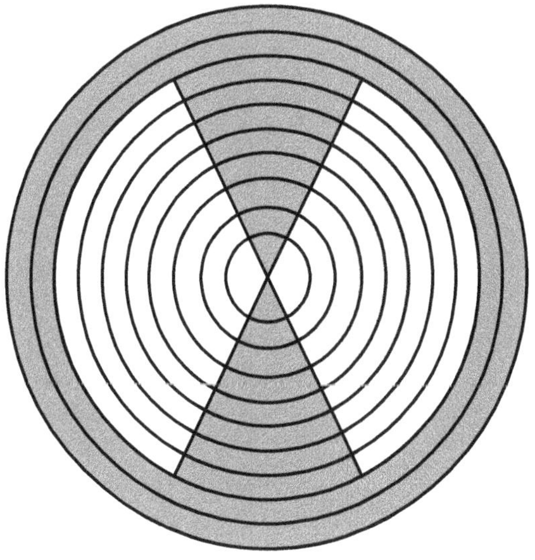

Red Path Cradle

The Red Path Cradle is identical in almost all respects to the Path Cradle style but with two red rings to mark the outer boundary and an added black fiber line border for the tipi triangle designs (diagram 1.2).[4] According to Warden's notes, the style symbolizes the duality of sun and moon through red and white, respectively. All other ornaments have the same symbolism as those of the Path Cradle (Warden-Dorsey 1903–1906: Box 2, Folder 13: 14–15).

Cornered Cradle

The Cornered Cradle is similar in design to the Path and Red Path Cradles, except that the head disk design features four black-bordered red arced rectangles as feet for the radii extending below the two central tipi triangles (diagram 1.3).[5] Warden's notes indicate that the cradle symbolizes the "[d]istribution of day when earth [was] being made," such that the red rectangles refer to day and the triangles to tipis. The crossbar array is again symbolic of the hair or spine of the child, with one hundred crossbars representing completion of the ideal life cycle of one hundred years. The seven pairs of ribs, he adds, represent the seven periods of creation, including four eras and three transitional stages in the epochal Arapaho history of the cosmos. The ten pendants on the head again connote the whirlwind (*neyóoóxet*) on the back of a child's head, associated with thought and will (Warden-Dorsey 1903–1906: Box 2, Folder 13: 12–13) and, as I discuss elsewhere, the motion of Whirlwind Woman (Anderson 2000: 17).

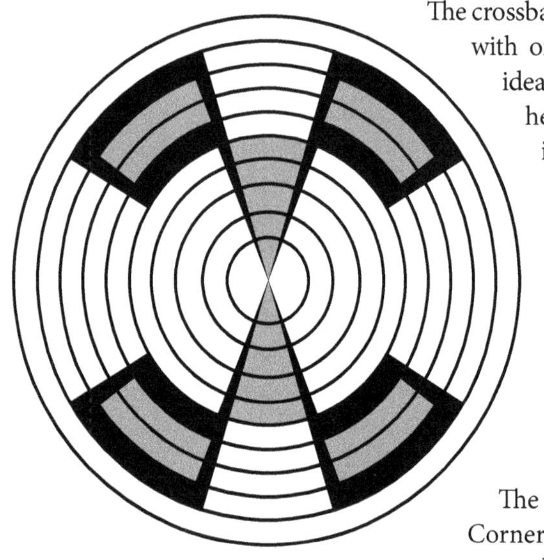

Diagram 1.3
Cornered Cradle Head Disk Design

Spotted Cradle

The Spotted Cradle style (plate 2) is very similar to the Cornered Cradle style but with the addition of four or five toes on each foot, and black only on the top row of each foot.[6] The crossbar ornaments for this type are identical to the Path, Red Path, and Cornered Cradle styles, but, like the Cornered style only, the loop ornaments, top bar pair, and seven rib pairs have five sections of two short red sections on the ends and three white sections with black dividers in the middle. The distinctive symbolism for the head disk relates both to bear's claws and to the marks on the red oblong tipi ornament style described in chapter 2. The triangles are icons of tipis; the dark lines bordering it, trails; and the white background, the snow of old age in the fourth hill of life (see the story of "Spotted Porcupine" in Dorsey and Kroeber 1903: 230–31). The four dual-looped pendants on the hood again symbolize the eyes and ears (Warden-Dorsey 1903–1906: Box 2, Folder 13: 18–19).

Lodge Cradle

The Lodge Cradle type of head disk (see figure 1.1) has eight narrow black radial sections together forming a cross of four equal-sized triangular "tipi" sections on a background of white and red alternating quilled rings. The center circle is white, while the ultimate ring is red on the ten-ringed example and white on a nine-ringed example from the Denver Art Museum (DAM 1939.366; see Bol 2001: 41). The remaining ornamentation is similar in most respects to that of all other red-white schema for the Path, Red Path, Cornered, and Spotted types.[7]

Adding to the symbolism covered so far, Warden notes that the center circle represents the sun, the white and red quilled circles are the sun's light, and the eight

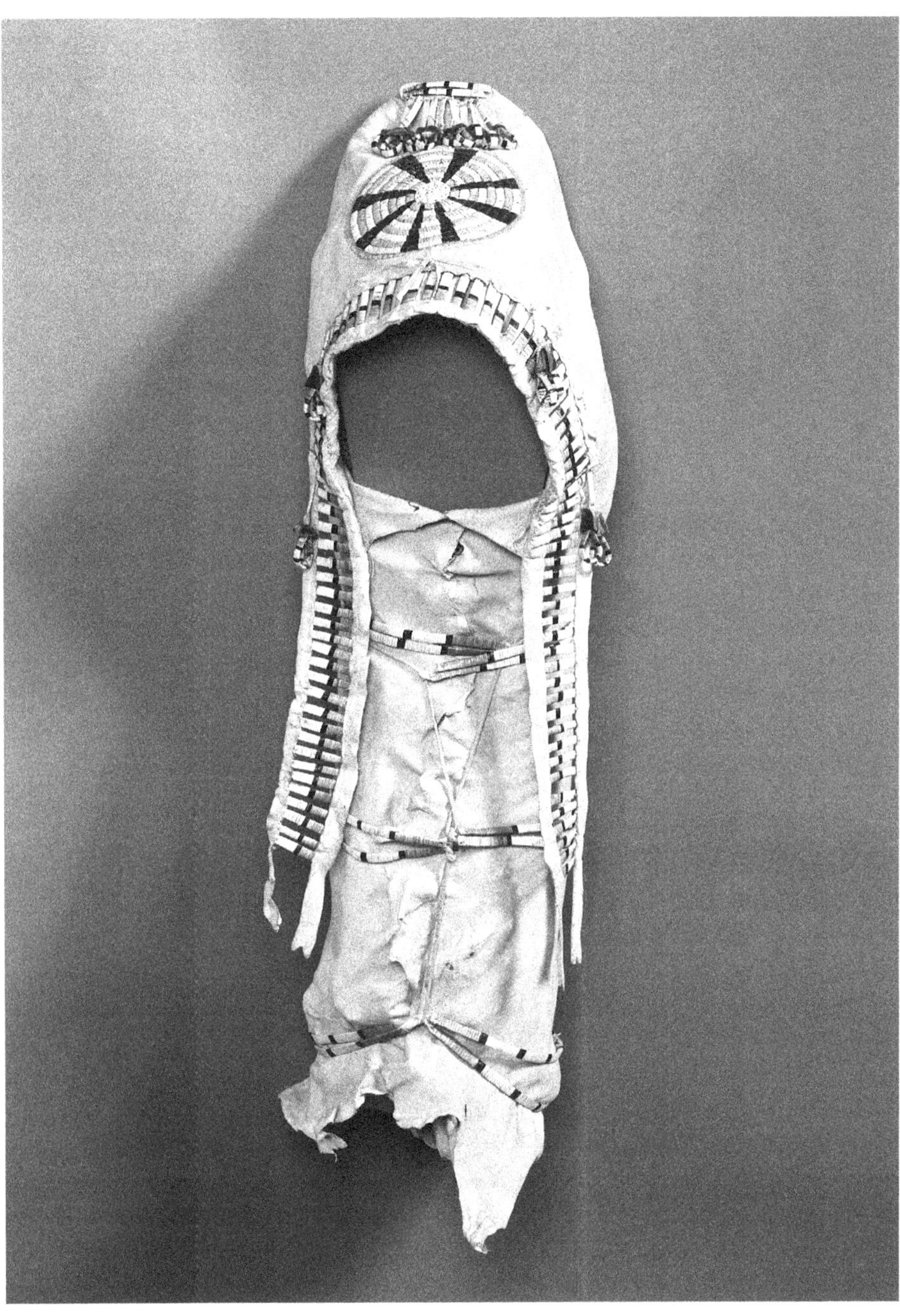

FIGURE 1.1
Lodge Cradle,
Arapaho, n.d.
Photography © Denver Art Museum. Denver Art Museum Collection: Museum Purchase, 1939.336.

dark radii are "the paths of numerous objects." The eight triangular designs formed altogether denote a lodge or the temple of the child. The five dark marks on the ribs and loops dividing the white and red segments refer to "humanity," as well as the child's whorl of hair, or the whirlwind. Warden notes in passing, too, that the entire design may be "called spider's web for its web" appearance (Warden-Dorsey 1903–1906: Box 2, Folder 13: 16).

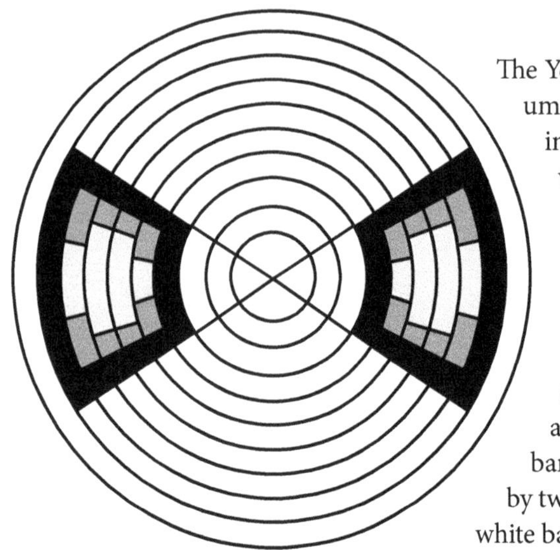

DIAGRAM 1.4
Yellow Crossed Cradle
Head Disk Design

Yellow Crossed Cradle

The Yellow Crossed Cradle style is one of the rarest and least documented in collections. Warden's description and drawing are incomplete and do not conform in all respects to the one surviving example of a head disk ornament (NMAI 04507) that approximates his description. The basic form of the disk includes two laterally symmetrically arcing bars bounded by black quills with the familiar morning star rectangular cross enclosed—denoting Little Star, which is the morning star, referred to as *nookoox* (cross). Warden's description is of "a red bar overlapped by yellow bar; surrounded by more yellow and dark quills of half-moon shape" (diagram 1.4).[8] Each crossbar on the hood fringe has a red half and a white half, divided by two black markers with a narrow white section in-between. The white background symbolizes the light of the sun on the earth or the face, while the dark boundary refers to night. Recalling the Arapaho Star Husband story (examined in detail in chapter 4), Warden notes, "This Little Star precedes the sun, therefore awakes people to prepare for the day, water, food, etc. Since he was the child of a human woman by the moon, all ceremonial sites for lodges are this [*sic*] laid: foundation of Little Star" (Warden-Dorsey 1903–1906: Box 2, Folder 13: 20–21). Little Star, the youngest of sacred beings, initiates and orients all sacred movements related to beginning all movement in the daily cycle and all ritual practices.

Ribbed Cradle

The Ribbed Cradle is also sparsely represented among existing quillwork examples.[9] As elsewhere, according to Warden, the two red triangles are tipis, but the unique yellow sections represent rays of sun and thus warmth for the tipi. The four white pointed needles connote paths. For this cradle, Warden identifies the overall symbolic meaning of the head disk (illustrated in plates 3 and 4 [left]) as relating to the centipede. The dark limbs extending from the tipi forms are the legs of the centipede. Warden adds, "Centipede is Lone Bull, who scattered his bones over the face of the earth, therefore 'many legged stone.'" In the story of "Splinter-Foot Girl," a buffalo herd lures a girl away from her brothers' camp, where she was using miraculous quillwork powers to bring quietude and prosperity to them. She marries Lone Bull, but when her brothers finally get her back and the herd retaliates with an attack that fails, her buffalo husband's body is scattered (Dorsey and Kroeber 1903: 161–78). The symbolism for all other parts of the cradle is the same as on other types discussed above (Warden-Dorsey 1903–1906: Box 2, Folder 13: 22).

Black Cradle

The head ornament of the Black Cradle style is similar to that of the Ribbed design, except with black rings that extend as arcs between the two red tipi forms in the center (diagram 1.5). The only remaining evidence of the Black Cradle is a drawing in Warden's notes and a pouch made from leftover cradle ornaments and a head pendant in the National Museum of Natural History (NMNH 200652).[10] In contrast to other cradle head disks, the Black Cradle style, Warden observes, "connotes night for the reason that they're all dark 'bows' touching four white pointed designs meaning paths." He adds that the alternating black and white arcs also symbolize the "path of four old men walking in file," as in the passage of the seasons in time. The Four Old Men are sentinels at the four corners of the earth but also send the winds as life-breath to mark changes in seasons. The meaning of the remaining ornaments is the same as on other cradles, but Warden notes that the twin bars at the top are the "paths of sun and moon" (Warden-Dorsey 1903–1906: Box 2, Folder 13: 24). In passing, Warden refers readers to the "story of twins who resurrected mother and killed Tangled Hair," which is taken up in chapter 4.

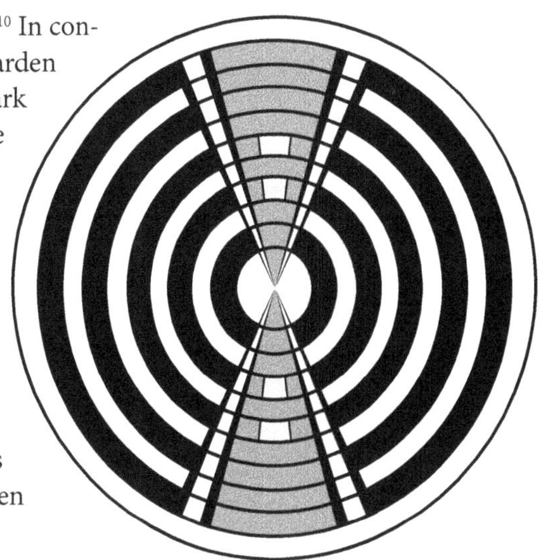

Diagram 1.5
Black Cradle Head Disk Design

Yellow Cradle

The Yellow Cradle style is similar in form to the Path Cradle but has a different color scheme and in most respects is similar to the Yellow Lodge design of tipi pendant described in chapter 2. No known examples or parts have survived, though. According to Warden's drawings, the head disk ornament had two central white triangular forms on a yellow background and yellow ultimate ring (diagram 1.6). Narrow black wedges set apart the tipi forms from the background. Nothing is known about the patterns of the ornaments, though the style does have the regular ornament complement of other disk-style tipis. Warden's notes indicate that the head disk design symbolized a sun beam shining into a tipi and the black borders "the shadows of all things" (Warden-Dorsey 1903–1906: Box 2, Folder 13: 26).

Half Yellow Cradle

There is even less evidence for the Half Yellow Cradle style, differing from the Yellow Cradle only by the addition of the common narrow white needle radii within the black dividers between the central white tipi forms and the yellow background segments on the sides (Warden-Dorsey 1903–1906: Box 2, Folder 13: 27). The head disk for this design appears to replicate the Yellow Lodge design for tipi ornaments (diagram 1.7).

Diagram 1.6
Yellow Cradle Head Disk Design

Green Cradle

The Green Cradle style Warden describes is also not represented in existing museum collections. The head disk had the common central hourglass red tipi forms but with two green squares in each (diagram 1.8). The background for the two lateral segments was white and enclosed two arced morning star rectangular forms, similar in shape to the styles above. The large rectangular section of each cross had three segments, including one central green portion and two outer red sections. The two smaller arm sections on each cross were yellow. Black borders divided each section and were added to the end of the yellow arms. All other pendants and ornaments were apparently the same as those for other disk cradles but with a green-red-white pattern throughout. Warden observes that the head disk represents "day in summer" and the green squares in the tipi triangles "vegetation," as well as the Four Old Men traveling in file with the seasons. The white background suggests "snow or light of day." The two cross designs in the white background are "frogs," in turn relating to wet weather "to make grass grow" and referring to an episode in the Arapaho story of "The Porcupine and the Woman Who Climbed to the Sky," in which the frog wife of Sun jumped into her brother-in-law Moon's face, thus becoming a permanent part of his appearance (Dorsey and Kroeber 1903: 321–41; Warden-Dorsey 1903–1906: Box 2, Folder 13: 28).

Diagram 1.7
Half Yellow Cradle Head Disk Design

Green and Yellow Cradle

The Green and Yellow Cradle head ornament is similar to the Green Cradle design but with a yellow background on the wing sections (diagram 1.9).[11] The loops and ribs follow a pattern of two outer yellow sections, two short green sections, and a middle red section, with each bounded by black. This pattern thus doubles that on the crossbars (diagram 1.10), a relationship consistent throughout almost all the styles.[12] Warden's notes give the meaning of the disk as "seasons, with everything in bloom; where baby disposes, etc., begins to walk." The central rosette denotes the sun; the two red triangles refer to tipis; the green and yellow are grass and day, respectively; and the two arced rectangular forms refer to frogs (Warden-Dorsey 1903–1906: Box 2, Folder 13: 32–33).

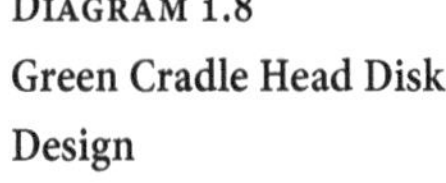

Diagram 1.8
Green Cradle Head Disk Design

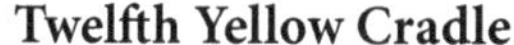

Twelfth Yellow Cradle

There are no known surviving examples of what Warden identifies as the "12th Yellow Cradle or Bird's Nest style." The head ornament has the common two red triangle tipi forms, along with two green squares on each, like those of the Green Cradle and Green and Yellow Cradle styles. The two background wing sides are yellow. On each side are two arced red triangles with terminating black sections (diagram 1.11). The disk itself, according to Warden, represents "all species of birds"; the two red triangles, tipis; the green, the paths of the Four Old Men and thus the passing of the seasons; and the four red arcs, the first parents, Father-Above and Mother-Above, and their sons, or "mysterious beings," Moon and Sun. The bodies are red and everlasting, such that each one refers to the night-path of day from twilight to dawn. The symbolism on the remainder of the cradle is the same as on other head-ornament types (Warden-Dorsey 1903–1906: Box 2, Folder 13: 30).

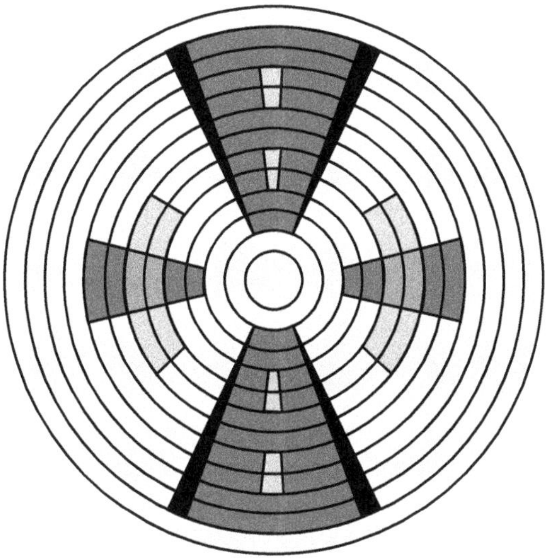

Diagram 1.9
Green and Yellow Cradle Head Disk Design

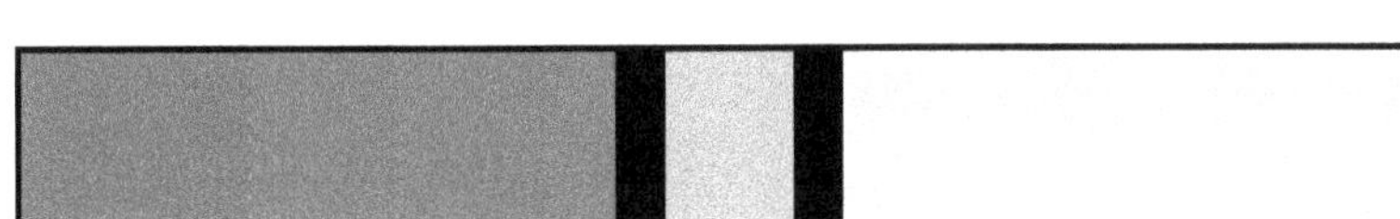

Diagram 1.10
Green and Yellow Cradle Bar Ornament Design

The Intricate Design

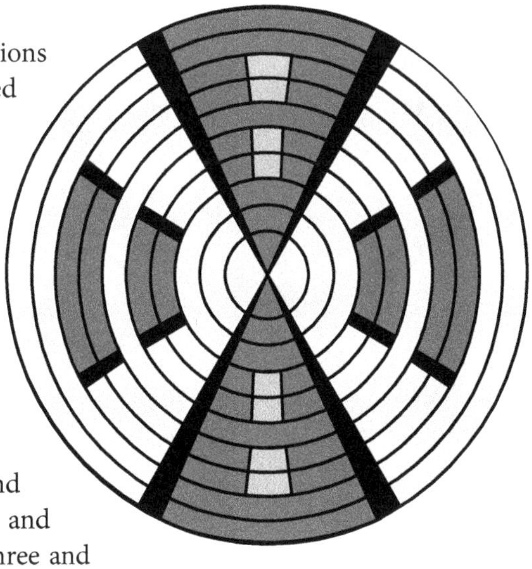

Two other disk cradle styles represented in museum collections with documented Northern Arapaho origins were not included in Warden's inventory or Kroeber's study. One is what I simply label the Intricate Design, represented by a full cradle in the Riverside Metropolitan Museum in California (RMM A1-589) and a pouch with one side remade from a rosette of identical style stored at the American Museum of Natural History (AMNH 50/1-1327) (illustrated in plates 5 and 4 [right]). The design is perhaps the most complex of all Arapaho styles. Both examples have twelve rings of quillwork with solid white in rows one, two, six, seven, eleven, and twelve. The two intervening three-part sections repeat a similar pattern. Rings three, five, eight, and ten have a black background interrupted by two white sections in what usually are the top and bottom triangular tipi sections along the vertical axis. Rows three and five have three white square dots on each horizontal side, which are two quills wide in row three and three quills wide in row five. Circles eight and ten have the same pattern but of four dots each, three to four quills wide. Rings four and nine are solid red with white sections in the vertical tipi sections. All these row designs thus form two lateral and two vertical triangular forms that altogether form the morning star pattern, similar to a Maltese cross. Other features are similar to the head-ornament cradle styles with red as the dominant color.[13] The unique symbolism associated with this style is unknown, though all general cradle meanings probably apply.

Diagram 1.11
Twelfth Yellow Cradle Head Disk Design

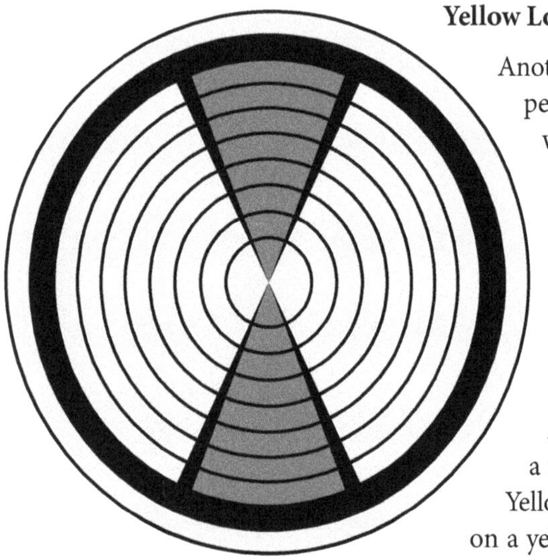

Yellow Lodge Cradle Variant

Another cradle style that Warden does not describe has a rosette head pendant very similar to that of the Yellow Lodge but lacking the somewhat larger black segment on the central cross formation.[14] Though the symbolism of the style is unknown, the same design for the central Yellow Lodge rosette represents Whirlwind Woman, who originated quillwork, and the cradle as a whole may represent the Yellow Lodge itself (diagrams 1.12 and 1.13).

Yellow Oblong Cradle

A second type of head-ornament cradle is the oblong style with a rectangular design, consisting of a yellow and red variation. The Yellow Oblong Cradle style (plate 6) has a head disk with a white cross on a yellow background.[15] Unlike the round-ornament cradles, it has ten pairs of quilled strips around the mouth of the hood instead of the array of crossbars. Kroeber (1983: 68–69) describes the meaning using Warden's evidence:

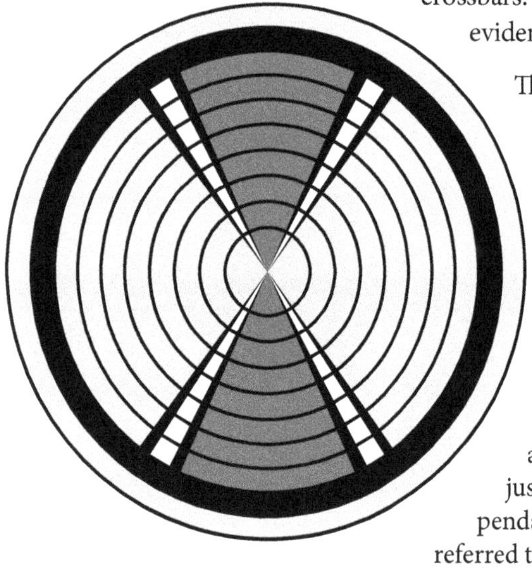

> The oblong ornament at the top represents the head of the child. Yellow wool embroidered upon it is hair. A stripe of blue beads surrounding this ornament represents face-paint. At the lower part of the cradle are the ribs of the child.
>
> The oblong ornament also represents a tent-ornament. The pendants above it are the rattles at the top of the tent. They signify that it is wished that the child may become old enough to possess a tent. Yellow strips surrounding the opening of the cradle represent the circumference of the base of the tent. Tufts of wool at intervals between these strips represent the places of the tent-pegs. The ornaments that are called ribs are also the pins used for fastening together the front of the tent, just above the door. Rattle-pendants attached to them represent the pendants on the tent alongside of these pins, lower down than those referred to at the top of the tent.

DIAGRAM 1.12
Yellow Lodge Cradle Head Disk Design A

DIAGRAM 1.13
Yellow Lodge Cradle Head Disk Design B

The main symbolism for the cradle is of Little Star, "with its brilliancy to the people," thus also associating the child's body and the tipi.

Red Oblong Cradle

Though not identified by name in either Warden's or Kroeber's accounts, the Red Oblong Cradle style (figure 1.2) is similar in overall form to the yellow type, though in white and red, along with some differences in ornamentation. The loops, bars, and crossbars of this type have a distinctive short white section just a few quills wide in the center, with a much longer red section and white section on each half, similar to the form on Path Cradles shown in diagram 1.1.[16]

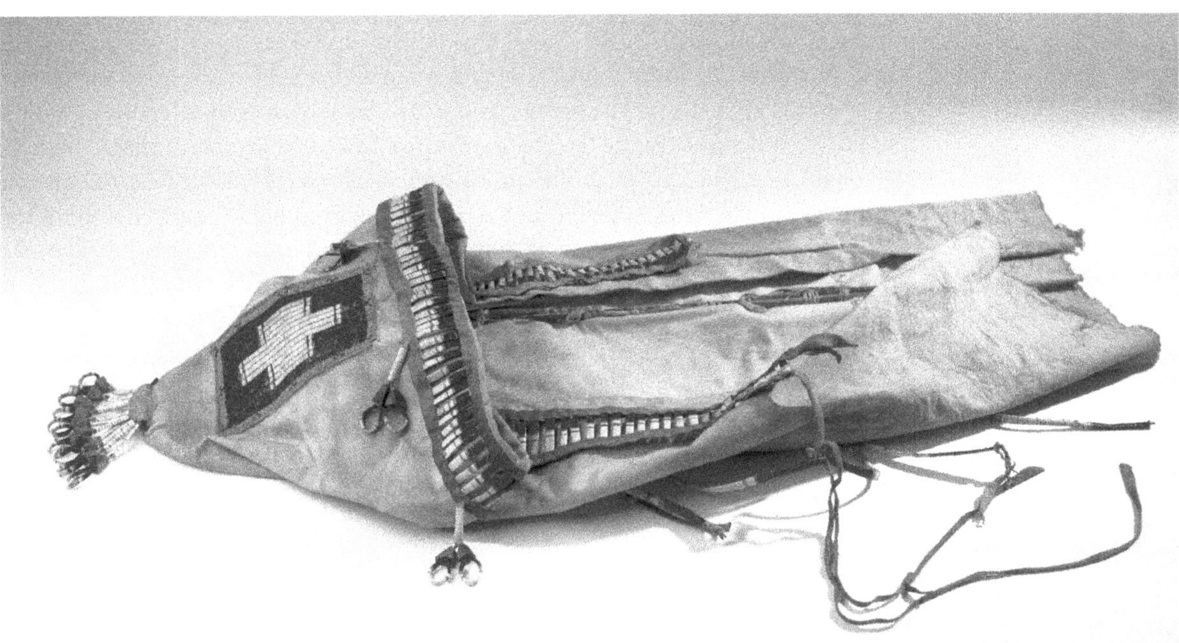

Figure 1.2
Red Oblong Cradle.
Courtesy of the Division of Anthropology, American Museum of Natural History (AMNH 50/1079).

White Path Cradle

There are four known lined-path cradle styles, each identified by a dominant color. The White Path Cradle, known only through Warden's notes, has a composite pattern of lined quillwork. He indicates that the red trapezoidal section formed along the top of the hood is the "path of sun," elsewhere called the sun road (*hiisiis bóoó*), and refers both to the part in a child's hair (once often painted red) and to the path of the sun each day as it passes from east to west over the tipi. The quilled white lines extending from the sun road are icons of "paths of people." The beaded design on each of the two triangular head pieces has five sections, including two larger outer sections of yellow, a narrow black section in the middle, and two narrow green sections paralleling it. The designs symbolize the "instincts of child," with black denoting "shades" and yellow "a bright future." The green line of beads refers to the horizon of the earth, and the red spots bounded by dark quills the Father and Mother (Warden-Dorsey 1903–1906: Box 2, Folder 13: 40). Unlike the other lined-path cradles, this style has only fourteen head rows and fourteen body rows (Warden-Dorsey 1903–1906: Box 2, Folder 19: 26). The color pattern of the rows on both head and body are the same, with a central red section paralleled by two white border sections set off by three black dividers, a yellow section, and a terminating black section (diagram 1.14). Each of the ten button loops follows the same pattern but without terminating black sections.

Diagram 1.14
White Path Cradle Hood Line Pattern

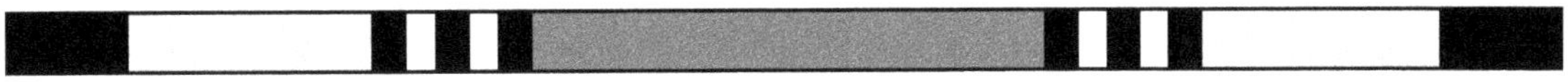

Green Path Cradle

The Green Path Cradle (figure 1.3) has twenty horizontal lines on the hood and twenty on each side of the body. The use of green in divider sections is much more common in quillwork designs among the Cheyennes, from whom, Warden suggests, this pattern may have been adopted. Red tufts overlie each green section. The red section in the middle increases in size from the back to the front lines toward the rim of the hood. The five pairs of bottom quilled loops all have red center sections but alternate green and white in the other sections as one moves from top to bottom. The top paired pieces, along with pairs three and five, have a pattern of white-black-green-black-red-black-green-black-white, while loop pairs two and four have a complementary pattern of green-black-white-black-red-black-white-black-green. The two head pieces have the common form of three radiating thongs terminating in pairs of tin cones. Three narrow green beaded sections have two wider white beaded sections to form the webbing in the middle portion between thongs. A green beaded line also borders the rim of the hood.

Green Cradle

Almost identical to the Green Path cradle is what Warden calls the Green Cradle (see diagram 1.8), which is known only from one example at the Carnegie Museum of Natural History (CMNH 3179-237), as well as through his notes there and at the Field Museum. It differs from the Green Path only by the lack of alternating patterns for lines and loop ornaments. The Green and Green Path types may indeed be the same style, for Warden also mentions that the design was acquired from the Cheyennes. The hood has twenty parallel rows of quillwork, each with one red central section and four white sections, altogether forming long isosceles trapezoidal forms from front to back. The large sections are divided by red tufts beneath which are short quilled sections of green bounded by black borders. As on other lined-path cradles, there are also two arrays of twenty quilled lines on each side of the body, though each has only three sections: one red central segment and two white. Each boundary between large sections is marked the same way. There are three ties on the front, each with a pair of quilled loops without dewclaws. Each loop follows the same pattern as on the Green Path style of a red central section and two white outer sections with divisions of green black-bordered short sections. The very peak of the hood has two triangular beaded pendants with three points. Each of the two forms has three strips of buckskin bridged by lateral strands of three green beaded sections in the middle against a white background throughout. The hood has a border of green seed beads with four white beaded designs of three stacked rectangles coinciding with the red tufts of the quilled lines (diagram 1.15).

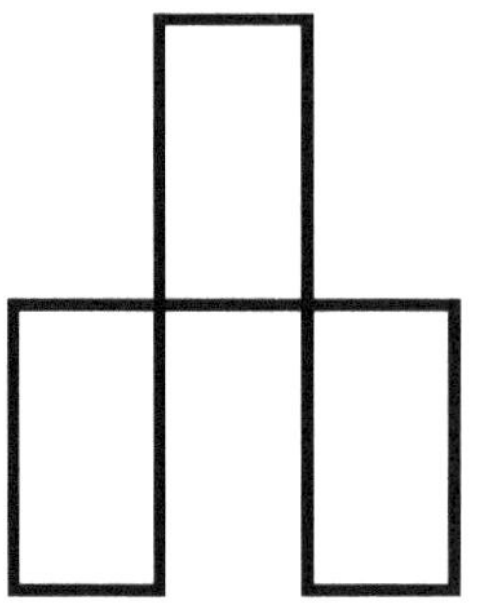

Diagram 1.15
Cradle Hood Border Beaded Design

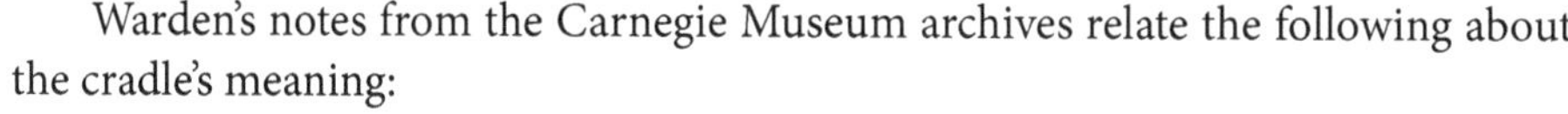

Warden's notes from the Carnegie Museum archives relate the following about the cradle's meaning:

> This cradle represents a buffalo. The parallel lines across the head and body are the buffalo trails. The red flannel denotes animal and human flesh. The red lines of quills in the center of the forehead represent a path of a baby. The parting of the hair symbolizes the path of the sun. The same designs on both sides of the body signify paths into the future. The two pendants at the top of the head denote the

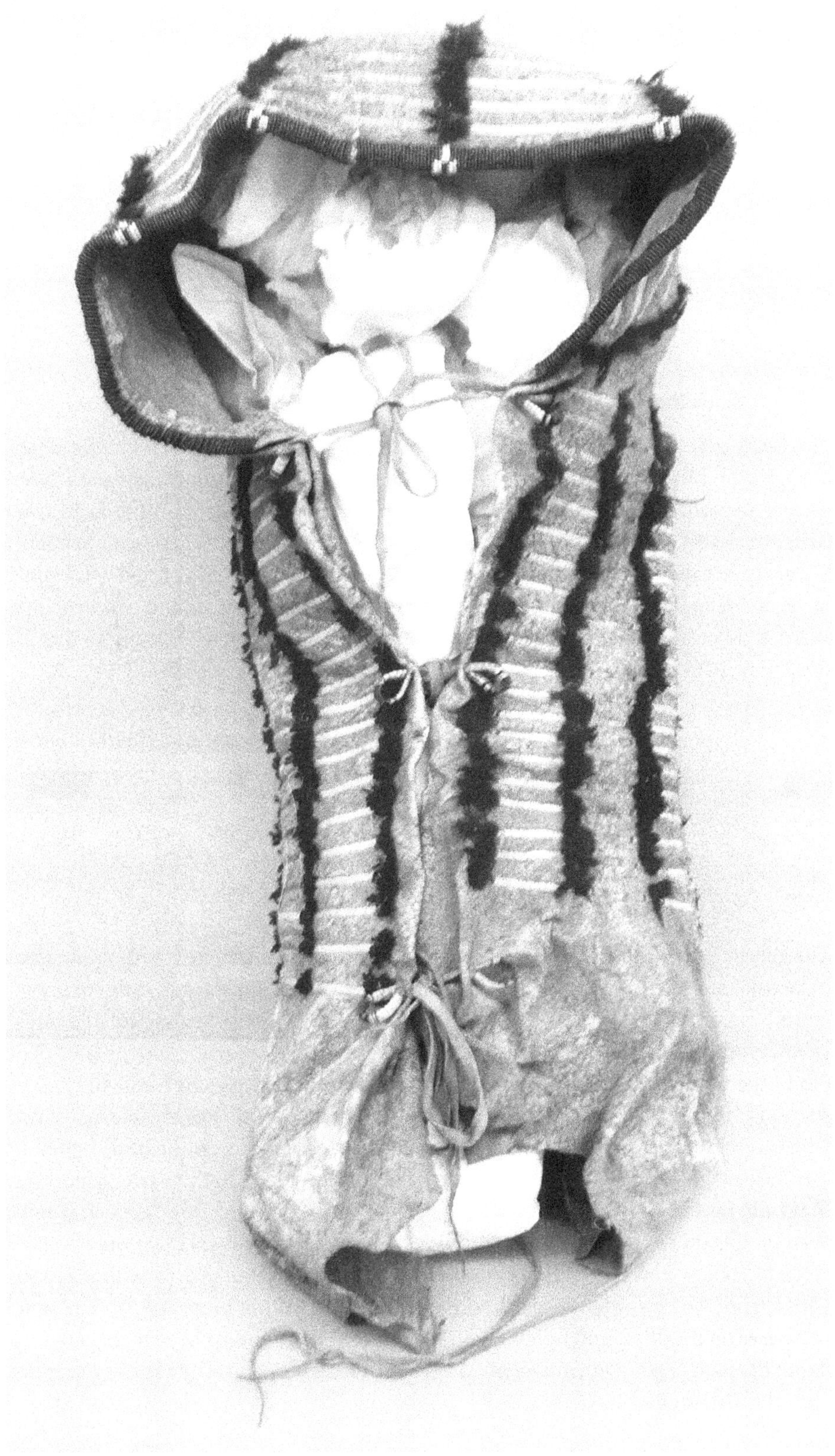

FIGURE 1.3
Green Path Cradle. Courtesy, Carnegie Museum of Natural History (CMNH cat. no. 3179-237).

> ears of an animal, or of a baby. The beads typify summer and winter; the bells, hearing, and should be of hoofs, which would then refer to the tepees and hearts of people. The beaded design at the mouth of the cradle (buffalo) represents the circumference of the earth, with representations of humanity and images of people, in white beads typifying cleanliness. The quilled loops represent the eyes of people, but are used in tying up the baby in the cradle. For the animal they denote limbs, ten in all. The red quills typify the sun; the white, winter, the green summer; and the dark, buffalo. The porcupine quill work on the cradle represents the different rays from the sun, from youth to old age. This kind of cradle marks one kind of degree. Similar designs are being placed on the buffalo robes, with variations. This cradle as it appears is called a green cradle, for earth. (Carnegie Museum of Natural History n.d.)

Black Path Cradle

The Black Path Cradle is similar to the Green Path Cradle and Green Cradle styles, though with black sections on the ends of the head rows and yellow instead of green divider sections on the body lines, while retaining green dividers on the head rows (diagram 1.16). As on the Green Path Cradle, the two three-pronged head pendants feature green and white beading. Again, there are twenty lines on the hood and twenty on each side of the body. There are no known examples of this style, and nowhere does Warden describe its symbolism. However, the meaning is probably similar to that for the Yellow Path, Green Path, and White Path Cradles.

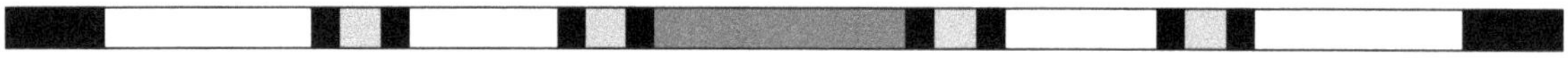

DIAGRAM 1.16
Black Path Cradle Line Pattern

Yellow Path Cradle

The Yellow Path Cradle (figure 1.4) is similar in form to other lined-path cradles but has a color combination for each line of yellow, red, white, and black in order of prevalence.[17] According to Warden, the trapezoidal red path is also the sun road. The black, yellow, and white sections leading to the red section are "trails or thoughts of people to the sun." The dark sections symbolize shadows (*betee3oono'*) and the yellow portions "a bright future." As on all quillwork, the red flannels or tufts are associated with the "blood or race of the people." The two beaded designs on the head represent the "instinct of [the] baby, used to guard [the] head." Overall, this style symbolizes "days and health" (Warden-Dorsey 1903–1906: Box 2, Folder 13: 36). In his drawings, Warden illustrates the body lines with one central red section and two outer yellow sections. Yellow and red sections are divided by the common narrow white sections with slightly narrower black dividers. Each of the ten button loops follows the same pattern as on the other lined-path cradles. The two three-thonged head pieces are similar to the Black Path and Green Path designs but with blue and white instead of green and white beading.

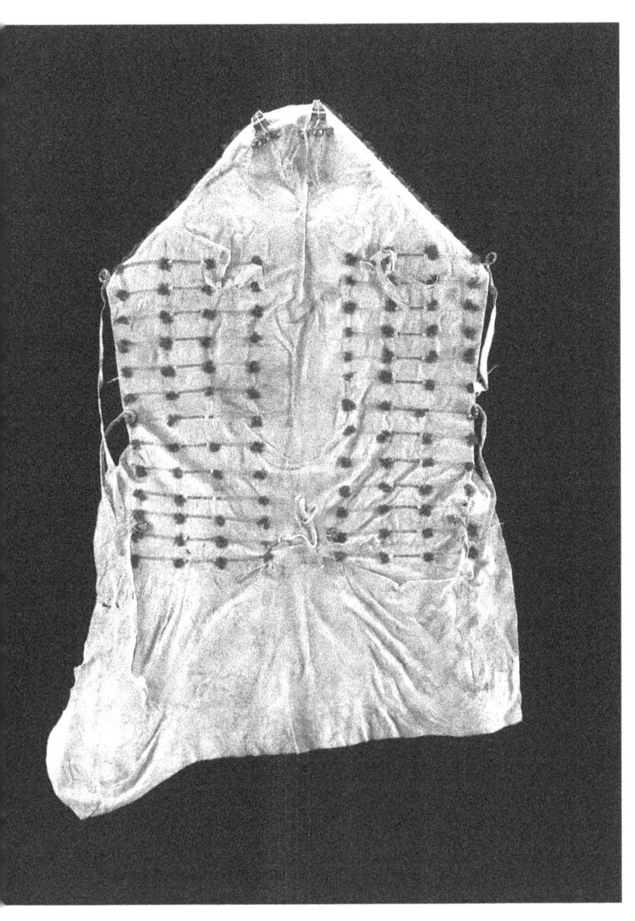

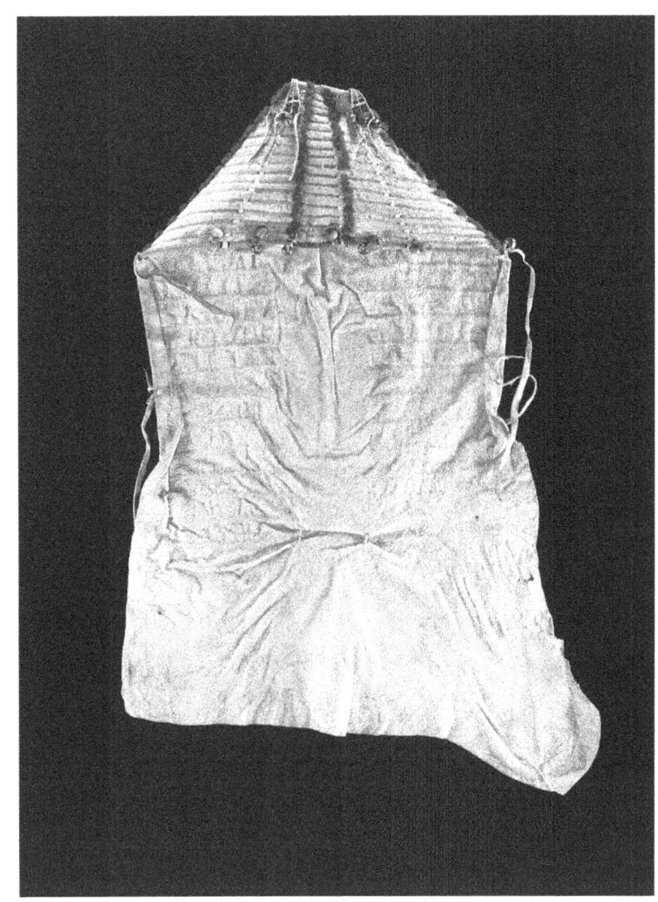

FIGURE 1.4
Front and back views of Yellow Path Cradle. Department of Anthropology, Smithsonian Institution, cat. no. 165774.

CHAPTER TWO

Tipi Ornaments, Robes, Leanback Covers, and Other Quilled Objects

Arapaho women made most other quillwork projects as gifts for adults to wear or use in domestic life. Tipi ornaments, robes, leanback covers, tipi liners, and tipi doors are among the larger projects known to require vows and ceremonies. Other items, for which less evidence is available, include moccasins, pillows, and bags of various sorts.

Lodge Styles

Warden categorizes a number of quilled tipi ornament styles, primarily by dominant color. Each tipi set included three types of ornaments, described here by Kroeber:

> 1. A circular piece of hide about eight inches in diameter, covered with embroidery of beads or quills. This is sewed to the back of the tent at its very top just below the place where it is fastened to the hiinana'kaya^{n} [*hiinonookoyoo'*]—the pole in the middle of the back which is used to raise the tent into position. To the bottom of this ornament are attached two buffalo (or cattle) tails. This ornament is called ka^{n}eibiihi [*ko'eibiiihi* 'round quilled'].
> 2. Four similarly embroidered pieces of skin considerably smaller. These are attached to the sides of the tent, several feet above the bottom, at the southeast, southwest, northwest, and northeast (the tent always facing east). To the middle of each of these ornaments is attached a buffalo-tail and a pendant consisting of three quill-wrapped strings which have at their ends the small dew-claws of buffalo and a quill-wrapped loop.
> 3. A series of pendants, each triple, with dew-claws and loops at the ends. These resemble the pendants just described, except that instead of strings, wider strips of skin are wound with porcupine-quills. When quills are not to be had, corn-husk or plant-fibres are used. These pendants, called xaxanää^{n}hihi [*xooxooneihihi'* 'small hanging'], are attached in two vertical rows to the front of the tent, where it is fastened together above the door; also to the edge of the two flaps or ears at the top (which give light and ventilation, but can be closed when it rains). (1983: 59–60)

Kroeber's field notes point out that the wife of Washington, a prominent Northern Arapaho at that time, told him that the large ornament was called "turtle" and the four other disks were similar to it. She also added information about their proper care: "They are hung outside, but can be taken in for rain, the 4 little ones are then hung over the head of the bed, large one over the foot" (Kroeber 1916–20: Notebook 11: 1).

All lodge styles had round disk forms, with the exception of one of oblong or trapezoidal shape. All round types included a central vertical hourglass double-triangle tipi section like cradle disks with variations of color and alternating or solid color rings on the remaining sides. The pendants on the front of the tipi were, according to one account, twenty-eight (seven times four) in number, because there were seven tipi pins on Arapaho tipis, each of which coincided with two ornaments, and, above those, a series of seven more on each side of the tipi ears extending to the top. Warden, though, identifies a total of thirty pendants for the Red Lodge style (discussed below). The various parts of a tipi ornament set coincided with ornaments on the pendant style cradles. The head or sun disk on both were similar, and the four small pendants were like cradle head ornaments. The front pendants on the tipi were identified with the row of ten ornaments on the top of the cradle hood.

Red Lodge Style

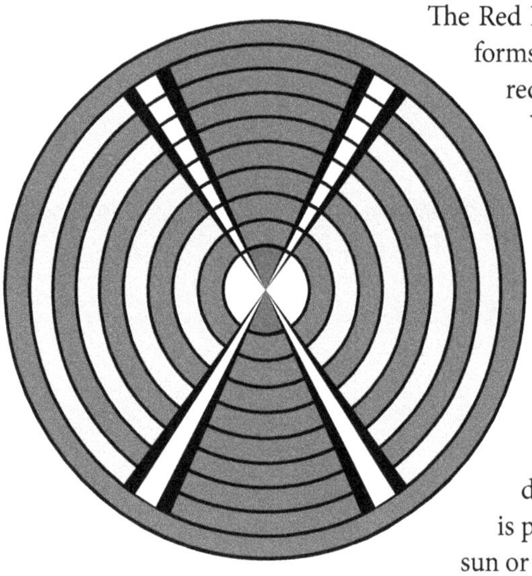

The Red Lodge style had a large disk form with two red triangular tipi forms along the vertical axis, white spokes with black borders, and red and yellow alternating arcs in the lateral sections (diagram 2.1; Warden-Dorsey 1903–1906: Box 2, Folder 13: 1). There are no known surviving examples of this style. As in all tipi styles, two buffalo-hair tails were attached where the lower white spikes terminated at the bottom of the disk. According to Warden, the large disk symbolizes the "sun as it rises early in the morning." The four white pointed designs are "paths" or the "ditches from old woman's tipi extending to her traps" in the Little Star story (discussed in detail in chapter 4). The narrower black border spokes "signify animals, buffalo and at the same time the dark rays in the sky." Warden adds, "The dark ring in the center of the disc does not mean anything, but is placed there to ascertain the other drawing. It really denotes the sun or center spot of the earth."

Diagram 2.1
Red Lodge Top Disk Design

Along with the one large and four side rosettes, there were thirty pendants running from the ear flaps downward to parallel the breastpins above the tipi door, thus including fifteen to a side, running vertically from the ears to flank the breastpins. Each pendant had three long quilled thongs with a pair of loop ornaments on each end. As elsewhere in Arapaho art, each such ornament included two dewclaws with quilled thongs and loops. Each loop had a yellow quilled section on the top half, a red lower half, and the common short black-white-black divider section dividing yellow and red sections. Within each dewclaw were twin red tufts, with the same meaning as the hair on the back disk. Each of the four side rosettes had four alternating red and yellow rings. Three pendants were attached in the center of each with a yellow quill-wrapped binding string, along with a length of red flannel. Each thong ended in a dewclaw and quilled loop, as well. For meanings, Warden remarks, "There are fo[u]r of these pendants located like the four old men and therefore the yellow porcupine bindings on this typify human people, because there are five fingers in each hand. The pendants denote rain drops, also tassels of cottonwood trees and others, also birds' feet. The hoops of course refer to buffalo. The red flannel extends from them and typifies the people" (Warden-Dorsey 1903–1906: Box 3, Folder 26: 12 [1905]).

Black Lodge Style

The Black Lodge style (figure 2.1) is said to be the "head of all" (Kroeber 1916–20: Notebook 7: 52–55), or highest in rank and oldest in age, originating in the above among sacred beings. The disks have only yellow and black rings with the typical white spokes and black divider sections on the main disk. In the large disk, the tipi and wing sections alternate two colors oppositely in the lateral and vertical sections, but with one solid yellow outer tenth ring. The tipi segments along the vertical axis begin with yellow in the center and end in yellow on the ninth row, while the wing portions begin and end in black. There are also white spokes and two divider black spokes between the tipi and wing sections, as on all round disk tipi styles. The four smaller Black Lodge disks have four alternating yellow and black rings, beginning with black in the center spot.[1] Warden describes the meaning of the central disk: "This design denotes a tipi at night, for the reason that there are dark rings or rays with yellow ones. The small dark circle in the center of the design indicates the night or dawn of day, while the white-looking designs are for paths" (Warden-Dorsey 1903–1906: Box 3, Folder 26: 1 [1905]). The four small disks are "eyes of four old men." There were also thirty ornaments for the ears and breast on the front. The Black Lodge was the first style of all lodges and perhaps all quillwork. It was the style for the home of Mother-Above, who made the first set, and her husband, Father-Above, the Creator, along with their sons Moon and Sun.

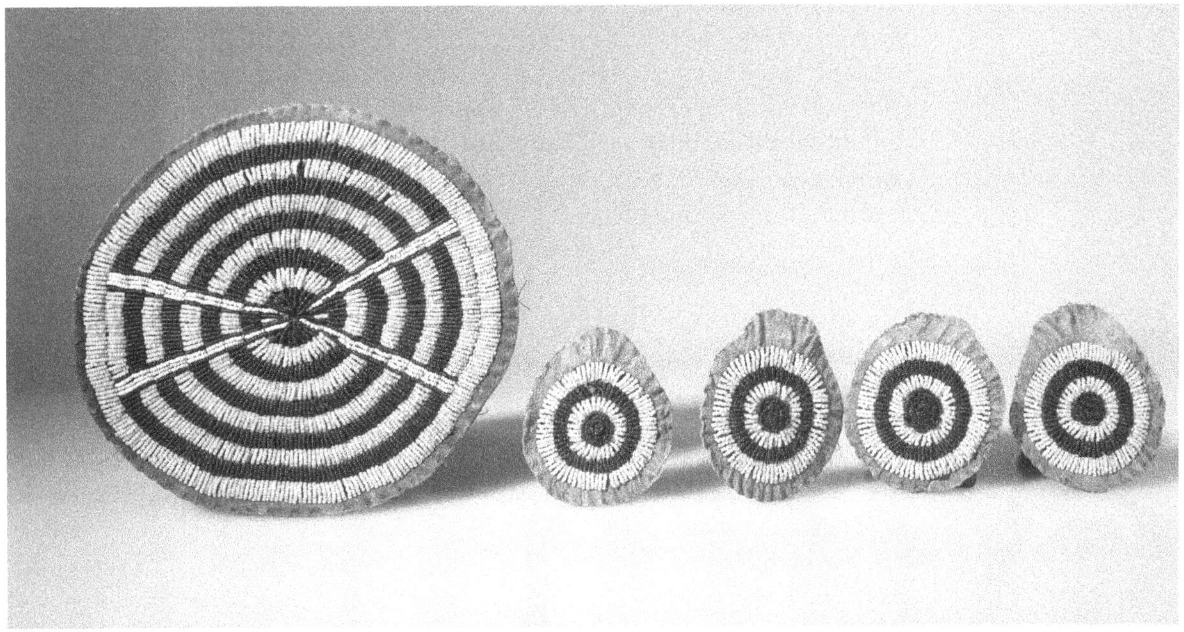

FIGURE 2.1
Beaded Black Lodge ornaments. Courtesy of the Division of Anthropology, American Museum of Natural History (AMNH 50/368A–E).

Black Lodge Southern Style

The Black Lodge Southern style (plate 7) is similar to the Black Lodge design and is likewise mentioned as the original and highest form. A beaded set of disks for this style collected from Southern Arapahos by Kroeber in 1899 is in the American Museum of Natural History collection (AMNH 50/298A–E). A large disk (AMNH 50/360) made from corn-husk fibers is in the same collection and of the same origin. The large disk for the complete set and the latter example have the same alternating black and yellow rings in the side sections but solid red in the vertical triangular tipi sections. Unique to AMNH 50/298A–E is the tenth beaded ring of a repeated pattern of triangular teeth or "sun rays." There are twenty-two of these in all, significantly arranged with four rays in each red tipi section and seven in each wing area. Example AMNH 50/360 has a solid yellow outer ring. There are also two quilled thongs with buffalo- or cattle-hair lengths beneath the lower white spikes. The four small disks are identical to the Black Lodge example, though with the buffalo hair and double thongs with dewclaw and loop ornaments attached in the center. Warden's drawings show each ornament with seven rings of quillwork and with the common triple thong hanging beneath each small disk ornament (Warden-Dorsey 1903–1906: Box 2, Folder 19: 21). Each thong has seven equal sections alternating between yellow and white, with yellow at the top and bottom. Each ends in a dewclaw and white-red-white pattern loop with black dividers. The loops on the existing example, as on other southern examples of this period, are made from corn husks or other fibers. The symbolism and mythological connections are similar to those of the Black Lodge, but Warden adds, "The buffalo tail pendants indicate dark streaky rays before the sun rises or before it sets." About the four side pendants he also notes, "The dark circle for men, the yellow ones for their glory. The hoof pendants from this disk typify humanity or birds' claws."

Earthly Tipi or Red Bottom Style

Another tipi style Warden identifies is the "Earthly Tipi or Red Bottom," for which there are no known artifacts. From his drawings it seems that this style was identical to the Black Lodge Southern style but without the white spoke sections on the large disk. The symbolism also seems to have been similar, though Warden remarks, "This design denotes the earth from the fact that it bears the two paints which are mostly used for the body painting" (Warden-Dorsey 1903–1906: Box 2, Folder 13: 6).

Yellow Lodge Style

The Yellow Lodge style (plate 8 and figure 2.2) is similar to the Black Lodge Southern style, but the large wing segments are solid yellow. Some examples have the serrated-edge sun rays on the circumference like that of the Black Lodge Southern example described above. Of all the styles, there are the most examples of this one in museum collections, though none in quillwork.[2] All of the known examples appear to have been made by Southern Arapahos. Each large disk has a central yellow circle, two red tipi designs along the vertical axis, a yellow background in the obtuse wing sections, one narrow black line along the red sections, wider white sections, and equally wide black segments bordering the yellow sides. The large disks all have an outer row of

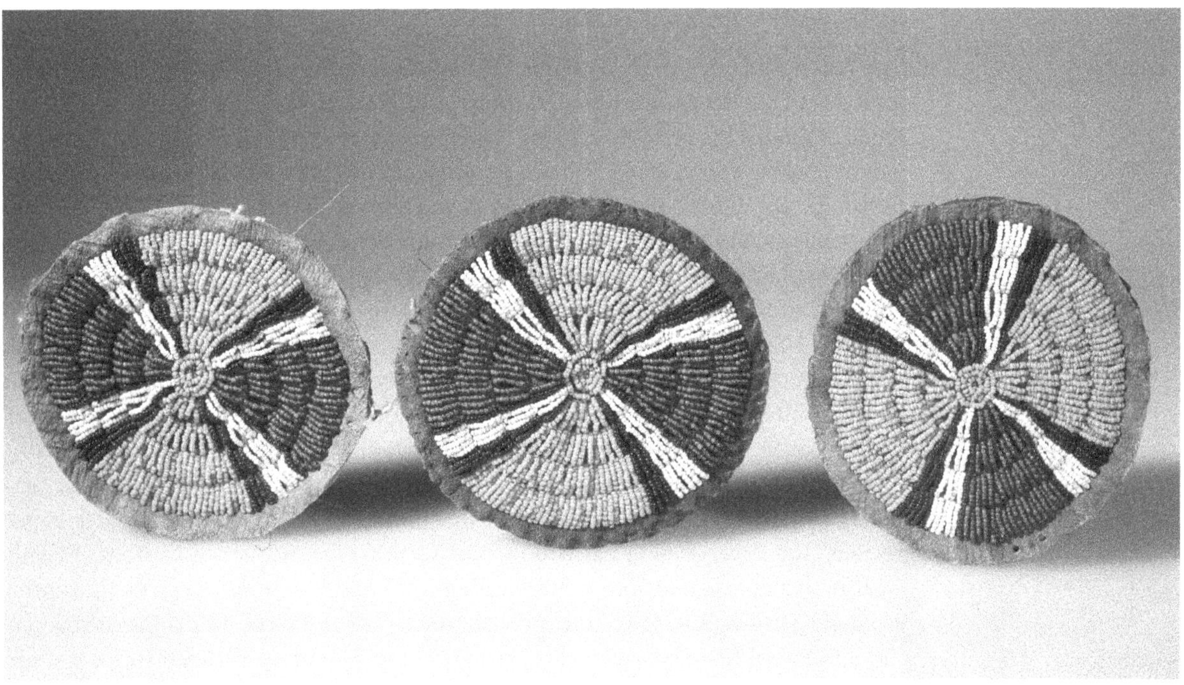

Figure 2.2 Beaded Yellow Lodge side ornaments. Courtesy of the Division of Anthropology, American Museum of Natural History (AMNH 50/360BCE).

teeth, though the number of these varies. The only available front ornaments (AMNH 50/360AY) associated with the style have three thongs, loops, and dewclaws, each consisting of a half yellow section at the top and a red section at the bottom and a short central green section bounded by black borders.

Kroeber (1983: 61–62) refers to this same style as "White" or "xanā^{n}kū'bää" (*xonookuube'ee'* 'straight-standing red') and offers this interpretation:

> It represents the sun, on account of both its shape and its prevailing yellow color. The two red sectors are tents containing persons (red sometimes signifies mankind in Arapaho color-symbolism). The teeth at the circumference represent persons.
>
> Another specimen of this third kind, worked in beads, was said to represent, as a whole, the sun. The red sectors, at the opposite sides (ends) of the circle, are the red of sunrise and sunset. The white and black radii bordering these sectors can be regarded as two intersecting diameters, forming a cross. Therefore they are the morning star.
>
> The four small circular ornaments going with each of the large ones that have been described are miniature reproductions of these, except that the small ornaments of the first two styles omit radii and sectors, consisting only of concentric black and yellow circles. (Kroeber 1983: 61–62)

Warden describes Yellow Lodge symbolism as "denoting the day, for earth and its inhabitants. The two red triangles traversing the disc denote tipis, while their white sides signify the brightness of day and the intersection or 'cross' formed by the paths of old woman in the Little-Star story. The dark ring in the center does not mean anything, but is to guide the woman in making the design. It is the place they begin it, finishing at the outside edge" (Warden-Dorsey 1903–1906: Box 3, Folder 26: 14 [1905]).

Yellow Oblong Tipi Style

The Yellow Oblong Tipi style (figure 2.3) has a unique top ornament in the shape of an isosceles trapezoid with yellow, red, white, and black designs. Kroeber notes that the name of this design is "nīhā^{n}xā'^{n}hayā^{n}" (*niihooxoohoyoo' 'yellow oblong'*) and thought it a more common form among Cheyenne quillworkers (1983: 64). Winfield W. Coleman (1980: 57, 68) reports that for Cheyennes this style is known as the Chief's Tipi and was considered exclusive to chiefs; it is the only ornament style in that tradition that is rectangular rather than round. The only Arapaho-derived evidence for this style is a beaded example of the top ornament at the American Museum of Natural History (AMNH 50/666). Drawings of the ornaments for this style also appear in Warden's field notes. According to Warden, the pendant was hung with the wider side up, but Kroeber illustrates it with the opposite orientation (1983: 64). Here I adopt Warden's version, since it is consistent with Arapaho symbolism elsewhere. The AMNH example is twenty-three centimeters long and thirteen centimeters wide with two main sections of beadwork, one in the bottom two-thirds and the other in the wider upper section. The lower section has two parallel vertical eight-sectioned swathes of beadwork on either side with four yellow beaded circles of increasing size down the central section. Each swath has two vertical outer yellow lines with two black lines demarcating the central section, which alternates from top to bottom between white and red beaded narrow horizontal sections. The yellow sections are from five to seven bead strands wide, the black line only one, and the alternating red and white two to three strands wide. The upper section repeats the tripartite basic form of each lower swath but spans the entire width and introduces an extra white line of beads within the two black border lines. There are eight somewhat narrower horizontal rows of beads that form two outer yellow sections and one inner section that alternates in the same red and white along the central section (Warden-Dorsey 1903–1906: Box 2, Folder 13: 7).

FIGURE 2.3
Beaded Yellow Oblong Tipi top ornament. Courtesy of the Division of Anthropology, American Museum of Natural History (AMNH 50/666).

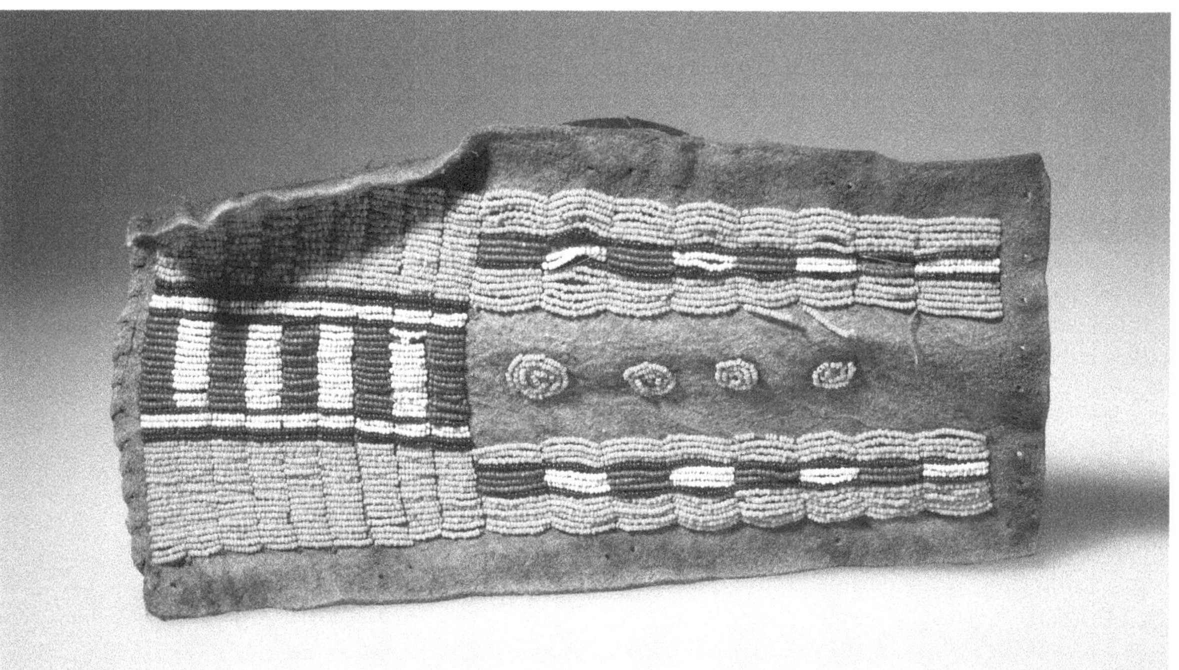

The trapezoidal pendant Warden describes and illustrates is roughly similar. On each end are fringes of yellow wool. Running along the entire length on both sides is a quilled line alternating between five yellow and four shorter white sections. Moving inward, this is followed by a solid yellow line, a white line, and another yellow. The lower half of the central section has six wider sections alternating in red and yellow. Above that, against a white background, are four yellow circles. Along the bottom are ten dark marks against a yellow background.

The overall symbolism is, in Warden's notes, "he-tan-nee" (*hiiteeni*), the life symbol referring to the Four Old Men, the watchmen of the four directions, seasons, and four-part order of time-space at all levels. Warden adds that the design is also in the shape of a buffalo. The dark straight lines are paths; the long yellow rows, rays of sunlight; the small dark checks, animals or buffalo. The alternating red and yellow horizontal bars in the central section represent the "heat or bright of sun." The four yellow circles below it are the four hills of life, or "struggle to old age." As in other contexts, yellow is a color of peace and prosperity. He adds that the short yellow circles are rays of sun, the hoof pendants puffs of breathing animals. In addition, "The yellow sections along the side on each edge are tipis in the camp circle. The yellow wool along the top and bottom aims to bring health or good prospects for tribe, no murders among the tribe."

With the set were twenty-two front pendants connoting "rain drops, tree tassels, or bird's feet." The front pendants Kroeber associates with the Yellow Oblong Tipi style are represented by two remaining pieces (AMNH 50/1060AB). Each has the three quilled thongs attached at the top with a pair of dewclaws and quilled loops at the bottom. Each thong has a yellow section at the top, a somewhat longer red section at the bottom, and a central white segment bounded by dark borders. Warden notes that the four side pendants were all yellow, though little else is known about them. In his drawings, Warden notes that there were twenty-two front pendants in all, including six on the side of each breastpin row and five on each ear (Warden-Dorsey 1903–1906: Box 2, Folder 19: 5).[3]

Council Tipi

One of the most remarkable artifacts adorned with quillwork art is the Arapaho tipi stored at the National Museum of Natural History (E18900-0) (plate 9), acquired in 1872 from Vincent Colyer, who was an artist, social reformer, and secretary to the Board of Indian Commissions. It is perhaps the oldest and best preserved Plains buffalo-hide tipi in museum collections, but no evidence survives about its place in women's quillwork traditions or the symbolic meanings it conveys. Accession records note that Colyer purchased it in 1869 from the Southern Arapaho Chief Little Raven, who described it as a "council tipi." Perhaps at times conjoined with another tipi to form an extra-large lodge, this tipi was probably used for the council meetings that included the Seven Old Men, the Old Men's society, the four chiefs, and the respective leaders of the men's age-grade lodges (Hilger 1952: 189). Among the four chiefs representing the four bands in either Arapaho tribe, one was recognized as the principal chief. By 1869 Little Raven would have been the principal Southern Arapaho chief, organizer of such meetings, and perhaps owner of the lodge.

The tipi is composed of fourteen hides and, unusually, has the quillwork ornaments sewn directly on it. As with other styles, there is one head ornament at the top rear and four small ornaments at the four directions roughly halfway up the side. The head ornament is uniquely ovate with a white background and a central red eagle or thunderbird figure. The entire ornament has fifty-two rows of quillwork and fifty-two black notches around the circumference, thus mirroring the number of peg holes and associated moons located on the circumference of robes and leanback covers discussed below. The bird form is similar, though without the set of markings, to the image on the red-style Eagle Design robe, also described below. At the top of the ornament is a thong of wrapped quillwork and at the bottom seven paired dewclaw ornaments with quilled loops and tufts of what seems to be buffalo hair. Each of the four side disks has the typical four rings of quillwork alternating between black and white. There are also seven of the typical triplicate ornaments with dewclaws and quilled loops on each ear. Below those, seven unique disk ornaments run parallel to the row of pin holes on each side, of which only four have dangling dewclaw ornaments attached. The tipi pin disks are more complex than the side disks. Each has seven quilled rings forming four tipi designs that together form the Morning Star cross. Between each tipi form, the rings alternate black and white.

All of the ornamentation conforms to the directional and number symbolism of the Four Old Men. The top ornament is a representation of either Thunderbird or the eagle, though in many instances in myth these two are referred to interchangeably. One can pray or pledge to Thunderbird, since he is one of the most powerful beings. He is most associated with the Spear Men and their habitus of quick and strong types of movement required of men in their roles of policing and defending the camp. It is significant that Dorsey (1903: 14) mentions that Thunderbird is also connected to the Four Old Men, since both he and they watch over the world and protect it from outside life-negating forces or beings. A parallel to the Eagle Design robe discussed below might also be relevant if indeed the tipi did serve for the chiefs' councils. Namely, the robe expresses overall a desire for a peaceful attitude or quietness, the type of motion and disposition appropriate to all council meetings and the fourth stage of life, as well as leaders in the second and third hills. The tipi seems to synthesize the two sides of Thunderbird and life itself: quick movements required for war in youth and stillness required in old age in general, for all who meet with elders, and as a type of strength in the face of approaching threats from outside. In all, like the highest-ranked robes and unlike some other forms, the tipi expresses colors and beings associated with the fourth hill of life.

Robes

Arapaho quilled robe styles are described in published works and unpublished documents, and several examples associated with these descriptions still survive in museum collections. A quillwork artist vowed to make a robe of a particular rank and style on behalf of a family member facing illness, going off on a war party, or in some other way being separated or challenged by hardship. Generally, robes were made for adult men, though one style was known as a child's robe and several were specific to women. As women advanced in quillwork apprenticeship and learning, they made increasingly more complex and higher-ranked robes requiring greater skill and time commitment for completion.

According to Kroeber, the two basic and most common robes had seventeen and twenty rows of quillwork, respectively, along the body length (1983: 29–30). The dominant color on the lines was yellow, with red designs interspersed. Solid red-lined robes apparently came later in history and were considered modern by 1900. The twenty-lined robe, called "niisa^{n}ûxt" (*niiso'ouht* 'it [animate] is a twenty robe'), had twenty single rows with another three sewn together along the bottom.[4] Another similar style had seventeen rows of quillwork with three rows together at the bottom. A Southern Arapaho quillwork artist named Mrs. One-Eye Left Hand told Kroeber in 1899 that the twenty-line style was for men and the seventeen-line type for women. Along the bottom of the twenty-lined robe were fifty or fifty-two dewclaw pendants. The seventeen-lined robe was apparently predominantly yellow and had only forty pendants at the bottom.

Small Red Painted Robe

This is probably the same style Warden lists as "Small Red Painted Robe" or "Small-Red-Pattern Robe" (in Arapaho, "Harechae-ba-hit-ho," which probably transcribes as *Heece[s]bee'eiht hou* 'it [animate] is a small red robe') (Warden-Dorsey 1903–1906: Box 3, Folder 26: 37a [1905]). Mrs. One-Eye Left Hand gave the name as *heecesbee'eyouhut* ('it [animate] is dressed/covered in small red designs') and contrasts it with another style called *heebesbee'eyouhut,* referring to large red designs. The distinction probably refers to the seventeen- and twenty-lined robes, respectively, but the precise difference is unclear from the evidence. According to Warden, the robe with the small red pattern has twenty lines apparently in yellow with red and white designs along them, as well as black fiber markers and red flannel tufts between sections:

> The twenty lines in colored quills reaching from one end to the other indicate trails or paths of people and animals. The red designs denote the effects of the sun upon vegetation and people. The dark fibres (water) signify moving creatures. The white designs in quills stand for holiness, love of nature. The red flannel is typical of the blood of people, but more especially of that of animals. One-half of the lines are quilled differently from the other half, for there is more glory or excitement some days than others. The robe derives its name from its small red designs. It referred to the life of fire. (Warden-Dorsey 1903–1906: Box 3, Folder 26: 37 [1905])

At the head, on the four leg sections, and on the tail of the hide are six designs each composed of five rows in similar quillwork. These are oriented more or less perpendicularly to the radial line of the hide and represent the "spreading seed of the people" (Warden-Dorsey 1903–1906: Box 2, Folder 13: 18). Each line has a larger red central section, as on almost all cradle lines and some other quilled lines. That section is bordered on each side by a white narrow square followed by a red narrow square, a longer yellow section, and an ultimate short section that alternates between red and white from one line to another, moving from top to bottom (diagram 2.2). All transitions are divided by black fiber borders. What is unique about the pattern is the recurrence of small red sections usually reserved for white in other quillwork lines. This perhaps accounts for the name of the robe.

Diagram 2.2
Small Red Painted Robe Line Designs

Yellow Calf Robe and Yellow Robe

Based on interviews with Firewood, a Northern Arapaho quillwork artist, Warden identifies and illustrates in his notebooks a style called "Yellow Calf Robe" or "Nehawnehit Waiho" (*Niihooneiht woo'(i)hou* 'it [animate] is a yellow calf robe'), also referred to as "Calf Robe." In his drawing notebook, Warden refers also to a "Yellow Robe," which seems to be the same design and was made only for a woman (Warden-Dorsey 1903–1906: Box 2, Folder 19: 27). The Yellow Calf Robe had sixteen parallel lines in yellow and red sections divided by two narrow white sections and thus three black dividers (diagram 2.3). The central red section was flanked by a yellow section on each side, followed by a red and then a yellow quilled section. There were somewhat wider black sections on the end of each line. Red tufts of flannel divided the sections of lines. As elsewhere, the quilled lines represented the paths of people and animals; the dark fiber dividers, the buffalo; the red tufts, blood of people and animals; and the bottom pendants, the tipi rattles as ornaments along the front ears and breast-pins of a tipi. At five points were yellow buckskin strings that connoted "blessings of the sun," with loop-hoof pendants referring to the "hearts of the people" or tipis of women, and yellow wool tufts hanging from inside the dewclaws meaning "excellence of people" (Warden-Dorsey 1903–1906: Box 2, Folder 13: 14–16). According to Warden, there were thirty pairs of hoof-loop pendants in a line on the bottom of the robe. Each pair had the typical seven sections of yellow and white on the top strings terminating in dewclaws and quilled loops with yellow sections on the top end of the loop followed by the double white/triple black marker sections, and a central red section on the bottom.

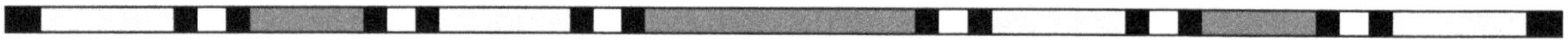

Diagram 2.3
Yellow Calf Robe Line Design

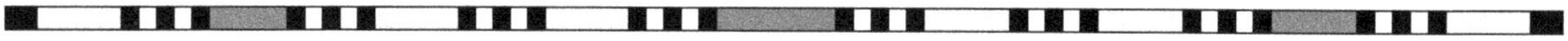

Diagram 2.4
Yellow Robe Line Design

Rattle Robe

Another style with twenty lines made for women was called Rattle Robe or Legged Rattle Robe, rendered in Arapaho in Warden's orthography as "He ah thi ka kŭ nare hit hō o" (transcribed into the modern Arapaho form as *Hi'oo3iikokounoohit hou*).

In Firewood's account of this style, she recalled one she made while visiting the Sioux that she gave to Bird Woman upon returning to Wind River. On this style there are no short-line designs on the appendages, head, or tail. The color sequence for lines is similar to that on the Yellow Calf Robe. The quilled lines in yellow and red are iconic representations of "trails or paths with blessings from sun." The black fiber boundary markers refer to moving creatures and the red flannel pieces, again, the blood of humans and animals. The long lines at both ends are for "beauty," according to Warden. Unique to this robe are two oblong rectangular pendants at the bottom, regarded as the legs of the robe and meaning the sun rays upon the earth. The quilled design of these oblong forms is in three equal sections, including a central red section and two outer yellow sections, divided by two narrow white lines. The hoof rattle pendants at the bottom as a whole suggest tipi rattles, while the pairs of strings in them are the "mercy of four old men." Each string has the typical four sections of yellow alternating with three white sections. The dewclaws at the ends are "hearts or tipis of people." The yellow wool tufts on them are the "glory or beauty" of the tipi (Warden-Dorsey 1903–1906: Box 2, Folder 13: 19-20; Folder 19: 10–11). As on most robes and leanbacks, there are fifty-two stake holes, representing tipi peg holes.

Double-Headed Green Robe

Firewood also identified to Warden a style called the Double- or Forked-Headed Green Robe, "Nare ne soo/nare-ate/cha net a nehit ho" 'forky/head/green/robe (*Neniisoo' noote' ceneeteeneiht hou*) (Warden-Dorsey 1903–1906: Box 2, Folder 13: 19–20; Folder 19: 22). This robe likewise had twenty rows of quillwork with the five short lined designs at the head and feet of the hide. There was also a quilled fork-shape design on the head portion of the robe. Each quilled line centered on a red section bordered by a green divider on each side, then a black section, green divider, red section, red divider, yellow section, green divider, black section, green divider, red section, green divider, black section, green divider, and terminating in alternating green and black from one row to the other. According to the Warden-Dorsey "Material Culture" manuscript (1903–1906: Box 3, Folder 26: 36–37 [1905]),

> The twenty lines on this robe denote trails. The designs at the extremities denote the scattering locations of both human and animal seeds. Each short line on the extremities had a pattern of red in the center, followed in each direction by a green divider, black section, green divider, yellow segment, and alternating green and black ends. The forky appearance of the head point[s] to the futures for men and women. All non-black sections or dividers were set off by black fiber borders. The designs in [black] quills or water fibres mean the earth's products. The red designs in quills refer to the sun's rays or heat from the sun. The green designs denote vegetation, while pieces of flannel typify race or blood of animals.

Ear-Pattern Robe

Another quilled robe style Warden classifies as "Ear Robe or Ear-Pattern Robe," or "Henaw-taln-nehit-ho" (*Hinotononeiht hou* 'it [animate] is an eared-robe'). On the neck of the hide are two painted dark, curved designs representing buffalo horns and, near those, two quilled designs representing the ears. Small curved designs in dark paint and yellow quills around the outside stake holes represent tipi pins, of which there were fifty-two, as on most robes. There are eight quilled lines from end to end representing trails of people and animals, and seven alternating straight black painted lines signify rivers. The quilled lines have yellow and red quills, only without black fiber borders. A narrow triangular tail was also quilled in the same pattern as the two ears, moving from the wide end to the tip from yellow to red divider, yellow to red section, yellow to red divider, and a yellow end. Quilled designs on the tails denote the path of a single animal, and the two hoof pendants attached to the tail symbolize victory of a chief or warrior.

Painted Robe

A robe style considered highest in value is simply called Painted Robe, translated from Warden's Arapaho script "Watha-nawhit-ho" (*Woo3onoheiht hou*), though it combines painted designs with embroidered quillwork forms. The style appears in the Arapaho story of "The Deceived Man and the Deserted Children" (Dorsey and Kroeber 1903: 286–93; see chapter 4), in which an abandoned girl acquires the power to make quillwork. Among all the items she makes, the Painted Robe is stacked on the top as the most valuable of all. Though of high rank, the overall design was a simple style and similar in overall form to the Ear-Pattern Robe, but without the head ornament. Like the Ear-Pattern Robe, this style had eight quilled lines alternating with seven black painted lines, but with no other ornamentation besides the fifty-two yellow arcs around the periphery of the hide representing tipi stakes. The quilled lines were also apparently identical to those on the Ear-Pattern Robe style, also lacking black dividers between longer segments of red and yellow only. Red tufts were dispersed along the lines at points of color transition.

Painted Circle Robe

Another style was the Painted Circle Robe, which had eight horizontal quilled lines alternating with seven black painted lines overlain by four disk forms in yellow and red. Each disk had a yellow background and red cross design (diagram 2.5). Like the Ear-Pattern Robe, the quilled lines on this robe did not have black dividers between colors. As on almost all quilled lines, a red section was central, followed by six medium-length yellow sections divided by six accompanying very narrow red sections. On the head of the robe there were also two black painted horns. Warden's notes on the design are as follows:

> Wathanahit, kawanenehit [*Woo3onoheiht koo'oneneiht*] (painted, round pattern). The two dark curves on the head denote horns of the buffalo (robe) the half-circles around the edge of the robe ornamented in yellow quills denote tipi pins (52 in all). The four discs in red and yellow quills on this robe typify the energy of Whirlwind-Woman, when she was enlarging the earth by making such designs. It also represents the rays of the sun

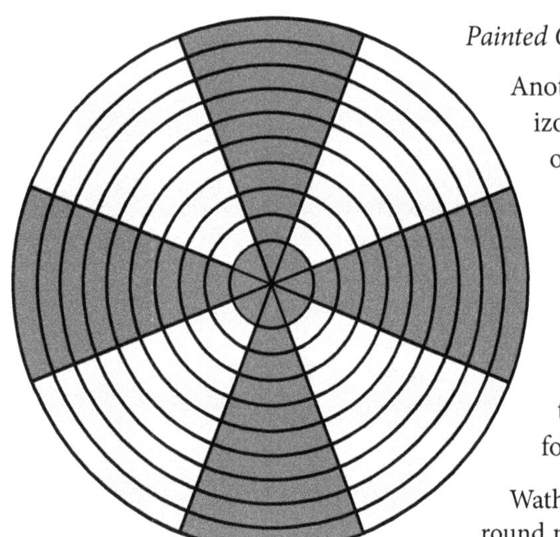

Diagram 2.5
Painted Circle Robe Disk Design

upon women and upon their works (see tipi designs in previous notebook). Seven dark straight lines in paint, reaching from one end to the other, denote rivers, while the eight yellow and red quill lines indicate trails or paths of human beings and animals. Pieces of red flannel attached to small red squares typify race of people. See story of woman ascending and the formation of old camp (circle) in the sky. (Warden-Dorsey 1903–1906: Box 3, Folder 26: 34 [1905])

The story cited is that discussed in chapter 4 titled "The Porcupine and the Woman Who Climbed to the Sky" (Dorsey and Kroeber 1903: 321–41) or "Little-Star" (Dorsey 1903: 212–28).

Eagle Robe

The Eagle Robe ("NareNē-ā-yo-hit" in Warden's script; *Nenii'ehiiyouhut* 'it [animate] is an eagle robe' in modern form) is one of the rare cases in Arapaho quillwork in which an actual being is represented in quillwork. Four eagles overlie the line pattern. Along the length of the hide are forty rows of quillwork in yellow, red, white, and black, framed by five quilled designs of five similar but short rows each at the head and in each corner limb section of the hide. This is thus probably the robe referred to in myth as the "fortieth robe" (Dorsey and Kroeber 1903: 217). As on other robes, the long lines are paths of people and animals, while the peripheral designs denote the locations of kindreds and radiating of blessings to them. Warden notes that the line pattern is the same as on the Yellow Calf Robe. From the center moving outward in both directions, the long line pattern's symmetrical center is a red section marked off by a double-white/triple-black divider section, followed by two yellow sections bisected by a single red square with double-black line divider, then a longer red followed by a yellow section partitioned by a double-white/triple-black line transition, and ending in a short black section (diagram 2.6). The quintupled rows on the neck, tail, and legs are shorter versions of the same line, consisting of a central red section and one outer yellow section, all divided by the double-white transition and with a short black segment on each end (Warden-Dorsey 1903–1906: Box 2, Folder 19: 2–3). The yellow quilled sections on both refer to the light of day; the red, the race or blood of the people; and the dark fiber dividers, the shadows of animals and the universe.

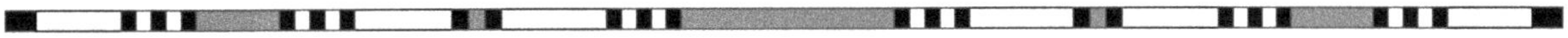

Diagram 2.6
Eagle Robe Line Design

The four large eagle figures that overlie the lines include two white eagles in the upper left and lower right quadrants and two red eagles in the upper right and lower left sections (diagrams 2.7 and 2.8). Similar to other Arapaho art forms in paint or beadwork, the four quilled eagles are geometrically formed with angular heads, beaks, and wings. In the modern Arapaho orthography, the two white eagles are called *Nonooku'eih3i' Nii'ehiiho'* 'white eagles' and the two red forms *Bee'eih3i' Nii'ehiiho'* 'red eagles' (Warden-Dorsey 1903–1906: Box 2, Folder 13: 8–11). Warden indicates that the two white eagles represent "Moon's powerful light" and the two red eagles "Sun's greatest light." All markings and designs on the white eagle form are of black fiber.

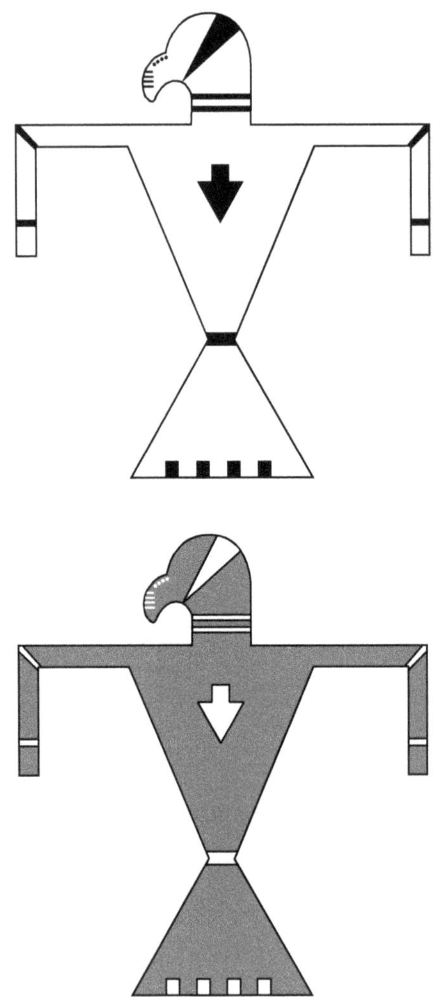

On each white eagle there is a black arrow shape descending down the throat and denoting a spear point, as well as the throat and heart of the animal. On the top of the beak are four dots indicating buffaloes in a row, referring to four stars in the sky. Four small horizontal lines near each beak's tip refer to the "collected or sitting council" constellation (the Pleiades) called in Arapaho *Benookuu3i'*, denoting old women sitting together doing quillwork. Four dark designs on the shoulders and wing tips represent the Four Old Men, which, together with three other designs, are the seven society lodges of the *beyoowu'u.* The four dots on each wing also symbolize the Four Old Men, in this case identified as "night, day, summer, and winter." The red eagle forms have similar symbolism but in white markings, connoting in total a "peaceable attitude" or what I have examined elsewhere as the "quiet life" toward which the ideal life road leads by the fourth stage of life (see Anderson 2001a: 73).

One Hundredth Robe

Another type of robe, called "One Hundredth Robe" (*Beteetesouhut* 'it [animate] is a hundred robe'), is mentioned in Kroeber's work (1983: 29–30) and the Arapaho story "Big Owl, Owner-of-Bag" (Dorsey and Kroeber 1903: 239–46). Warden indicates "Noisy Robe" as another name for the style and notes that it was made only for a man (Warden-Dorsey 1903–1906: Box 2, Folder 19: 31a). In the Big Owl story, the robe is identified as the highest ranked of all robes and quillwork. It apparently had one hundred parallel rows of quillwork, thus requiring a vow of one hundred days for a quillwork artist to complete it, at a required pace of one row per day. A robe with approximately one hundred rows is stored at the Field Museum (FMNH 87248), but it is in arsenic quarantine and thus inaccessible to researchers. However, Warden mentions in his drawing notes that there are actually only forty lines of quillwork on the robe. From a photograph in the Field Museum collections catalogue I was able to see yellow quillwork on the majority of each line with red tufts dividing yellow sections from sections of four dots together, one dot, and four more symmetrical to the other side. On each leg and on the head is a pattern of three staggered groups of four approximately seven-inch-long rows of quillwork in a pattern in approximate lengths of two inches of yellow, a red tuft, four inches of yellow, a red tuft, and two inches of yellow. From Warden's drawings, the pattern of quillwork on the line is, moving from outside to center from either end, a short black outer segment, followed by a yellow part, then a double white spacer with three black border lines, next a unique section of three red sections divided by two very short yellow segments only several quills thick without black dividers, then another double-white/triple-black lined divider followed by a yellow section, then a red narrow section with black line borders (diagram 2.9). In the center is another three-segment red design divided by two short yellow segments. Fifty single pendants surrounded the lined design. On each collarbone there were five pairs

Diagram 2.7
White Eagle Design

Diagram 2.8
Red Eagle Design

of dewclaw loop pendants. On the neck were two pairs of loops. All pendants had the typical seven alternating yellow-white sections on the thong, with a quilled loop of two yellow sections next to the dewclaw, followed by a white-with-black-line border divider and then a red section in the middle (lowest) point of the loop. As on several other higher-ranked robes, there were fifty-two painted yellow arcs around the peg holes originally used for staking the hide to stretch it.

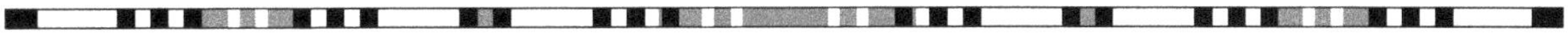

Diagram 2.9
One Hundredth Robe Line Design

The symbolism can only be drawn from what applies to other robes. The five extremity designs usually mean the seed of the people or desire for blessings extending to all the kindreds in the camp or tribe. Parallel rows are commonly paths of people and animals multiplied by the number lines, which in this case would seem to make the strongest statement of that recurring theme. The dominance of yellow generally refers to sunlight and hope for the future.

Arapaho Robe of Unidentified Style

A robe identified as Arapaho but not fitting Warden's or Kroeber's descriptions is held in the collections of the Peabody Museum of Archaeology and Ethnology (99-12-10/53120) (figure 2.4). The robe combines elements of known robe styles with those of leanback covers. There are thirty-one long rows of quills and five short rows, above which, near the head of the hide, are ears and a head disk. Recognizable designs of Yellow Lodge and Yellow Cradle styles are dominant, including oblong morning star figures. A unique fringe of ornaments around the top edge somewhat resemble the lattice on cradles (as well as leanback covers, discussed below). Unusual designs of yellow squares and three-pronged foot forms are possibly *hiiteeni* and bear-claw symbols, but no interpretation can be offered with great precision.

Leanback Covers

Another ranked object that women quillwork artists vowed and created under the guidance of the Seven Old Women is variously called a buffalo-skin pillow or leanback cover. Like other Plains peoples, Arapahos built beds with four tree-fork pieces for legs supporting rails and a willow-rod frame. On the each end was a leanback made of willow rods tied together in a tapered trapezoidal form set at an angle. Covers of buffalo hide with the hair on and quillwork designs were draped over the leanback and bed surface. Kroeber describes the cover as follows:

> Buffalo-skins, from the head and neck of the animal, were used to hang over the head of the bed. One of these skins seen by the writer was ornamented in the following manner.
>
> 1. The horns were not attached to the skin. Where the eye had been there was sewed one of the small circular tent-ornaments consisting of yellow and black concentric rings. 2. The place of the top of the head was covered by a quill-work ornament called the "brain," which was nothing else than one of the large circular

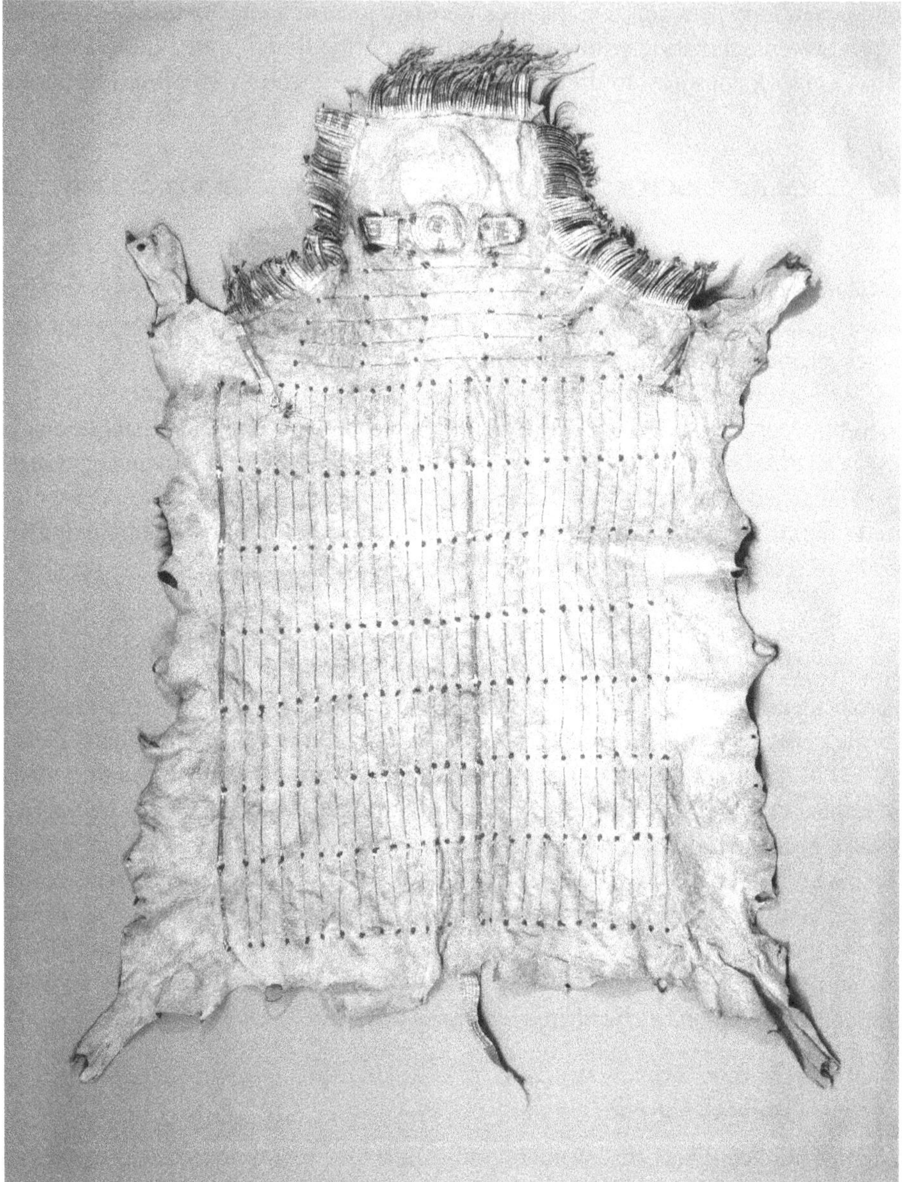

FIGURE 2.4
Arapaho robe of unidentified style classification. Courtesy of the Peabody Museum of Archaeology and Ethnology, Harvard University, 99-12-10/53120.

tent-ornaments of the style that lacks the black concentric rings. 3. The place of the ear was covered by a figure embroidered in beads and quills. This was trapezoidal, the smaller of the bases being convexly rounded. Most of it is yellow. The middle portion is red; this is bordered by two white stripes, which are edged by black lines. 4. Along the "throat," that is, along one of the sides of the piece of skin, was a fourth ornament. This consisted of two strips of hide extending the length of the skin, parallel to each other at a distance of about six inches. Connecting these were about thirty short strips of hide, each about half an inch wide. These strips were wound with corn-husk of the four colors,—red, yellow, black, and white. The arrangement and proportion of colors on these strips were identical with those on the ornament representing the ear. In addition, three or four smaller strips, with the same color-pattern, were put on each of the long pieces of hide, extending in the same direction as these; that is, vertically. (1983: 65–66)

In his notebook, Kroeber identifies the owner as Howling Man and the maker as his mother (1916–20: Notebook 7: 63). This is the object Kroeber mentions in a letter to Franz Boas discussed in chapter 6, asking for clarification as to whether he should buy things in such poor condition.

Although Kroeber comments, "It is probable that the last specimen of this kind has now perished" (1983: 66), one set of quilled ornaments and one nearly complete specimen are known now to exist in major collections. The two examples represent the two types Warden identified as "white-quilled," associated with the buffalo bull, and "yellow-quilled," which, though not indicated explicitly, is probably associated with the female buffalo. A leanback cover of the yellow type (figure 2.5), though lacking the brain ornament, is preserved at the National Museum of the American Indian (NMAI 101936), but it is identified as Cheyenne in origin. The evidence for Cheyenne quillwork is small, so this could very well be a style shared with Arapahos, but no description of such a leanback cover is provided by George B. Grinnell (1924) or Winfield Coleman (1980). The color pattern of yellow-black-white-black-red-black-white-black-yellow is also uniquely Arapaho. Further, the array along the "throat" of this magnificent specimen is exactly how Kroeber describes it and is similar in form to those described only for Arapaho cradles and leanback covers.

The second style is called *Heneecee bee'iitóoó*, derived from Warden's transcription *Harenarecha-bai-tall* (1902: 9–10), and meaning literally 'buffalo bull blood-bed.'

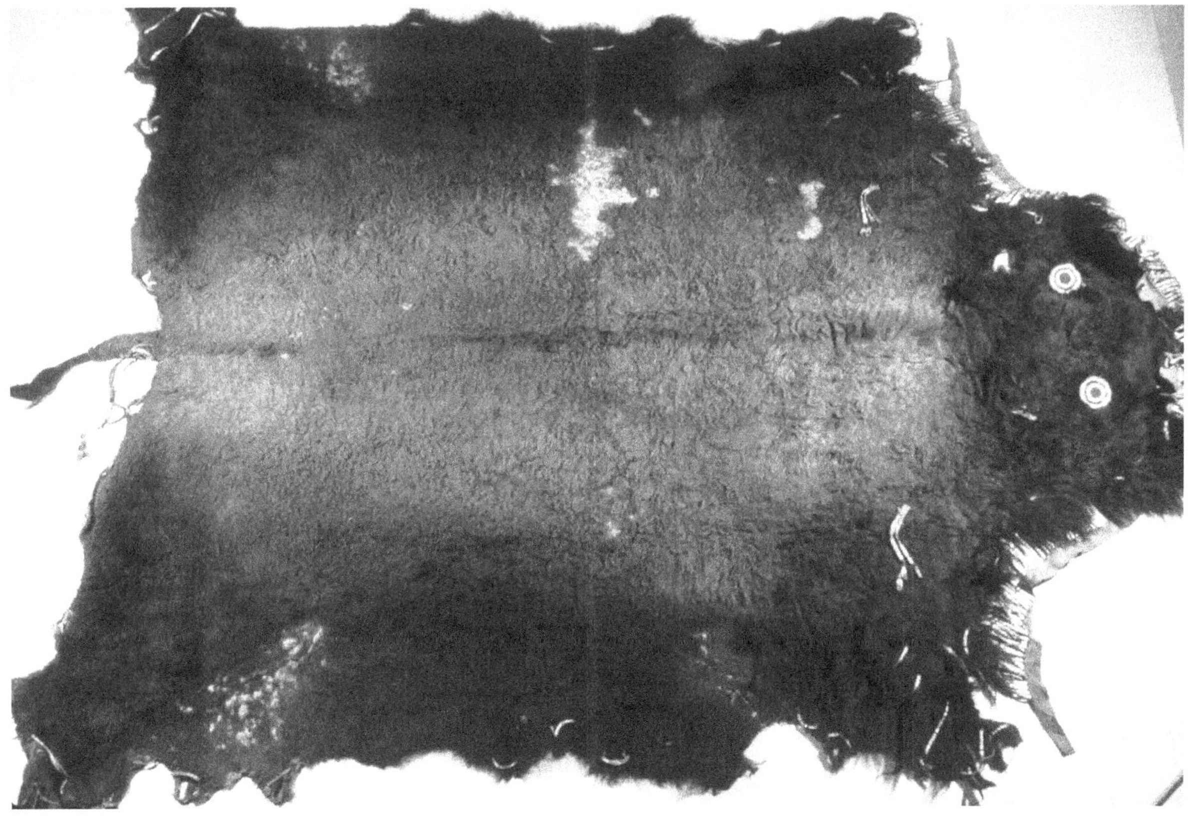

Figure 2.5
Yellow Style leanback cover. Courtesy of the National Museum of the American Indian, cat. no. 101936.

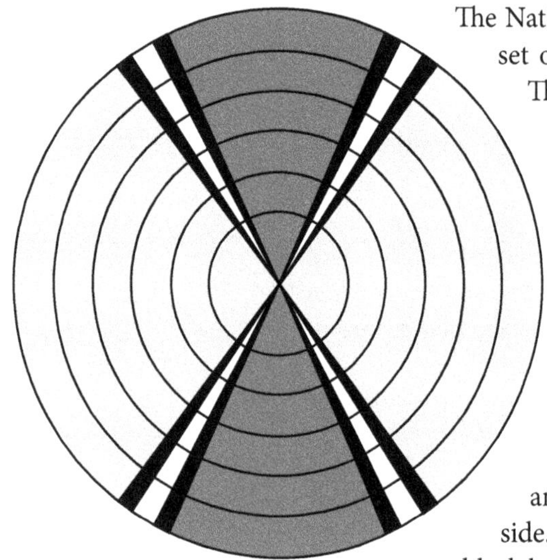

The National Museum of Natural History (NMNH E165791-0) has a set of eye, brain, and ear ornaments that conforms to this style. Though identified in the catalogue records as "tent ornaments," the set is described as "Quilled ornaments used on backrest of tipi owner" on an accompanying card. The pieces of the set are sewn together. The museum acquired the set in 1893, six years before Kroeber's field research, from H. R. Voth, a Mennonite missionary among Southern Arapahos, though its original owner is not identified. The red sections on the ears and brain disk have faded to brown, and all but the dark sections, done in black fibers, are made from porcupine quills. The brain disk is similar in form to, but smaller than, both tipi and cradle disks. It has the common red tipi triangular forms along the vertical axis and a larger field on either side. The difference is that the spokes of the cross are yellow with black borders and the field is white, a unique combination for quilled disks.

Diagram 2.10
Yellow-Quilled Leanback Cover Disk Design

Following the same pattern as the disk in the set (plate 10) but in a line, on the ears are two white outer sections and a central red section divided by two yellow segments with black fiber borders. The pattern is thus white-black-yellow-black-red-black-yellow-black-white. The small eye disks have four rings alternating from black in the center ring to white on the outer ring. The width of all quilled rows and rings on the two available examples is somewhat wider than on cradle or tipi ornamentation.

Warden learned about this style from the accomplished quillwork artist Firewood, based on one she once made for her son (with the Anglicized name William Shakespeare). The cover was eventually sold to whites. This style of leanback, she explained, was made for a young man by a senior woman. Warden gives this full account about the symbolism of the Buffalo Bull Blood-Bed type:

> The tipi stake pins are called "jaysaw[ ]ana" (baby-lump-hair—which is seen tied on the forehead) [*ce'iisoono'* 'lump of hair babies'], there being 52 in all. Work begins with the disc, eyes, ears, and the rest until it is cleansed for use. The central disc on the forehead denotes the sun with its rays in different colors. It also signifies the brain of the robe (animal). All the triangles in the disc mean tipis (see symbolism on tipi designs on former notes, 1903, which took also various kinds of cradles). Small rotary discs in white and dark quills denote the eyes of the robe (animal). Just at the right of the eyes are two quilled designs which denote the horns of the robe (animal).
>
> The seven dark quills on white quills at the end of the nose of the robe (animal) denote periods from creation, and the quilled bars which are fastened to the front end of the buffalo also denote ages of the people, but in this place they signify the beard or hair of the animal. The whole design is one piece which has two pieces of rawhide or tanned pieces of buckskin or elk skin to which these quilled "bars" are sewed or fastened, as indicated in the drawing. The curves in white quills denote tipi pins, of which there are 52. The four quilled designs at the extremities typify locations of people as well as referring to the Four-Old-Men. The design, which is broader towards the center, on the tail of the robe signifies

a path. The pendant hoofs from shoulders represent the instinct, voice, beauty of the animal (robe). The dark field represents the hide (hair) of the robe. (Warden-Dorsey 1903–1906: Box 3, Folder 26: 21–21a [1905])

As on cradles, the brain disk is associated with the sun. As on tipi and cradle disks, the acute triangular forms in the disk represent tipis. As for tipi ornaments, the small similar disks are associated with eyes. Continuous with robe symbolism, the fifty-two peg holes made when stretching the hide are decorated and represent tipi peg holes, as well as baby's hair. According to Warden's drawings, there were also four loops above the rows on the front legs in the same pattern found on the ears and tail piece (Warden-Dorsey 1903–1906: Box 2, Folder 19: 18–19).

Other Quilled Items

At one time, women also vowed to apply rows of quillwork to a tipi door (figure 2.6) with a round or rectangular willow structure to support the hide. Warden notes that a Southern Arapaho woman named War-Path vowed to make a door for the safe delivery of her child (Warden-Dorsey 1903–1906: Box 3, Folder 26: 15 [1905]). The door symbolism as a whole was said to represent *hiiteeni,* the life principle associated with the Four Old Men and the four directions.

A woman could also vow to make a tipi liner that would form a wall inside the tipi, primarily on the west side, as an extra break against the wind. No quilled tipi liners exist in major collections, but several beaded examples have survived. The Field Museum has three (FMNH 58011, 58012, 58097), all of which Warden acquired in Wyoming in 1905. Each is a scraped hide with a series of rows running along the length, much like robes, though fewer in number in all cases: one has eight rows, another six, and the last four. All rows follow the familiar pattern of five sections, including one middle red section, two yellow sections on either side of that, and two outer red sections. On one (FMNH 58011), this pattern is inverted for yellow and red in alternating rows. Two red tufts mark transitions between the large sections. One (FMNH 58012) has a series of ornaments with red feather tufts and tin cones instead of dewclaws along the top. Another (FMNH 58097) has a row of morning star cross designs with paired black feather pendants between the second and third lines, a row of small circles with quill-wrapped tuft pendants between the first and second lines, and another row of circles but with black feather ornaments between the third and fourth lines. A beaded canvas tipi liner with typical quillwork patterns was on display in 2005 at Matthew Chase, Ltd., in Santa Fe. It has twenty parallel rows of beadwork in the typical Arapaho pattern. Each row has a central red section bordered on each side by two somewhat longer yellow sections followed by another red section of the same width, two more yellow sections, a red section, and two outer yellow sections. All sections are bordered by the traditional white with black bordered dividers, each with a red tuft. Across the top above the lines are fourteen small disks in yellow, black, and red beadwork patterns. Hanging from the center of each disk and between each disk is the common pair of thongs, each terminating in a dewclaw-loop pendant. The disk pattern is somewhat unusual (diagram 2.11).

Each dewclaw also has a yellow tuft hanging beneath it. The loops appear to be wrapped with corn-husk fiber in the Arapaho style of a red bottom section and

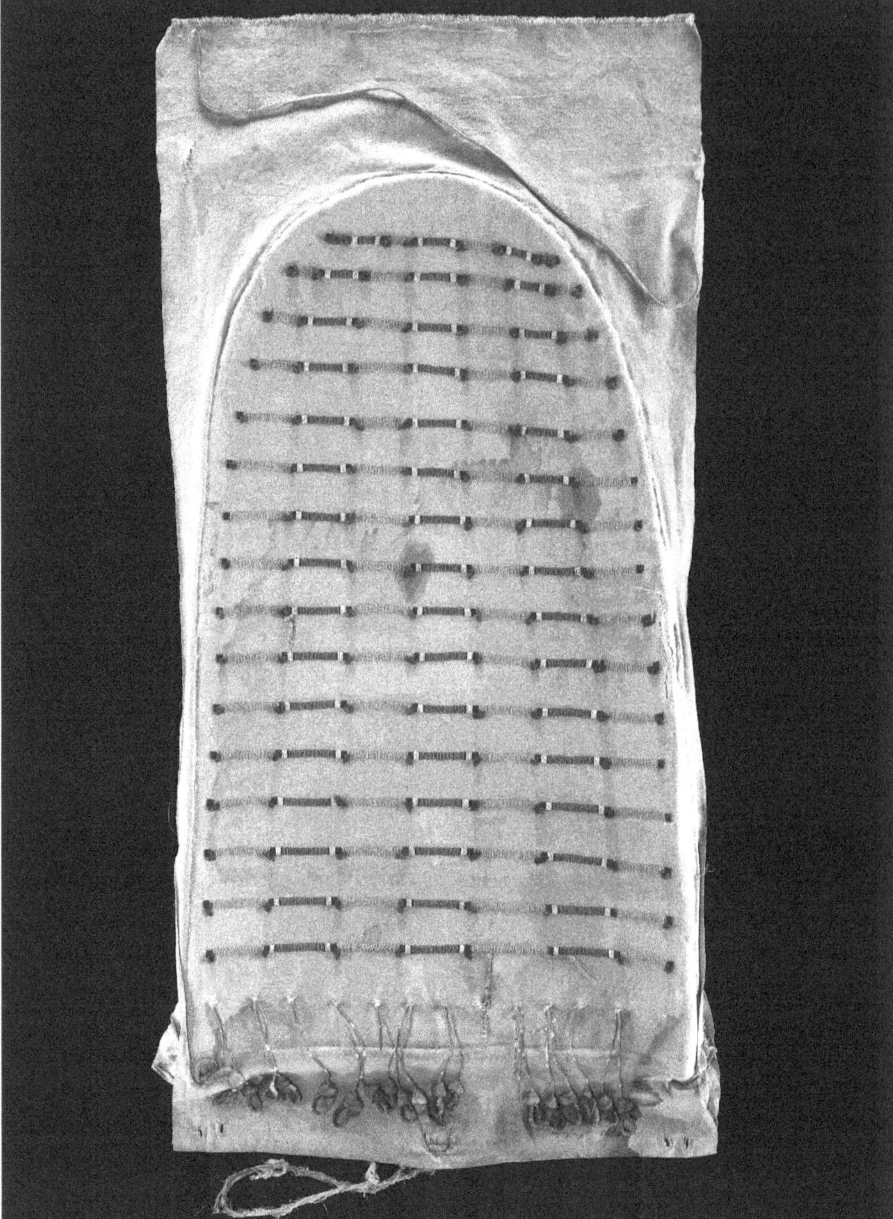

Figure 2.6
Beaded tipi door in quillwork style. Department of Anthropology, Smithsonian Institution, cat. no. 165793.

two outer yellow ones, divided by the black-white-black divider. There are a total of thirty ornaments, including the fourteen on the disks and sixteen others. Beneath the central pendant above the central red section of lines are three more pendants arranged vertically. Given the beadwork and corn-husk material for loops, the liner was probably made in Oklahoma. The only information about its origin is that it was acquired by a man named Myers in the 1880s.

Quill decorated shirts are a great mystery in the Arapaho case. They were apparently intermediate in rank to and transitional on a quillworker's learning path between beginners' projects, such as moccasins, and larger projects, such as robes (Dorsey and Kroeber 1903: 239–46). Apparently, there were two styles: (1) a short style with quilled swathes along the tops of both sleeves and two stripes running down both sides of the chest; and (2) a scalp-lock style, with two quilled disks, one on the front and another on the back. There are no known verifiable examples of Arapaho men's quilled shirts in major museum collections, though two beaded Arapaho shirts with scalp-lock ornaments supported by quill-wrapped bindings are in the Carnegie Museum collections (CMNH 279, 285). One of these (CMNH 285) conforms roughly and in some respects to the style called "short shirt," but the designs on the shirtsleeves from neck to cuff are in beadwork. These cannot be correlated to the two quilled styles, for which no descriptions are given in either Kroeber's or Warden's published or unpublished materials. Quillwork artists consulted around 1900 do not mention shirts in their counts of the various projects completed in their lifetimes.

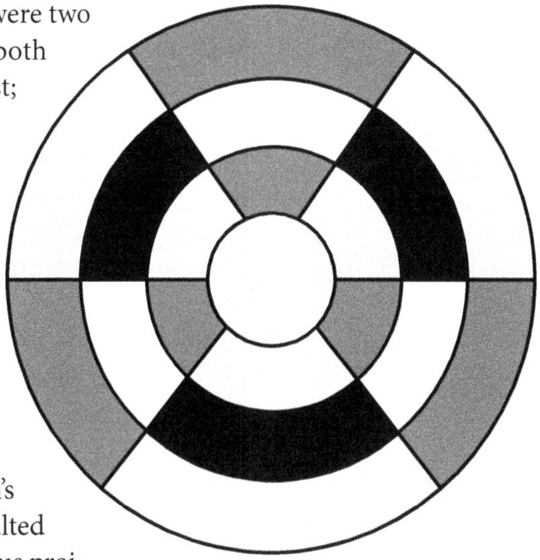

DIAGRAM 2.11
Tipi Liner Disk Design

Quillwork also appeared on moccasins, pillows, possible bags, navel amulet bags, various items in most of the ceremonial lodges, and many other everyday objects. Moccasins are mentioned in several myths as the first in the sequence of projects a women quillwork artist was required to complete in her career, but there is no mention of a required vow or ceremony. A few quilled Arapaho moccasins survive in existing collections. The basic style (plate 11) has horizontal rows of predominantly red quills across the instep, often broken with segments of yellow or black, as well as red tufts. Some pairs have a line of beadwork around the lower border of the entire upper portion and, less frequently, another line of beads on the top of the instep above and parallel to the quilled lines. Kroeber's account (1983: 44–46) is the only published interpretation of the symbolism for any examples of this style. A pair of children's moccasins at the American Museum of Natural History (AMNH 50/1031AB) has seven rows of quillwork across the instep, each consisting of a short yellow section on each end, and a blue section in the center segment that tapers in length from the top to the end line on the instep.[5] The black segments combined, then, form the isosceles trapezoidal form common in so much Arapaho quillwork design. Kroeber notes that the white background for the beaded border is the "ground" and the green zigzag line on it a snake. White is often the ground or background in nonritualized art forms, and the snake design is homologous with the Plains sign language gesture for the animal itself. Two green squares at the heel of each moccasin in the white border connote the covers of the sweat lodge. The quilled lines represent the poles of the sweat lodge, while the different colored quills symbolize the stones of the sweat lodge, which for Arapahos are flat, round stones gathered from a river.

The Field Museum (FMNH 61393) collection includes a much more elaborate pair of lined-path moccasins that Warden collected in Wyoming in 1900. Quilled parallel lines extend along the entire length of each moccasin, including twenty rows on the instep section. The red central sections of the rows on the instep form the recurring long, isosceles trapezoid, while predominantly yellow lines extend along each side of the red segments all the way back to the heel. In the center of each lateral yellow segment are black-bordered squares that alternate between red and white from line to line. Red tufts divide the red and yellow sections of the lines and border the entire design. A white beaded line runs along the bottom of the upper section, with a pair of blue squares at the toe and red and blue squares spaced throughout.

Warden's unpublished notes about this pair indicate that they were made of elk hide. The meaning of the parallel quill lines, he relates, are paths of life. The red section in total symbolizes the owner's skin. Red tufts on each side of the red center section signify heat. The yellow scheme as a whole relates to a young fawn. The black and white alternating centers denote a mature fawn, and the black breaks in each line, buffalo bugs. The two little blue squares at the toe refer to the life principle of *hiiteeni,* while the two small strings of elk hide at each heel symbolize paths of life (Warden-Dorsey 1903–1906: Box 3, Folder 26: 47 [1905]). A similar pair at the Denver Art Museum (DAM 1951.362) has ten rows across the instep with the red central pattern forming a trapezoid bounded by red margin tufts from a yellow quilled segment on the outside, also terminating in red tufts. There are thus four tufts to each line, forty in all. A white beaded background line with blue designs marks the bottom of the upper section. Another pair at the Field Museum (FMNH 61262) has ten quilled rows on the instep in colors appearing as orange/red for the central segment and yellow for the outer segments. Red tufts and short black dividers mark the transition between yellow and red segments. Triple quilled rows on the top and sides are presented in orange, black, blue, and yellow that form a rectangle at the toe, and there are rectangular morning star forms on the sides and top of the instep. The circumference is beaded with blue mountain symbols against a white background.

Quilled pillows are another item that women quillworkers made to furnish lodges. The only surviving pillows are found in the Field Museum and Carnegie Museum, and the only descriptive material is available in notes from Warden and Dorsey supporting the latter collection (Carnegie Museum of Natural History n.d.). Most pillows in those collections acquired around 1900 are beaded, but several apparently older examples are quilled. Pillows are rectangular and about twice as long as they are wide, with a one-piece white hide cover stuffed with deer, antelope, or buffalo hair. Typically, only one side is decorated, leaving the other for resting the head. Most have a series of evenly spaced quilled or beaded lines running parallel or perpendicular to the length of the pillow and paired pendants at the four corners.

CMNH 3179-204 (figure 2.7) is one of the most spectacular quilled pillows. Sewn with sinew, it appears to be quite old. The embroidered side has four pairs of quilled lines running across the width of the pillow, forming three sections. Each outer section has two five-pointed stars above and below a central cross in the middle. The lines in each pair are about an inch apart. The line pattern has five yellow sections divided by four shorter red sections with black dividers. Each red section and star has a red feather tuft as well. At each corner of the pillow is a pair of red and yellow striped quilled thongs, each ending in a cone ornament securing a yellow tuft. According to Warden's notes, the pillow was made for a young girl with the following meanings: "Parallel lines running across the body of pillow denote trails of crawling insects. Colored porcupine quills signify their wanderings, some long and short. Red feathers mean the heat from the sun. Four spotted stars typify human hands, because they have five points, five fingers on each hand. Colored crosses at

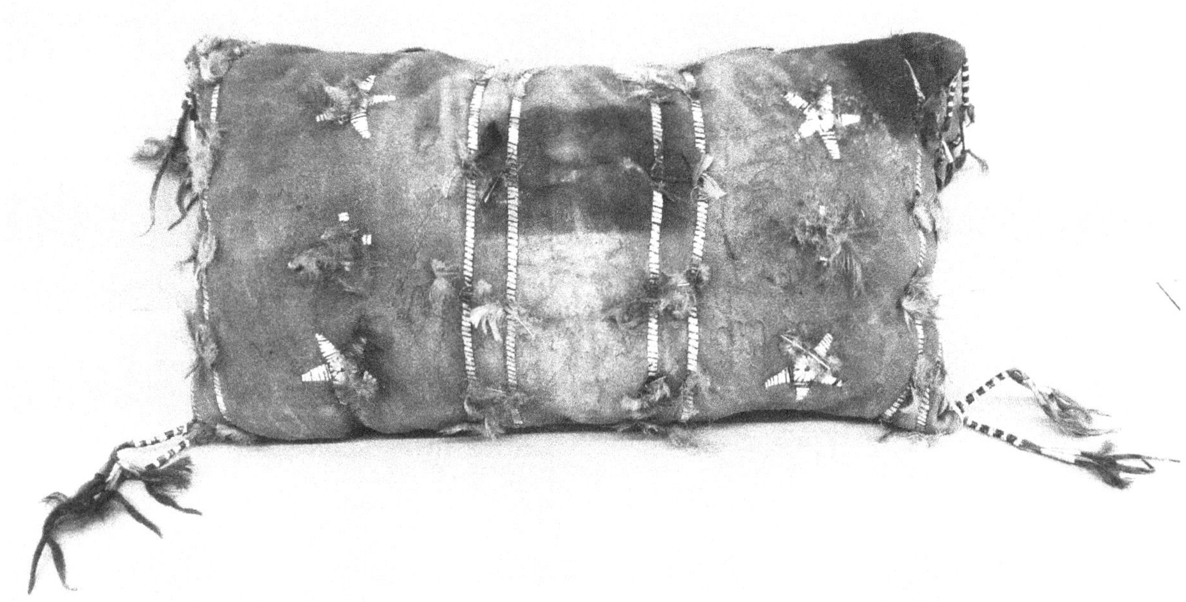

FIGURE 2.7
Pillow. Courtesy, Carnegie Museum of Natural History (CMNH cat. no. 3179-204).

each end signify the brilliancy of Morning Star, called "Now kaw k" (*Nookoox*) or Little Star. Pendants at corners are sun rays, and the notches at ends denote hazy atmosphere" (Carnegie Museum of Natural History n.d.). Insects, reptiles, amphibians, and small mammals are commonly associated with childhood, as on navel bags made for infants.

Another excellent example from the same collection (CMNH 3179-243) has seven quilled longitudinal rows, each with a central red section and two outer yellow sections (plate 12). The yellow and red segments are divided by a short white section with black borders. At each corner are a red quilled square and a pair of red-quilled thongs with hoof pendants and red feather ornaments. Warden offers the following interpretation of the designs: "The seven parallel lines in colored quills denote buffalo trails; the hoof pendants, hearts of people; the orange [faded red] feathers, a gentle disposition and good conscience; the red binding, the blood; the four orange [faded red] spots, sunbeams; the red quills, heat from the sun; the yellow quills, light of day; the white quills, peace and snow; the dark quills, buffalo. The pillow represents a young calf" (Carnegie Museum of Natural History n.d.).

Two other less elaborate quilled pillows from the same collection have longitudinal lines of quills in red and green. CMNH 3179-203 has five horizontal quill lines in red, blue, and green. There are paired tin cone ornaments with red feathers at each corner. Notes from Warden and Dorsey state, "This pillow represents a mole & at the same time the earth. The tin pendants at the ends denote the feet of the mole & the red painted feathers the dirt that the animal throws up. The five parallel lines on the pillow are symbols of sun rays. The dark fibers denote the charcoal produced by intense heat, the red and green are the colors of fire when blazing. This pillow is for a boy under 10 years of age. Its contents consist of antelope and deer hair" (Carnegie Museum of Natural History n.d.).

The other similar example (CMNH 3179-206) has six solid red horizontal lines and, at the ends of these, two vertical alternating yellow and green lines. There are six pendants on the outside seam, including four on the corners and two on the short sides. The notes indicate that this was a young boy's pillow and that it "denotes a ground squirrel from the fact that its back is specified by red parallel lines. These lines also denote human trails ending at glorious days. Green & yellow for good seasons. Green pendants, as parts of animal, means [*sic*] the head, tail and four feet. White clay of pillow for health and purity of person" (Carnegie Museum of Natural History n.d.).

The various pillows at the Field Museum are similar in form but employ beadwork of a much wider range of colors than on quilled types, which tend to stay within the four basic Arapaho colors. This suggests that the shift to beadwork brought greater variation in the use of colors, though the shapes and overall composition tended to persevere. The same shift applies to many other items, such as moccasins, various bags, and clothing styles.

Drawing general conclusions about Arapaho quilled pillows is difficult, given the small number of remaining examples and the complete lack of information about adult styles and symbolism. Children's pillows seem to have combined some of the stylistic elements of bags in general and symbolic aspects of navel bags, such as the representations of small animals or insects.

One type of quillwork not mentioned as part of ritualized production are bags variously called saddle bags, soft bags, toilet bags, or women's work bags. These bags were probably made in identical pairs, a custom among other Plains groups. For example, bags 50/25 (plate 13) and 50/26 at the American Museum of Natural History are identical in every way except that the former has fourteen rows of quillwork, the latter thirteen. Each bag usually has five sets of four pairs of horsehair with tin cone ornaments: four on the ends and one along the top flap. Kroeber mentions that the parallel red lines on the front of quilled bags connote paths, as similar lines also symbolize on robes. The tufts of hair with tin cones, he adds, symbolize pendants or rattles and tents associated with quilled ornaments (1983: 101–102). Typically, there are three or four sections of beadwork on each side and along the flap. These generally refer to campsites and trails. Lined bags are nowhere mentioned as part of ritualized quillwork. Whether these required supervision or marking by one of the Seven Old Women is unclear, as is whether a vow was required. Such bags were likely a part of the wedding gifts made by a wife's aunts and mothers for the new couple (see FMNH 61256, 61386, 67323, 67321, 67325).

CHAPTER THREE

Many Paths to Meaning

The aims and methods of early ethnographic studies of Native American cultures, such as those that produced the results in chapters 1 and 2, have been subjected to ruthless revisionist critiques both from inside anthropology and from indigenist perspectives. Such critiques tend to caricature past interpretive anthropological approaches by reifying simple binaries and generalizations about ethnographic encounters without considering the specific facts of each particular case. The greatest sources of distortion are to misread such early ethnography, including that about quillwork, as (1) reducing all the evidence to a solely imposed, even colonizing external view that denies local agency and voice; (2) "merely" descriptive and thus lacking conceptual sophistication; (3) based on a static and closed concept of culture; or (4) restricted to the mission of interpreting one-to-one referential connections between designs and meanings and failing to complete that mission.

Responding to the second criticism, the material here is indeed primarily descriptive, but it is richly so, and perhaps this is a lost skill in ethnographic writing. Alfred L. Kroeber's descriptions of objects and ceremonies are highly detailed, remarkably empirical, and, I believe, humanistic in tone. At no point does he insert statements of a superior moral or epistemological position, and in almost all cases he is simply relating what consultants told him. His observations are also not confined to regaining a gaze on past traditions alone, for he includes records of then-newer traditions, such as the practice and arts of the Crow Dance, Ghost Dance, and Peyote religion. Kroeber's descriptions of the quillwork ceremonies themselves (included in full in chapter 5) are among the best ethnographic observations of that generation. One of the reasons for this is that Cleaver Warden was there, too, not simply as an extra pair of eyes, but with eyes trained in Arapaho ways of observing and learning. Kroeber and Warden were probably the only men ever allowed into quillwork ceremonies, and the former the only non-Indian ever to observe them. Other contemporary anthropological views may diverge, but I do not believe that Kroeber was intrusive or exploitative. Following the protocols of Arapaho conservatism, all such issues would have been deliberated and decided by consensus among the very senior elders of the time before permission would have been granted. Clearly, Kroeber, Warden, and Dorsey were denied permission to enter some other contexts or acquire some sacred objects. The irony remains, though: Arapahos are perhaps the most religiously conservative people in the Plains area and among the most conservative in North America, yet they freely shared vast amounts of information about religion.

Unlike some other groups, by 1900 Arapaho elders and chiefs had embraced literate forms of knowledge and education in such knowledge as having the power to preserve the present and give direction to the future (see Anderson 2001a: 288–89). In this case, Warden served as the intermediary and translator between not only languages but also ways of knowing. As introduced at the outset, one unique aspect of the evidence is that it is saturated with an interpretive eye and voice that are uniquely Arapaho and not just those of Euro-Americans or trained anthropologists. The sweeping generalization that salvage ethnography was based on the observer versus observed binary or Euro-American versus indigenous opposition does not apply here. Though at one level it could be assumed that Cleaver Warden merely followed George Dorsey's directions and at times Kroeber's Boasian mandates about what information and objects to collect in the field, he clearly took an active role in the interpretive process. Warden and those he interviewed offered a uniquely Arapaho way of seeing and talking about language, art, and ritual practice. While critics of the ethnographic mission are anxious to dismantle colonizing gazes that reify alterity, they are still reluctant to recognize indigenous perspectives as actual theoretical orientations commensurate with academic ones. I agree with Marsha Bol (1996: 120) when she suggests, about early anthropological studies, "Perhaps the flaw was not in the information that was transmitted, however, but in the way the information was analyzed by the receivers." Bol has been successful in showing that both Warden as researcher and women as quillwork artists had a fair share of agency in published and unpublished knowledge about quillwork. Returning to the opening narrative for this book, one can read in Warden's work a unique Arapaho way of seeing, voicing, and understanding motion, shape, and connections in language, art, and narrative that is still very much alive today in Arapaho communities. In fact, Warden was an ethnographer of a part of his culture that he had never seen or known before but used his general knowledge to make sense out of it all. For one thing, almost all of the allusions in the evidence that connect quillwork to mythical narratives come from Warden and quillwork artists themselves, such as Firewood. To mainstream anthropology, the type of research Warden conducted has been discarded to the past, but my field experience in the Northern Arapaho community makes clear that this is exactly the type of inquiry in which local scholars, elders, and educators are engaged and for which much more work needs to be done for developing cultural education. At Wind River, Warden remains a role model for bringing cultural and formal education together.

As Bol reflects (1996: 120), the mission of Kroeber and some of Boas's other students has been caricatured as a simple referential semiology: "In the last twenty-five years scholars have begun to discount the results of these early field investigations because . . . the effort to assign one-to-one relationships between design motifs and meanings did not prove successful." Critics who hold such a standard have made at least several errors. First, they have reduced the range of symbolic meanings to a referential or denotative function. While not always named as such, the evidence reveals other, various levels and dimensions of meaning for the forms, colors, numbers, materials, ritual practices, and contexts of quillwork. Kroeber and Warden also provide many residual comments and notations about symbolism in Arapaho quillwork, as well as myriad nascent connections for a rich contextualized understanding of multiple symbolic functions.

Beyond the expression of conventional symbolic meanings, quillwork also functioned, for example, as icons and indexes, to borrow Peircian terms. Many quillwork forms and total creations express direct iconic connections to the things themselves, such as tipis, the human body, and celestial beings. Quillwork creative production and created objects were also indexes with a causal or volitional connection to the recipients, as embodied in women's vows to complete them for the life movement of others. In Roman Jakobson's (1960: 355–56) terms, quillwork functioned beyond referencing concepts to include an extended type of the phatic function by interconnecting kinspersons and families through ongoing exchange; the conative function, such as in the condition that compelled a woman to make a vow and the subsequent supplications in quillwork ritual production and embodied in the objects themselves to compel sacred beings to generate long life for the recipient; the emotive function, as in the maker's pity, love, respect, and charity for her kin that are core Arapaho psycho-social emotions; and even the poetic function in visually conveying paradigmatic meanings in syntagmatic sequences of lines, cycles, parallelisms, and symmetries.

Quillwork in all its phases and forms was not just a detached form of art immobilized and sequestered from lived time and space like a text, exhibit, or framed work. Throughout their life history, quill-embroidered objects were touched, worn, heard, smelled, and slept on. As such, their meanings were embodied and pragmatic. They conveyed not only general meanings but also what to the makers, owners, and others were tokens with unique meanings about their life experiences. For the quillwork artist Firewood, each creation told a story and drew a particular connection to a relative who was the object of the vow (Bol 2001). Quillwork carried collective and individual memories about life histories and tribal history as well. Thus, quillwork had much meaning beyond the referential functions of the object considered as text. As is evident but generally not explicit in Warden's and Kroeber's interpretations of symbolism, quillwork was largely about processes for generating movement in time and connectivity. Misreadings tend to reduce quillwork creations to synoptic Euclidean geometric two-dimensional forms or static configurations like texts, without placing them in larger contexts of space and time. If you read Warden's and Kroeber's works carefully, there is more in the meanings about motion than about essences and more about connections than about boundaries. Quillwork creations interconnected human, natural, and other-than-human realms and both moved and generated movement in the Arapaho lived world.

Another critique of interpretive approaches in the anthropology of art is that for the meanings to have empirical validity they must be identified as belonging to particular individuals or types of individuals. Some concerns do remain about the validity and reliability of interpretations from Kroeber, Dorsey, and Warden, because in published works the owner, maker, or other source of interpretations is not always specified. A thorough reading of both Warden's and Kroeber's unpublished notes, though, does indeed provide direct or probable identification of consultants for many symbolic interpretations. Moreover, symbolic interpretation cannot be restricted to inductive methods and inside perspectives alone, for deductive associations to other evidence about Arapaho culture and society reveal many valid connections. As mentioned at the outset, too, despite the prevailing critique today that early Boasian anthropology defined and studied culture as a total, closed system, the work toward this aim with respect to Arapaho symbolism was never finished, despite the wealth of evidence available. In fact, only rare examples remain among Boasian ethnographies of total, systematic analysis of even cultural subsystems, let alone totalities. As in Kroeber's work, single strands of connectivity appear here and there that allude to a total system, but that is where the analysis ends. For example, no analysis to date has ever followed the trail blazed by Warden to associate quillwork with the rich, mythological context from which it drew vitality and depth of meaning.

Another way of misreading the evidence is the often ignored or at least confused distinction Kroeber drew between the two orders of individualistic and sacred art forms. Interpretation of symbolic meanings for the individualistic forms varied with the maker, though the meanings for sacred forms, including quillwork art designs, were highly conventional and consistent from one object to the next. The lines and proportions of individualized forms are also generally less geometrically precise than forms made in quillwork. While geometric forms in beadwork or painted creations may represent any number of things, the same forms have relatively fixed meanings in ritually produced quillwork productions. As Kroeber realized, sacred designs associated with ritualized quillwork were not open to free interpretation, combination, or improvisation (1983: 150). Many researchers since Kroeber's time (see Anderson 2001a; Fowler 1982; Starkloff 1974) have recognized that Arapahos were and are among the most religiously conservative peoples in native North America. To improvise with sacred things is potentially life-threatening for self or kin. Concerted studies of quillwork and supporting evidence show that the forms and symbolic meanings of ceremonial quillwork are fairly consistent and constrained by definable core mythopoetic relations (see Bol 1996; Greene 1992). Many quillwork designs, the motion they convey, and connections they radiate were chartered by sacred beings in mythical time (see chapter 4 discussion).

As the previous chapters reveal, elements of quillwork carry multiple meanings. Polysemy, though, should not be confused with methodological flaws in defining clear and distinct meanings, for those multiple meanings are not open to random or individualized associations but are constrained by a distinctly Arapaho logic of visual tropes. Connectivities of meanings tend to follow vertical and horizontal relations of inclusion according to shared shape, color, number, and values, to achieve interdimensionality between space and time and homology among levels of each. A cradle disk, for example, can interconnect an infant's body, the tipi, the sun, and the four directions/stages of time on the earthly plane. Finally, all such ethnopoetic contiguities and metaphorical associations are part of the language and pervade Arapaho religious contexts beyond quillwork, both past and present.

Other symbolic dimensions of Arapaho quillwork are likewise constrained by definite rules, patterns, and conventions of placement and combination. Careful review of all the evidence reveals many tacit rules for quillwork composition that defined meanings of proportions, colors, and positions of elements. Some of these applied only to specific types or styles of quillwork, while others cut across many or all styles and types. Candace Greene's distinction between the paradigmatic and syntagmatic symbolic meanings of cradle quillwork designs applies here. The former refers to the simple one-to-one connections that designs, numbers, and colors make to objects, processes, persons, and sacred beings in the Arapaho world. Syntagmatic meaning, though, is a function of contextual position in relation to the whole work or parts of it. As Greene observes, "Cradle elements appear to gain meaning primarily from their position within the overall composition rather than as isolated features" (1992: 111). Colors, shapes, and number acquired meaning as much by context as by being discrete symbols with single meanings. The large primary disk or oblong ornament must be placed on the top or head, for example, of the cradle, tipi, and leanback cover alike.

Symmetry is one of the most obvious principles of composition. Almost all quilled lines, bars, and loops, for example, were symmetrical such that one half was a mirror reflection of the other with respect to at least one point or axis, and in most cases, two or more. All disks for tipis, cradles, robes, and leanbacks are symmetrical along both the vertical and horizontal axes in a double symmetry that Franz Boas recognized for many art forms ([1927] 1955: 36). Beyond these two axes, there is also the radiant symmetry Boas identified for circular forms, such as disks, and at times, diagonal, repetitive parallels along lines and even chromatic symmetry of colors. In turn, the whole of each quillwork object iconically represents the symmetry of an experienced totality, as well as spatiotemporal orientation and movement in it. Forms of the human body, the sun, a tipi, the life cycle, the sky, or the cosmos share the same orientation or pathways of motion in the design compositions.

Relations between placement and meanings of colors are also conventional and consistent in quillwork forms. In the sequence of making quillwork designs, one color must follow another in the right proportion and shape. The four colors of yellow, red, black, and white that predominate in women's quillwork art are not just static mappings of directions, meanings, or stages. Taken together, they express life movement and other forms of movement within and among levels of space and time. The four core colors themselves, along with their relative proportions and positioning for different styles, are part of the sacred technique and symbolism tied to the core of Arapaho religion. Other colors (such as dark blue, light blue, pink, purple, and orange) found in quillwork elsewhere on the plains are negligible or absent in sacred Arapaho quilled forms. Green appears only on several cradle line-path designs and one robe, as well as on some beadwork accompanying quillwork. The cradle styles that incorporate green in most cases suggest borrowing from Cheyenne traditions, in which green is more prevalent. Blue appears only as rock or mountain forms in beadwork border designs for quilled moccasins and a few examples of disks. Beadwork using blue or green is generally peripheral and in some cases seems to have been added later to quillwork forms.

The colors themselves are also not wholly arbitrary but are based on natural processes and basic experiences. For example, blood and flesh are in fact red; the sun is indeed yellow; and winter and old age share a color shift to whiteness. These are also, incidentally, basic color terms encoded by the human visual apparatus, as described in the classic work of Brent Berlin and Paul Kay (1969). The four main colors are most often associated with the central number four, though in quillwork it is not always simply a matter of the four directions or four time periods (Kroeber 1983: 416–17).

In Arapaho cosmology, the four colors together, along with shapes consisting mainly of squares, circles, and rhombuses, articulate movement through turns to the four directions, the four stages of life, the four seasons, the Four Old Men, and the life-symbol of *hiiteeni* described below. The vital formative role of colors was thus not simply a matter of synoptically mapping time in space, for each color and combination of colors also conveyed types and shapes of motion. First in the sequence, yellow is the color of the east, childhood, and morning. Red follows as the south, youth, and summer. Black is the color of the west, sundown, adulthood, and night. White in turn is the color of the north, winter, and old age. Yellow and black were thus part of a duality of sunrise and sundown on the east–west axis, while red and white as north–south represented the seasonal duality of winter and summer.

Yellow is probably the most common color for quillwork overall and, when other colors are present, the largest in proportion. Yellow conveys meanings of daylight, a bright future, the sun, and radiance. Red is almost always centrally located and connotes blood, flesh, humanity, the earth, summer, and daylight. The red of Arapaho quillwork is distinctively deeper than the more brightly hued red of most other Plains quillwork traditions. Outside of quillwork, Arapaho red was the most common color, associated with the ochre and tallow paint worn as face and hair paint, increasingly as one moved through the life path (see Anderson 2001a: 192). It survives today as the preferred shade of red in various Arapaho art forms and is thus deeply tied to collective identity.

Black, usually a dividing color, is associated with night, shadows, dark rays showing through clouds, buffalo, boundaries, transitions, and shades. It was also used on robes and leanback covers for horns, ears, and lines. As discussed in chapter 4, the Black Lodge tipi was the first to appear in Arapaho mythical time: it is the lodge of the first family. This makes sense in terms of black as a dividing color, since one important act of creation associated with this style and Father-Above is the establishment of periodicities that govern the human and natural worlds at the same time (see Lévi-Strauss 1978: 222).

In terms of color positioning on quillwork designs, although yellow is generally in the largest proportion, red appears most frequently in the central position or axis on quilled lines, disks, and overall compositions for robes, cradles, and leanbacks. Red is most common along the vertical axis of many forms, including both lines and circular forms (the circle is also a linear axis as viewed from the horizontal plane, as in the Sun Road connection). In Arapaho color logic, red and black often form a duality associated with internality and externality, respectively. Red is the color of blood, flesh, and all things inside enclosed space or in the center, while black is the color of things outside or brought from outside. Black is also the color of blessings moving into the camp circle from outside. Thus, returning war parties painted themselves in black from charcoal upon returning from a successful raid. The black fiber used in quillwork is also associated with things from the margins, which is paralleled in their source, since they are not quills but derive from a plant that grows at the edge of the water. Black is rarely a main color or the color of forms themselves; it is often in the position of marking borders between other colors.

Yellow is more prominent on cradles, probably because it connotes youth, the rising sun, daybreak, the morning star, and all beginnings. As I discuss elsewhere (Anderson 2001a: 192), yellow is the color most strongly associated with the first hill of life, or childhood, as the color of growth, spring, bright futures, and fertility. On quilled lines and circular pendants in general, yellow often flanks red when both colors are present. Overall, yellow is the color associated most with various kinds of movement, including the path of the sun, the morning star's path, radiance outward from a center, and expanding the multiplicity of blessings.

White is the color of winter and of the fourth hill of life and marks completion of any four-part cycle. The whiteness of undyed quills approximates a natural ivory hue and luster. White can be a focal color, too, on some quillwork styles, and can symbolize the morning star, winter, old age, snow, and the light of day. Among the four colors on quillwork designs, it often serves as a background color, as it also does in other Arapaho art forms in general. White hides or canvas formed the background for most cradles and tipis, as well as some other quilled objects, though most robes and some cradles seem to have been made of tanned hide. Among Plains groups, Arapahos and Cheyennes were known for the brilliant whiteness of their prepared hides. On many lines and pendants, white is bounded by black dividers and functioned to mark the transition between red and yellow. White is often the color of transition in other contexts, such as in the men's Crazy Lodge or women's Buffalo Lodge. It is the color of stopped or paused motion, as in camps along a trail, winter's stillness, the quietness of old age, death, paralysis, and so on.

In most quillwork styles, two of the four colors are generally dominant, including one for background and the other for figuration. Yellow-white, red-white, red-yellow, and yellow-black contrasts are most common. White and yellow tend to alternate as the dominant background colors for disks and lines, contrasted with red and black for figures. When white is dominant, yellow or red is the main contrast. When yellow is dominant, white is minimal on lines and disks. However, white appears in greater proportions on some quillwork, such as the Eagle Design Robe, lodge paraphernalia, and a few cradle styles. As illustrated in the previous chapter, the pattern of colors for each style of cradle, robe, tipi ornament, or other form is generally consistent throughout all ornamentation and embroidery.

The spatial positioning of forms was also intimately connected with paradigmatic meanings as types of motion, that is, references to natural, celestial, or sacred beings, processes, or ideals. Some designs functioned as appeals to sacred beings in the form of prayer-like future-oriented requests for longevity, completion of cycles, recurrence of daylight, bountiful subsistence, and other blessings. The best textual analogy for quillwork is that it is a visual prayer for movement. As in prayers throughout Arapaho and many other Native American traditions, quilled objects called together into themselves all of the most sacred beings. No sacred being, form, or design related to quillwork was just a static form on a map of meanings; all were enlivened with movement.

Sacred beings were also associated in this way with different parts of the body as human or animal capacities to be realized. The four quilled-loop pendants on the cradle's hood and the four small tipi pendants at the four directions, for example, represent the Four Old Men, and their eyes or vision in particular, thus ensuring that they watch over the child, that the child's life extend through all four hills they represent, and that the child acquire and maintain sharp vision. Eagle or Thunderbird is also associated with sharp vision of senior people. At the top of a cradle, tipi set, and leanback there is usually a primary disk associated with the position of the brain or head on the body, thus as thinking itself, as a form of motion, and as the Sun in the sky or, in some cases, Whirlwind Woman. Multiple parallel lines represent trails of humans and animals as symbolic multipliers of offspring, perhaps even alluding to the symbiotic relationship between human and animal prosperity. Thus, throughout all quillwork is a general ordering of elements that interconnects the body of humans or animals with the lodge and the universe, as well as with the forces that generate life in the time frames of the day, life cycle, and history.

As for all Arapaho ritual actions, quillwork aimed to generate what I have elsewhere called "life movement," meaning a straight and long life through all four stages or hills (Anderson 2001: 31). For this purpose, the multiple meanings associated with sacred quillwork designs were not arbitrary but tended to effect homology among multiple levels from the small scale of what could be held in the hands to the larger scales of the body, the tipi, animals, the earth, and the cosmos as a whole. This homology in turn both symbolized and effected life movement. Shape or form was a core dimension for affecting homology and life movement through quillwork. Geometric forms—including lines, circles, triangular forms, rectangles, arcs, and trapezoids—are the most frequent and consistent shapes in quillwork designs.

Quillwork symbolism combined geometric and imagistic shapes with conventionalized forms of motion, number, color, size, and totality. All these dimensions in turn connected to multiple levels of space-time, from the nearly microscopic sinew stitching of the quills to the hands and body of the maker and wearer to the tipi, the earth, the land, and the world above. All dimensions combined for vertical symmetry and homology among those levels and thus moved toward cultural ideals of sacred beauty.

All of the sacred quillwork practices and forms conveyed temporal dimensions on several levels of movement, from the microscopic motion of the hands in making objects to the epochal time of the four ages of the cosmos. All shapes thus contain types of motion, and these are inextricably interrelated. Elsewhere I have called this fusion "motion-shape," paralleling approaches to space and time that recognize their interdimensionality by referring to "space-time" (Anderson 2001a; Munn 1992). Some forms of motion-shape in cultures take on multiple tropic connections. These can thus be considered basic, sacred, or ideal forms. In Arapaho cosmology, sacred beings and animals are defined as much by their shapes of motion as by their appearance or dwelling place. Blessings in human life are related to the shapes of motion in turn associated with sacred beings.

Straight lines are associated with one core Arapaho value aiming toward long life, expressed in supplications, prayers, and vows, as well as art forms. All ritual actions aim to generate life and direct it in a straight path. In Arapaho language, according to Kroeber's notes, there are two contrasting terms to refer to human actions: *xouubee'*, meaning "straight, open, upright, right," and *ceibee'*, conforming to craziness and denoting "crooked, bad, wrong, foolish" (Kroeber 1916–20: Notebook 6: 63). This contrast, he adds, is "used on account of the milky way [*bóoó*], part of which goes straight, part branches off + gets lost." Straightness also applies to walking or movement on land. Standing straight, walking straight, and flatness of surface are all associated with good life direction. The following prayer from a Southern Arapaho Sun Dance shows the place of "straightness" and its vertical equivalent, "flatness," among other values for perfectibility of performance, long life, harmony, and removing life-negating elements to a distance. Like prayers, quillwork aimed to generate such a motion-shape:

> Listen to me, please, Four-Old-Men! You are the people to whom we look for daily protection and seek for good breath of life! We ask of you to be near to us upon this occasion. Oh, give us gentle breezes and cleanse us from impurities! We are obliged to call upon you for help, in order that we may obtain good paint and stand by your teaching. If we shall make any mistake, have pity upon us, for we are yet children! May our road lie straight, and give us peace of mind! Please help me, for the burden is heavy! Make it light, and cause the people to rejoice with thanksgiving! If there is any evil in the camp, take it away from the sick one! Have mercy upon us, you Four-Old-Men! Be good to us and put our steps on good, hard ground, toward the level road, a road that is not soft. Let us follow your ways, for we want to be old! Protect this sacred ceremony, and cause these children to remember the routine work of the lodge! (Dorsey 1903: 106)

In some contexts the Four Old Men are mentioned as walking in a single file as the seasons, thus representing a straight path to follow across the long duration of time. Each is regarded as a past keeper of the sacred Flat-Pipe, and together their file is symbolic of the succession of Arapaho care and mercy for all that is sacred across generations. A road that is straight is also lighter, solid, good, and generative of blessings and life. Illness and other hardship are associated with an uphill climb or other burdensome travel without good breath, such as carrying heavy loads or walking through soft ground. Also opposite to a straight, flat road is a crooked road, which is "crazy" (*hohookee-*) or foolish, that is, not followed in a good way with the right knowledge. In Arapaho values, craziness is associated with childhood, lacking common sense, and to an extent non-Arapaho cultural ways.

Vertical straightness was also a core value expressed in quilled objects. The infant's cradle aimed to make his or her body erect and vertical and road of life straight and flat. In the beginning, humans were defined by their ability to stand upright and rise in the morning, as in the Arapaho term *3owo3neniteeno'*, "rising people" (Dorsey and Kroeber 1903: 6), a term now applying only to American Indian people. An admirable tipi was also straight and tall. Among Plains groups, Arapahos and Cheyennes took pride in their distinctive vertical white tipis. As Carl Sweezy reminisced, "The tipis of the Cheyenne and Arapaho were taller than those of other Indians. Anyone traveling the prairies long ago knew one of our villages as soon as he saw it, even before he was near enough to recognize the people or the designs on the chief's tent or the shields and trophies hanging outside. The low, round lodges of other tribes were never so beautiful as ours; they never stood so white and tall, with the poles crossed so high against the sky, as ours" (quoted in Bass 1966: 13).

Vertical straightness was also inscribed in robes worn with the hair inside, which would have shown the multiple lines following the vertical form of the body. Multiplied, geometrically straight parallel lines on robes, bags, moccasins, tipi doors, tipi liners, and many other items are among the oldest and most widespread form among Arapaho quillwork. The plurality of roads, trails, and paths convey blessings for multiple types of beings, whether kin groups of people, herds of buffalo, or other living beings.

The circle is another recurring motion-shape in quillwork design. It can refer to the sun, head, brain, or desire for completion of all four hills of life. The circle can be associated with completion of four stages or with radiance from a central point. As mentioned above, the circular disk form, where it occurs, is generally the prominent symbolic form and central feature of a cradle, leanback cover, tipi set, or robe. Circles usually replicate the sequence of color on the lines of the same quilled design. Circular and linear movements are thus rendered homologous. Elsewhere in Arapaho culture, the circle is both a common and a sacred form with multiple connections of meaning and types of motion conveyed. It was the shape of the tipi floor, bowls, men's shields, berries, beads, and so forth. Hoops were common in hair decorations and other adornments. Quill-wrapped hoop forms are also common in the men's lodges and women's Buffalo Lodge paraphernalia. According to Dorsey (1903: 12–14), the sacred wheel, second only to the Flat-Pipe in importance, has various meanings including the sun, the water snake, and the earth island with surrounding water. Because the snake it represents is harmless, the wheel connotes "gentleness and meekness." The circle was also found in gaming wheels, rolled as boys and men threw darts or shot arrows at them to hone their hunting skills. The circle was also relevant in men's shields, used for protection in battle.

The rectangle, square, and isosceles trapezoid all denote a core Arapaho principle of *hiiteeni,* which Kroeber translates as "life-symbol": "The writer is unable to give the exact meaning of the word *hiiteni,* mentioned above. This symbol is said to signify life, abundance, food, prosperity, temporal blessings, desire or hope for food, prayer for abundance, or the things wished for. It may be best described as a symbol of happy life, or, since in Arapaho symbolism the representation of an object or condition usually implies a desire for such object or condition, a symbol of the desire for happy life. Briefly, it may be called a life-symbol" (1983: 40).

Dorsey (1903: 14) and Warden generally refer to the same term and symbol as identical to the Four Old Men, as well as the four directions, four seasons, and four hills of life they evoke. The life-symbol is thus an expression of the desire for life to extend to all four hills or stages. The shape of the design likely refers to the butte, hill, or monument upon which each of the Four Old Men sits at one of the four corners of the world's rim. Etymologically, the word for life-symbol is related to a root word also common to "heart" (*betee*) and "person" (*hinenitee*). A literal translation of the term is probably "our heart." The trapezoid *hiiteeni* design in particular has multiple iconic connections. From Warden's and Kroeber's evidence, it is associated with the heart, the tipi itself, bird's claws, the Sun Road, bear's claws, buffalos, raindrops, and the buttes upon which the Four Old Men sit. The square or rectangle as a *hiiteeni* form is considered equivalent in some respects to the circle, since all are considered four-sided or four-phased things (Kroeber 1983: 413).

Another common geometric form in quillwork is the cross with arms of equal length, known in Christian typology as the Greek cross. In all contexts, the cross refers to Morning Star, who is the messenger of the Four Old Men and son of Moon and Woman Who Climbed to the Sky. In some contexts the vertical line of the cross is widened to form a central rectangle. The cross can also appear in arced form on circular disks. It is associated with dawn, youth, the beginnings of motion, and the convergence of roads.

The triangle is another basic form, both in quillwork and throughout other types of Arapaho art. The narrow isosceles triangular shape is generally a representation of the tipi. In nonquillwork designs, a flatter, wider triangle form usually denotes a mountain. The most frequent place for tipi triangles is on quilled disks as generally paired along the vertical axis in hourglass form, with the base of each design rounded by the radius of the circle.

Some representative forms are also present in quillwork design or in accompanying decoration. Animal forms are represented on quilled items, by either a whole animal image or a body part in quilled forms or accompanying nonquilled forms, such as paint or ornaments. Eagles are represented on one robe style; buffalo are commonly referred to by ears, horns, or the totality of a robe or leanback cover. Animal paths are also represented in quills or paint on robes.

As meaningful to quillwork as shape and color are principles and patterns of numbers and counting, which are likewise about creating connections and movement. The nature of sacred vows in Arapaho generally entailed commitment to a counted length of time to extend and straighten others' or one's own life path. For all the lodges, a vow to participate involved commitment as an encumbrance on one's life from the time of the vow until its completion in the ceremony. If circumstances intervened to prevent completion, there were various alternatives, such as elders recognizing a substitute to stand in for the pledger. For fasting alone, men vowed for four or seven days. For sacrifices of flesh, men vowed to sacrifice a specific number of pieces of skin in exchange for the suffering of a kinsperson: "When any member in the family is taken severely ill suddenly, one of his relatives makes a vow in the presence of the family. He says to them: 'In order that my brother may get well soon let it be known to all spirits that early in the morning I shall cut seven pieces from my skin, and in lieu of my brother I will bury them'" (Dorsey 1903: 182).

After the ceremony under the authority of one or several of the Seven Old Women owners of the quillwork bags, the pledger of a quilled robe had to complete one line each day. The count of lines was thus a count of the days of a woman's vow and the time of the receiver's life-threatening experience. Each quillwork object thus contained the count of days for completing a vow, a fact that would be known to the Arapaho community. The rank in importance of each quillwork project that women vowed was defined, among other qualities, by the number of quillwork lines. The perfectibility of form in all projects was classified by the length and number of rows of quillwork, too. The symbolic connections between the motion of the making and the resulting art form were also tied to mythical beings through number. On a smaller scale, embroidery itself involved counting quill widths bent and tacked. Numbers were related to the nature of the prayerful aims of each project to extend long life. In each quillwork project and resulting work, there were layers of numbers applied on top of each other. Each object combines several different numbers. As one example of this, a possible bag at the American Museum of Natural History (AMNH 50/322) has ten horizontal rows of red quills, each line broken by red puffs into five segments, and five sets of four paired horsehair and cone pendants tied along the borders of the beadwork design on the top and side, each with a four-part form. Fringes, beadwork, and other nonquill materials tend to be on the periphery of quillwork. All large numbered forms (ten or more) are generally arranged in crossbars or lines, while those occurring in small numbers (ten or less) tend to be pendants, strands, loops, and dewclaws.

Four is the most frequent and perhaps the most sacred Arapaho number, "to an extent and inevitability that may be equaled by certain peoples, but is perhaps scarcely surpassed by any, even in America" (Kroeber 1983: 412). Compared to southwestern cultures, Arapahos have an even greater rigidity of adherence to four as the beginning and end of all things, as Kroeber observed. The number four sets boundaries on all Arapaho times and spaces. It also expresses the desire for moving all life toward fulfillment and for performing all actions toward completion. It thus expresses the vow for which quillworkers made and gave away the items they completed. All forms and lines in four, and the coordinated four-main-color sequence of yellow, red, black, and white in lines and circles, are related to the four stages of life, both for the human life cycle and for the history of the world. The positioning of four quill loop-dewclaw pendants at the four corners of cradles, rosettes, robes, tipis, leanback throws, and almost all other ceremonial quillwork embodied multiple levels of meanings. The four points on a circle, line, or square refer to the Four Old Men at the four directions, who send life as breath to the people and guard the world from threats beyond its borders. Taken altogether, the symbolic meaning is often referred to as *hiiteeni*. Four represents the circle and the circle fourness, both a desire for completeness in life movement (Kroeber 1983: 413): "A circle is to him a four-sided or four-ended thing: it is *per se* four-determined and four containing. The rhombus, the rectangle, the cross, are all equivalents of the circle." Tipi rosettes, cradle head disks, pillows, liners, leanback covers, and robes are all oriented to four in shape, color, configuration, and meaning. The ritual practice of quillwork itself was multilayered with repeated movements to the four directions in the sequence of east, south, west, and north. In Arapaho stories, actions are repeated four times until some resolution or transformation follows. Characters, such as the trickster Nih'oo3oo, who overuse certain powers do so by reaching or exceeding the limit of four, upon which life-negating events follow.

Duality may indeed be as basic as four, or even more so. Among colors, red and black are the core Arapaho color duality. In the southern Arapaho Sun Dance described by Dorsey (1903: 14), red and black are respectively associated with two halves of the lodge, north and south, left and right, inside and outside, and gentleness of life and strength in war. In fact, a recurring interpretation in Warden's and Dorsey's work is the association of the Four Old Men and fourness in general with two dualities in time. The Four Old Men are associated with day, night, summer, and winter, as well as the four stages of life. Dualism associates homologously with time and space on various levels. Quillwork dualities reference the dualities of eyes, ears, gender, parenthood, and the solar-lunar difference. Each of the four paired quilled pendant loops on most rims of cradle hoods represent the eyes of one of the Four Old Men, who watch over the entire world (Warden-Dorsey 1903–1906: Box 2, Folder 13). The two parallel strips at the top of each head-pendant-style cradle, Warden (Warden-Dorsey 1903–1906: Box 2, Folder 13: 25) states, are the paths of the sun and moon, while Kroeber suggests that they represent a man and woman who are married and own the tipi together (Kroeber 1983: 58). Duality is not only about gender difference but also about complementary male and female roles in nurturing life movement. Similarly, there are two three-pronged claw-form pendants on the top of each lined-path cradle style, including Green Path, Yellow Path, and Black Path (Warden-Dorsey 1903–1906: Box 2, Folder 19).

Four is occasionally combined with dual and triple forms of quilled art. At the back of the hood for each cradle were two tipi strips, representing man and woman, and thus their co-ownership of the tipi (Kroeber 1983: 68). Some cradles also had four pairs of dewclaw-and-quilled-loop pendants around the opening for the child's head, which according to Kroeber signified the "holes in the bottom of the tent [tipi] through which tent-pegs pass" (Kroeber 1983: 68). According to Warden's evidence, the four pendants are the four corners of the earth, the four sets of eyes of the Four Old Men, the Four Old Men themselves, and accordingly the four periods of life in the history of the world (cited in Hilger 1952: 33). Each pendant for a tipi had three lengths with three loops and dewclaws. Combined with the ten similar pendants at the top of the cradle mentioned below, the dewclaws functioned as rattles for a child's amusement (Hilger 1952: 36). On the lined-path cradle styles of Black Path, Yellow Path, and Green Path, there are ten quilled-loop buttons along the front and bottom of the body associated with the ties to secure the two body sections together.

Five was an extension of the four-part sequence with the addition of a return to the center. In a sense, four and five were basic and sacred. Four was related to the number of fingers on the hand, and five to the fingers with the addition of the thumb. Seven, as in so many other Native American contexts, was also important as a sacred Arapaho number, for it included the four directions with the addition of above, below, and center on the earth. This was represented by the sacred beings of the Four Old Men, Our Father or Man-Above, Mother-Earth, and the pipe in the center. Seven was also very sacred as a reference to the Seven Old Men (the oldest and most influential in the tribe) of the sweat lodge and their female counterparts, the Seven Old Women bag owners, who directed all quillwork.

Beyond the numbers two, four, five, and seven, ten, and products of it up to one hundred were also important for counts of rows and lines on quillwork. Ten is a basic number for much quillwork, though its significance has not been fully explored in existing works. The head rosette of a cradle should and in most remaining examples does contain ten rings: "The disk over the head of the child was always 10 successive rings of quillwork, counting the center piece as one. All rings were alike in width" (Hilger 1952: 36). Most existing cradle disks do have ten rings, but others have as many as twelve or even thirteen. In these cases, it seems that an extra outer ring or center piece may not have been counted. The number of top-hanging loop pendants on the tops of cradles is universally ten in number, though less on toy cradles. According to Kroeber, these "represent the pendants or rattles above the door of the tent" (1983: 67–68). Ten is also associated with the human body. Warden mentions that the row of ten pendants of quilled strips typically at the top of cradles is associated with both the whirlwind of hair on the back of child's head and the fact that humans have ten fingers and ten toes (Warden-Dorsey 1903–1906: Box 2, Folder 13: 27). Many beaded items in quillwork style, I observed, also use ten beads in each cross-strand row for lazy-stitching. One example of a large tipi ornament acquired by the Field Museum from Southern Arapahos in 1905 contains ten rings with ten beads for the width of each row. The rosette is part of a complete set of five composing a variation of the Yellow Lodge style but with four green instead of white spokes.

There are several other associations with the number ten. Arapaho numbers are decimally based. Counting moves from one to ten, then, with the multiple of ten and associated ones. Sister M. Inez Hilger observed that when numbers were in question, all her Arapaho informants invariably counted using their hands, beginning with the little finger on the left hand and ending with the little finger on the right, folding each finger with the index finger of the opposite hand (1952: 88–89). In the

Arapaho Little Star myth, too, Father-Above (Sky or Man-Above) did not like that his son Moon's first child (Little Star) was born unexpectedly, so he established the human gestation cycle of ten moons, to be counted in the manner described above from the little finger on the left hand to that on the right (Dorsey 1903: 178). This association for the number ten may have had some relevance to quillwork symbolism, though women may have been unlikely to discuss such things with outsiders or men, since there was a general taboo barring talk about matters related to birth.

Twenty was basic to numerous forms, too, including quilled bags and robes. An accomplished Southern Arapaho quillworker told Kroeber in about 1900 "that the usual buffalo-robe had twenty lines of quill-embroidery across it, and was called niisa^{n}ûxt [in modern orthography, *niiso'ouht* 'it (animate) has twenty']. There were seventeen lines, and then three more close together along the bottom of the robe. The lines were ordinarily yellow" (Kroeber 1983: 29). Kroeber describes one example from Southern Arapahos: "This robe made by Yellow-Woman had twenty lines of quill-work. The lowest three, as already described, were close together and somewhat separate from the rest. The lines represented buffalo-paths. The greater part of each of these lines was yellow. On each were three red marks, each of these red lengths being bordered by a shorter white portion, and each of these again being bounded on both sides by still shorter black marks" (Kroeber 1902: 34–35). Cleaver Warden refers to this as the "Small Red Painted Robe," which he adds is the foundation of all other robes, the basic pattern from which all others derive. On all lined-path cradle designs, including the Black Path, Yellow Path, and Green Path styles, there are twenty rows of quillwork along the hood running horizontally, as well as twenty rows on each body section side. Firewood made three types of robes (the Small Red Painted Robe, Legged Rattle Robe, and Forked-Headed Green Robe) with twenty lines of quillwork for her brother Bird's-Head. Each robe has a similar central pattern of twenty lines running the length of the hide, but the robe styles differ in the colors, forms, and pendants surrounding the central pattern (Warden-Dorsey 1903–1906: Box 3, Folder 26: 36 [1905]). Twenty-lined arrangements also appear on some tipi doors, liners, and work bags. With a similar pattern to the lined-path cradle style, a pair of quilled moccasins from the Field Museum (61393) collection have twenty horizontal rows, too.

The number one hundred was associated with the desire to live one full generation or one hundred years. A Northern Arapaho quillwork artist explained that counting was also associated with measurement using the hands and fingers: "The band which was attached over the face of the child and which reached down the sides of the cradle cover was to have 100 crossbars of quill work. Some makers made fewer, but bands that contained 100 were prettier. Each crossbar was to be as wide as the maker's thumbnail is long. The length of the crossbar was from the tip of the first finger to just beyond the second knuckle of the same finger" (Hilger 1952: 36). The highest-valued quillwork projects in robes and leanbacks contained one hundred rows. The one-hundredth robe is mentioned as the most valuable in the Deceived Man and Big Owl stories. In the former, the woman made two leanback covers. For the first, a yellow style, she said, "On the throat let there be a hundred bars of yellow quills. Let the ear be a yellow cross of quillwork. The head should be round and the tail also should be round and the tail should also be embroidered; and in four places let there be embroidery loops, two of them in front and two behind. All around the edge let there be fifty bars of quill work, and for the nose two bars of yellow quills" (Dorsey and Kroeber 1903: 290). In turn, for herself, the woman made a white lean-back cover with white and black quilled designs and one hundred bars around the throat. Next the woman commanded and made a small calf robe with only fifty bars of yellow and red quills.

Fifty seems to have been the second-ranked number, with forty the next in rank. On the basic twenty-lined robe, "Fifty small dew-claws of the buffalo were hung as pendants or rattles along the lower edge of a twenty-lined robe. If the robe had only seventeen lines of quill-embroidery, forty hoof-pendants were attached. She had made a robe for every member of her family but one" (Kroeber 1983: 29). The number fifty-two applied on almost all robes to the number of stake holes around the edge, decorated with black painted and yellow quilled half-circle arcs. These represented both tipi pin holes and "baby-lump-hair," referring to the way a baby's hair was tied up on the forehead. Apparently there were fifty-two stake pins on a tipi. After becoming frayed with pounding, each stake perhaps shared a likeness to the bunch of short hair tied up on a baby's forehead.

Counting completed quillwork projects was a source of meaning for women's lives and paralleled the counts men made of war deeds, rituals, and other feats they achieved. Women counted hides scraped, types of quillwork projects made in their lifetimes, years in their children's lives, days of a quillwork vow, and lines and even quills on quillwork projects. Quillwork counts were expressions of ideals for long and complete lives. Counts projected a desire for blessings into the future in exchange for the suffering or sacrifice experienced at present through ritual action.

In all, numbers and counting were an expression of the homologous relationship between linear and cyclical time, as in the complementary symmetry between lines and circles in quillwork forms. Time should make the complete cycle of the four phases of life, seasons, daytime, and all ritual actions but should also project along straight, flat paths on the road of life. On many quillwork types, the same color sequence is followed in both lines and circles. Numbers and counting thus connected the past to the present and future.

Pragmatic meanings of quillwork were also experienced as embodied knowledge. Woman quillworkers used their hands to measure lengths and proportions. Recipients of quillwork objects also wore them, slept on them, and lived inside them. Sensory experiences extended beyond the visual perception of form, number, and color that is often given primary attention in the anthropology of art. For women quillwork artists, the tactile experience of applying quills was a meditative form of ceremony synchronizing the motion of hands, eyes, mouth, heart, and mind. To wearers and owners, quilled clothing or furnishings conveyed an awareness of protection of the body and the immediate social space around it. In daily life, hoof pendants on cradles and robes emitted rattling sounds as their carriers or wearers moved about the camp and tipi. Wind blowing tipi ornaments also rattled ornaments heard by occupants and passers-by. By contrast, the lodges of women doing quillwork added to the loci of sacred quietude in the camp deserving of reverence and respect. Because they were smudged in a ceremony, quillwork items also likely retained an aroma of cedar smoke and sage.

A few other works have paid attention to some of the social and symbolic functions of quillwork that extend beyond what the objects themselves express (Bol

2001a; Santina 2004). Arapaho women did not just make ceremonial quillwork to express collective or individual meanings to a general audience. First of all, the ritual process for making quillwork served a supplicative, life-generative function by intending to make and maintain real communicative connections with sacred beings and forces. All ceremonially quilled objects were animated with life connections through smudging, prayer, purification, medicine application, and presentation to sacred beings. The very making of the objects was sacredly symbolic in that it replicated the motion of sacred beings and forces.

Second, quillwork generated, maintained, or redefined social relations among human beings. Women who made cradles for their brother's children or robes for their brothers secured bonds of respect across the distance often referred to as "avoidance" between brothers and sisters. Although in young adulthood, brothers and sisters should not speak directly to each other or stay in the same informal social space, as their lives moved along, exchanges between them could narrow that distance. Quillwork was also part of marriage in forming bonds through the exchange of goods and horses between bride's and husband's family. As a young woman became initiated to quillwork, she formed bonds with older women in an ongoing teacher-apprentice relationship, which also required exchanges of gifts, food, and knowledge. Through this education, women learned not only quillwork skills and designs but also the traditional stories, songs, medicines, and oral history. Though women's age-ranked relationships were less publicly formalized than those for men, quillwork, along with the women's Buffalo Lodge, maintained a ceremonial age hierarchy among women, about which less is known than the male counterpart. For teachers, makers, and receivers of quillwork gifts, the objects also carried meanings of personal memory, shared history, kinship, and exchange.

Third, a woman's quillwork defined both her own and others' life histories and trajectories within the Arapaho path of human development. Through quillwork projects counted by type and progressing along the graded series, a woman's status grew in life in a way parallel to that of men's achievements in war. Women kept count of their quillwork achievements, and these were considered similar to the counted coup and other war deeds of men. In turn, the status was extended to her husband and kin as an expression of the highest cultural values of generosity, self-sacrifice, beauty, purity, and prosperity. A woman's social self and her family's identity were extended throughout the tribe through the cradles, robes, and tipi furnishings she gave to others. Success was not the intention of accumulated quillwork as the extension of one's personal relations, influence, and legacy throughout a broader social space (see chapter 5 discussion). By the time women reached the fourth hill of life in old age, their influence would have become omnipresent in the community, though at this stage older women would display little or no quillwork, beadwork, or painted designs on their own clothing or bodies, save for the paints they wore for ceremonial roles. As men and women moved through the four hills of life, the extent of their influence over others' movement in life became greater as they increasingly became mediators with sacred beings and forces. As mentioned previously, all quillwork was done to ensure that a specific recipient would receive blessings, a bright future, long life, success, growth to maturity, and security from harmful forces.

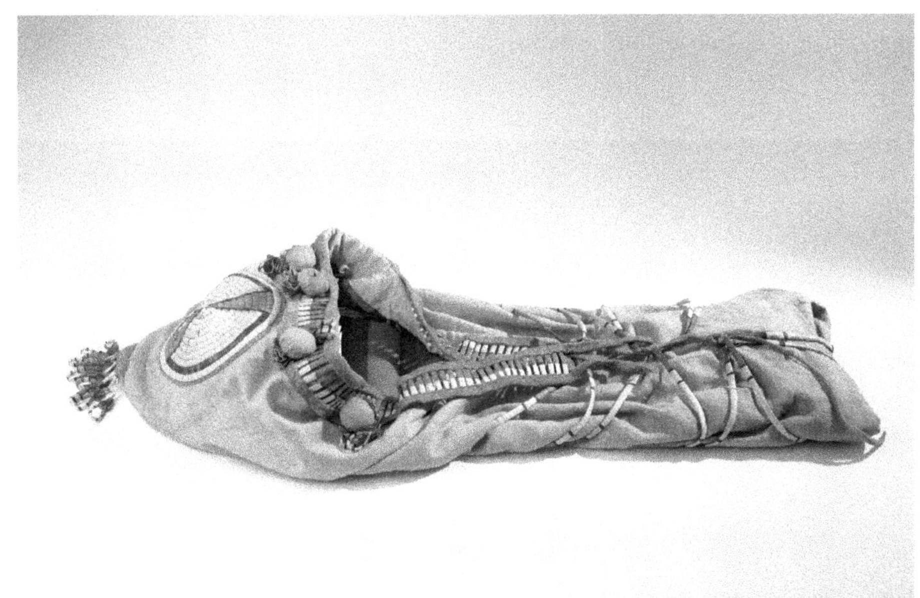

PLATE 1
Path Cradle. Courtesy of the Division of Anthropology, American Museum of Natural History (AMNH 50/958).

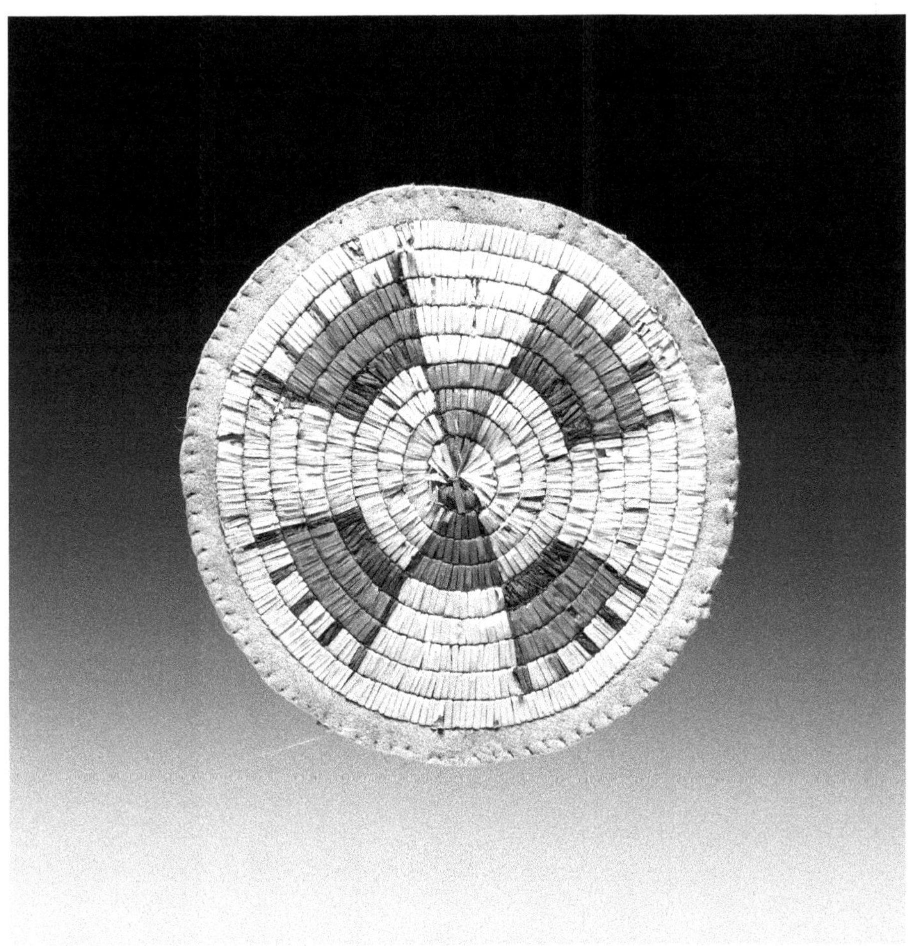

PLATE 2
Spotted Cradle head ornament. Department of Anthropology, Smithsonian Institution, cat. no. 200604.

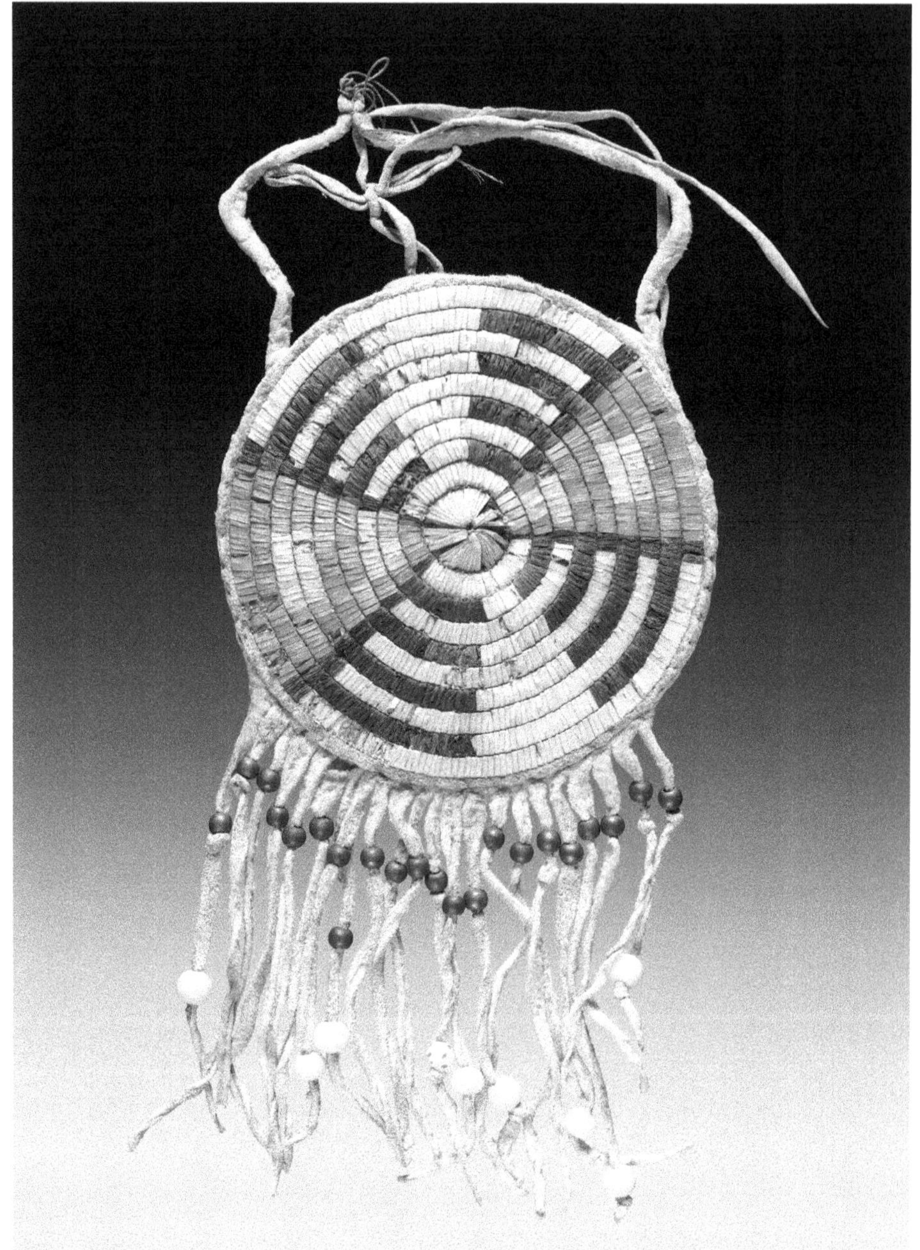

PLATE 3
Ribbed Cradle head ornament necklace. Department of Anthropology, Smithsonian Institution, cat. no. 200651.

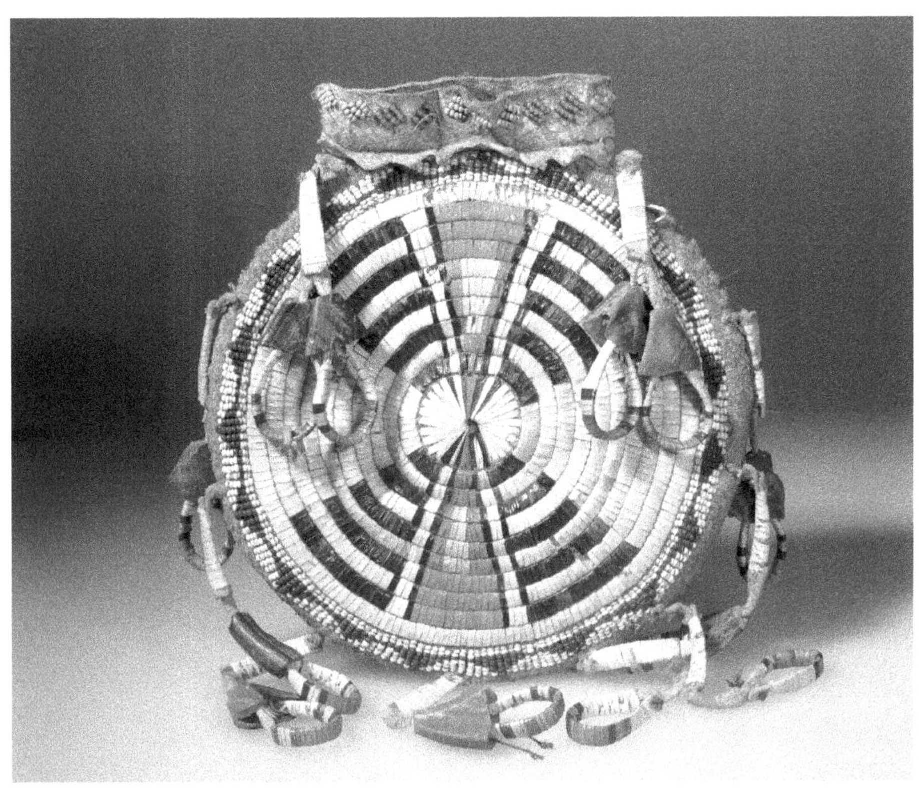

PLATE 4
Ribbed Cradle and Intricate Cradle ornament sides of pouch. Courtesy of the Division of Anthropology, American Museum of Natural History (AMNH 50/150-1327).

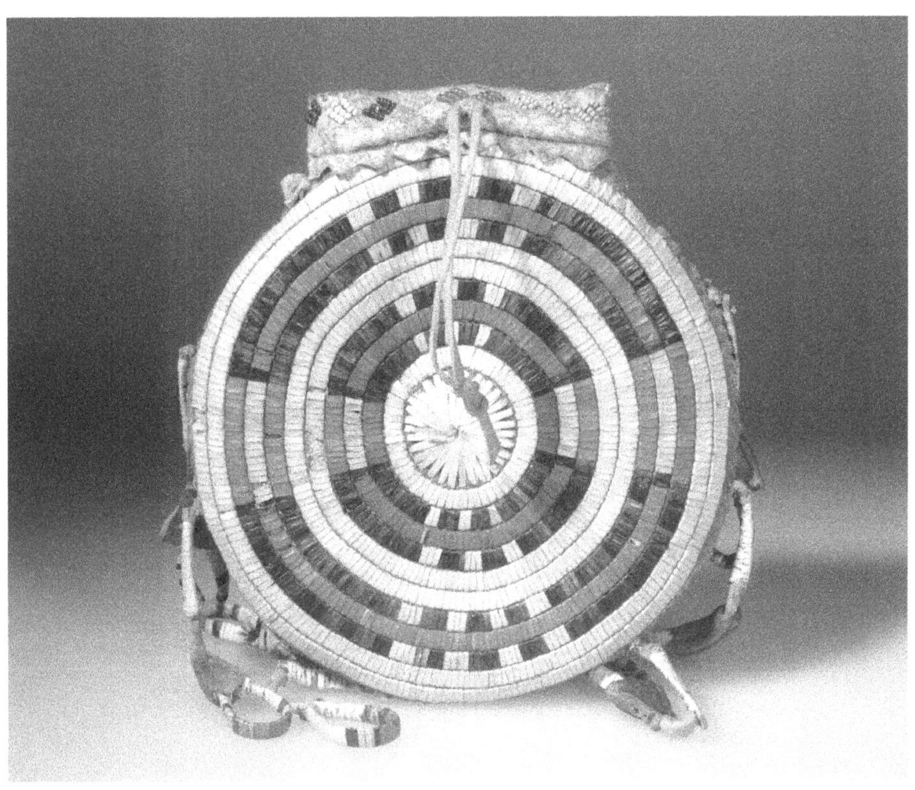

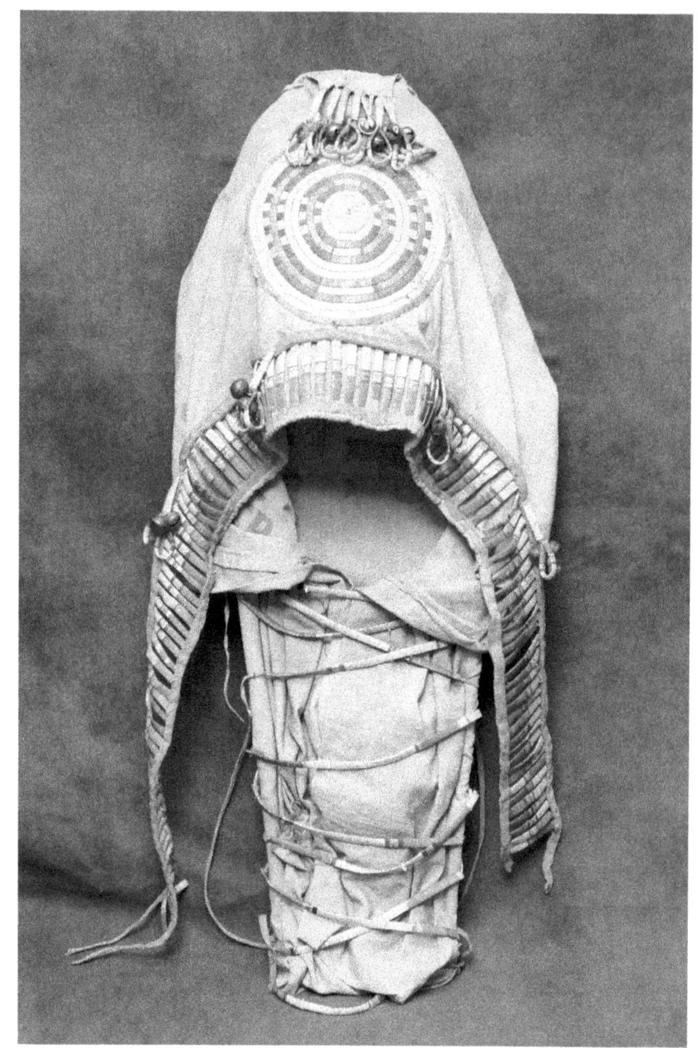

Plate 5
Intricate Design Cradle. Courtesy of the Riverside Metropolitan Museum, copyright 2011 Chase Leland/Chase Photography, cat. no. RMM A1-589.

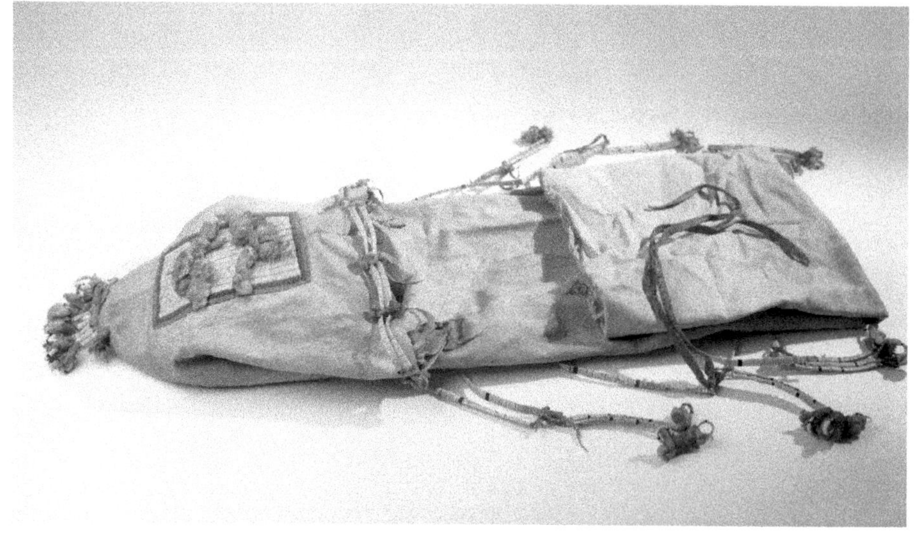

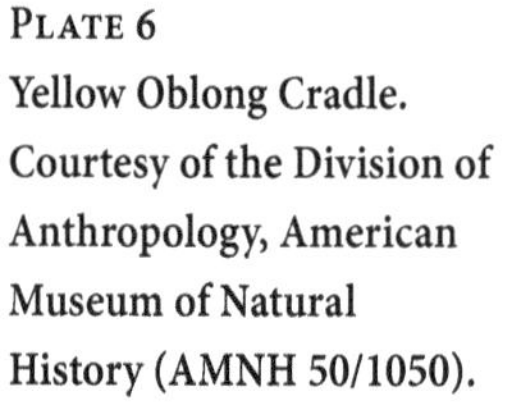

Plate 6
Yellow Oblong Cradle. Courtesy of the Division of Anthropology, American Museum of Natural History (AMNH 50/1050).

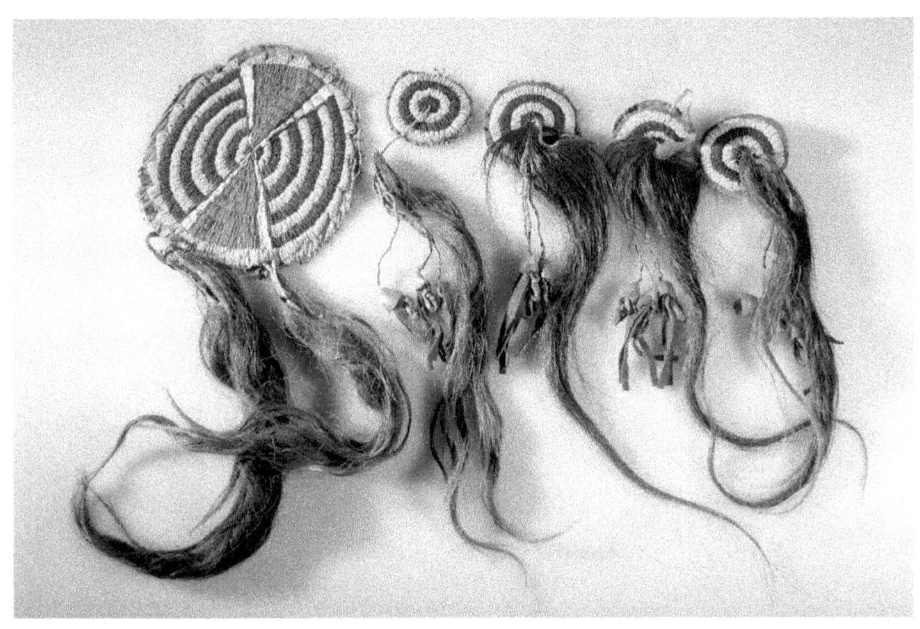

Plate 7
Beaded Black Lodge Southern style tipi ornaments. Courtesy of the Division of Anthropology, American Museum of Natural History (AMNH 50/298A–E).

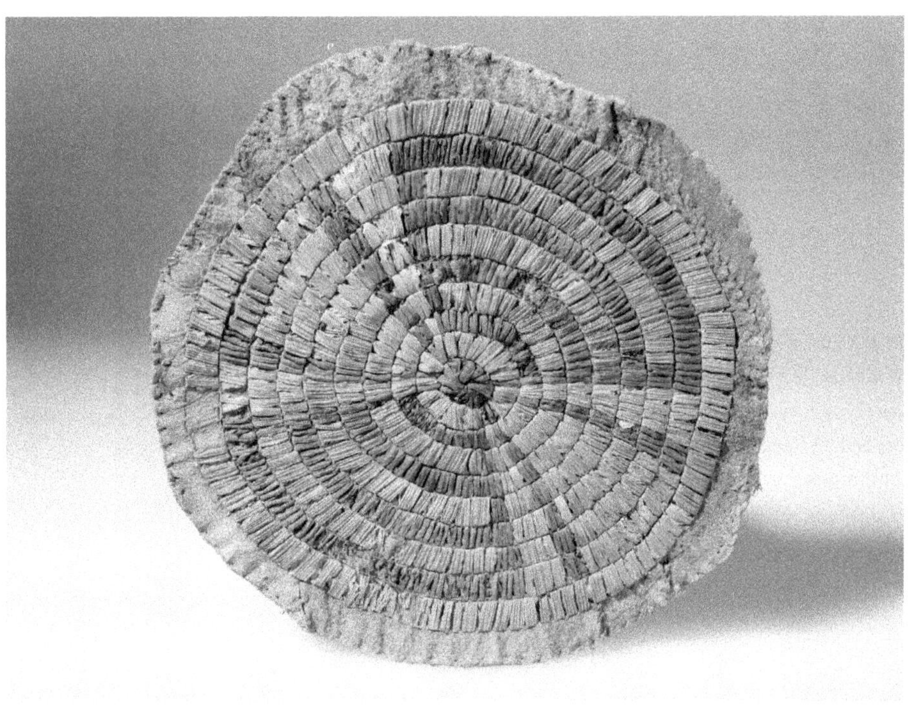

Plate 8
Yellow Lodge top disk head ornament. Courtesy of the Division of Anthropology, American Museum of Natural History (AMNH 50/360A).

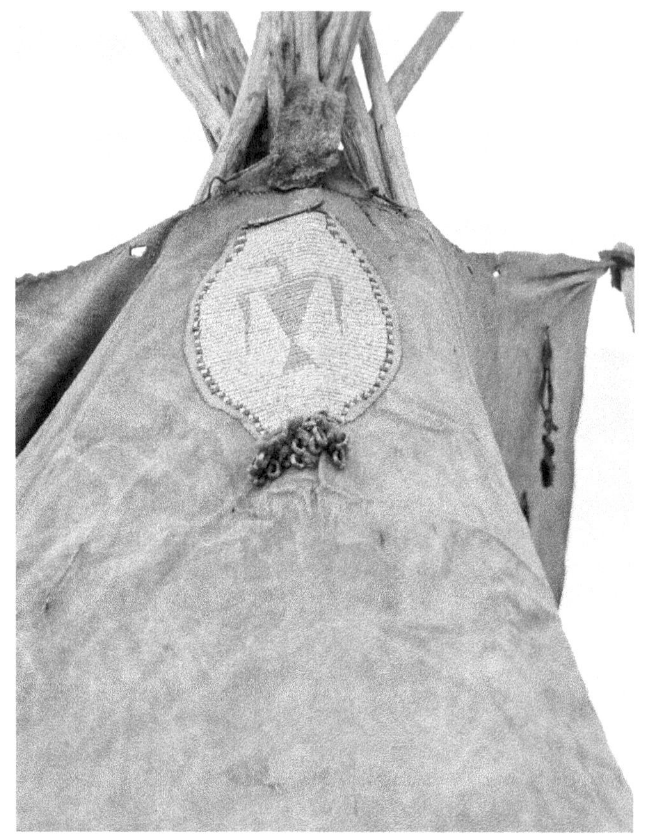

Plate 9
Arapaho tipi top ornament. Department of Anthropology, Smithsonian Institution, cat. no. E18900-0, photograph no. 76-8978.

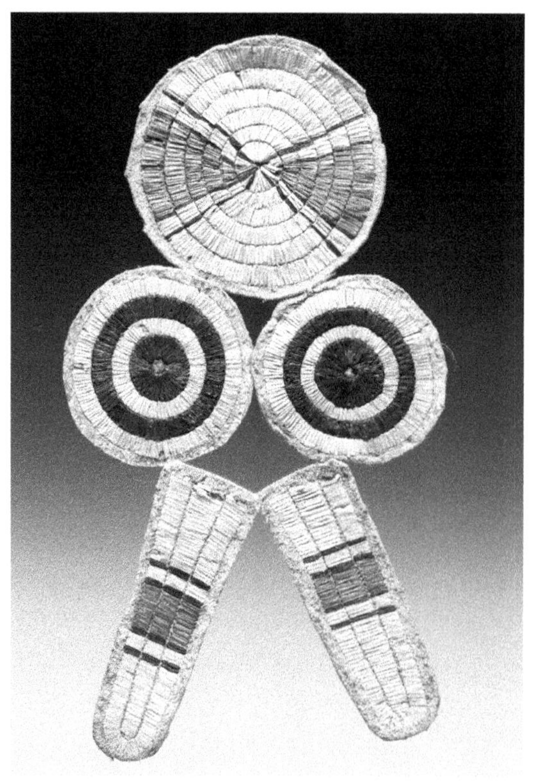

Plate 10
White-quilled leanback cover head, eye, and ear ornaments. Department of Anthropology, Smithsonian Institution, cat. no. 165791.

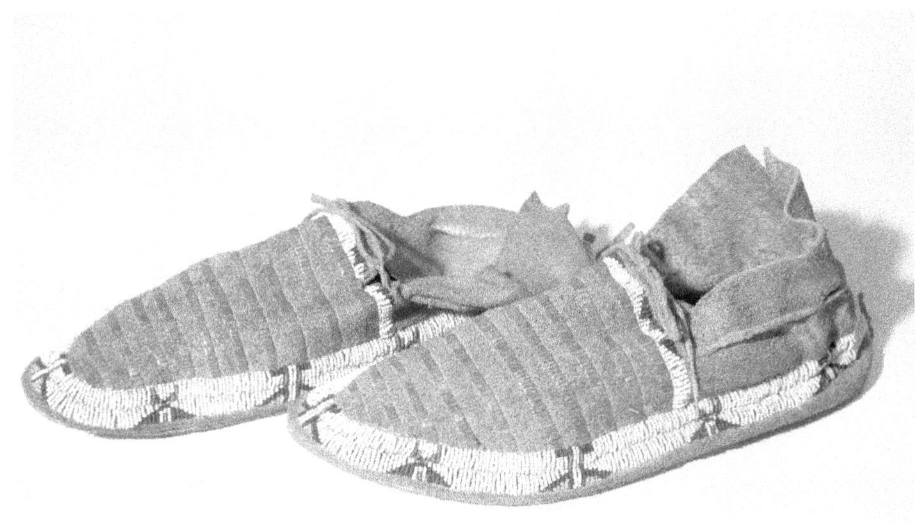

Plate 11
Quilled moccasins. Courtesy of the Division of Anthropology, American Museum of Natural History (AMNH 1/5708AB-2).

Plate 12
Pillow. Courtesy of the Carnegie Museum of Natural History (CMNH cat. no. 3179-343).

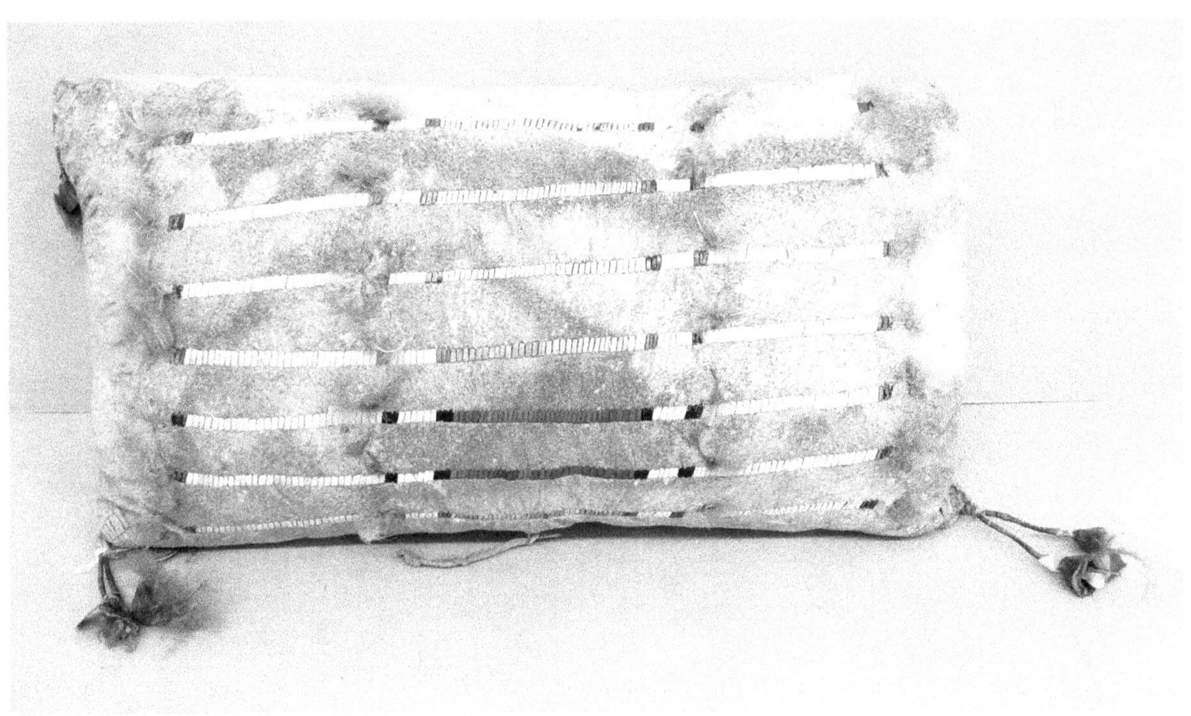

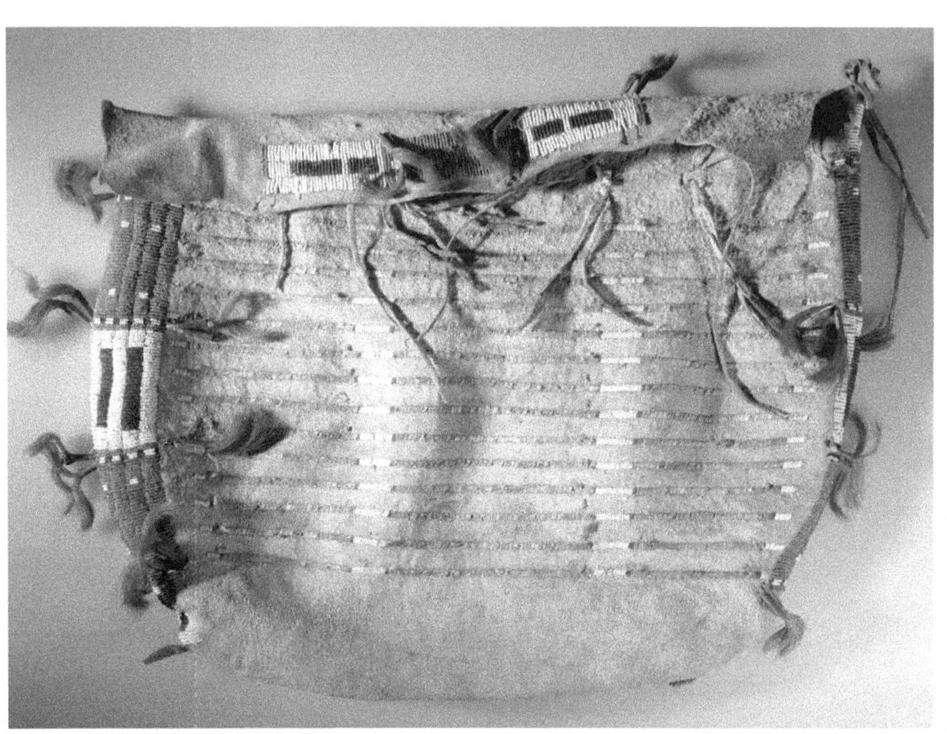

Plate 13
Women's work bag.
Courtesy of the Division of Anthropology, American Museum of Natural History (AMNH 50/25-1).

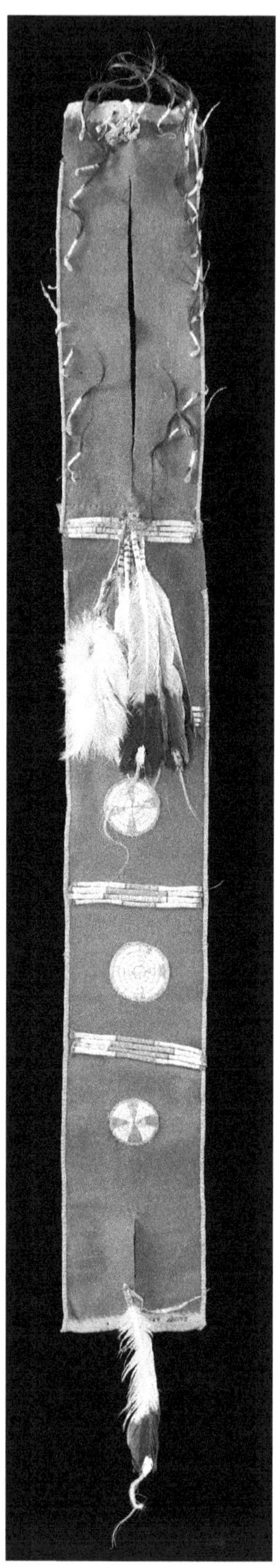

Plate 14
Dog Lodge sash. Department of Anthropology, Smithsonian Institution, catalogue no. 200789-1.

CHAPTER FOUR

Quillwork in Mythical Traditions

Women's quillwork as both practice and product brought the mythical past into the present, as well-projected prayers and hopes for blessings of life into the future. Moving about in day-to-day life, people of all ages saw, wore, and touched quillwork designs, colors, and patterns that carried core Arapaho symbols and meanings set in motion in mythical time. Compared to other modes of expression, quillwork was the only ongoing, publicly visible medium expressing mythical beings, powers, and events. Children heard stories only in wintertime. Adults were initiated into increasingly sacred knowledge as they entered and moved through the lodges in the hills of life, but only a few were admitted to narration of the most sacred myths. Likewise, the most sacred objects were displayed only in brief, ritually circumscribed events. Though not all of what was distinctly Arapaho in prereservation life was expressed in ornamentation on tipis, cradles, robes, leanback covers, and other quillwork projects, many core connections and patterns of language and culture were conveyed or reinforced through them. The messages conveyed to younger people were not necessarily text-like forms carrying meanings but also derived from predominantly direct visual forms that transcend words. They shaped ways of seeing that precede words, to borrow from the title of John Berger's *Ways of Seeing* (1972).

The meaning of quillwork thus extended beyond the objects themselves to enduring ideals established in the time of creation for relations among humans, as well as among humans, sacred beings, and animals. Deeper roots of American Indian women's arts planted in myth and other sacred narratives have, as Janet Berlo suggests (1993: 31), long been ignored by art historians, anthropologists, and folklorists. Analysis of these deep roots is all the more conspicuously absent in this case given the available body of Arapaho oral literature and ethnographic evidence for drawing connections between women's quillwork and mythological events, beings, and forms. Throughout Cleaver Warden's notes, in particular, there are numerous allusions to Arapaho myths by way of understanding the meaning of designs or objects. Several works address particular aspects of these deeper relations (Anderson 2000; Lévi-Strauss 1978; Santina 2004), but to date no study has examined the full range of connections between mythology and quillwork. Among Arapaho art forms, quillwork is the most pervasive in traditional mythology and was thus deeply linked to core practices and qualities for constituting womanhood, personhood, family, tribe, and humanity in general. Women's movement toward perfectibility through art in turn enacted the spiritual power to generate life, conveyed the highest form of beauty, and maintained the most respectful social relations. Quillwork, specifically, moved across social, cosmic, temporal, and physical boundaries. Study of the deeper connections between quillwork and myth reveals the transcendent power of women's art to effect meaning beyond their individual, gender, and even human contexts of identity to form vital relations across the borders of male and female, animal and human, below and above, and human and sacred powers.

At the outset it is necessary to challenge a premise that pervades almost all prior studies of mythology. In early folklore studies discussed below, as well as Claude Lévi-Strauss's inclusion of Arapaho myths, the analyses cannot seem to shake the preoccupation with women as a source of danger or complication for men. This is misplaced in the Arapaho case. Berlo's (1993: 41) more recent generalization that American Indian women's artistry in myth is ambivalent by stressing both its nobility for maintaining cultural ideals and the dangers it poses to men deserves qualification and contextualization in the Arapaho case. For one thing, all human actions in myth are ambivalent in this way by definition, and the dangers are not necessarily gender-specific in agency. Women's or men's dangerous or "crazy" actions can bring harm or blessings to the entire tribe or human race. On the surface of the stories, at least, no mythical incidents of Arapaho quillwork pose or bring any specific harm to men.

In myth and in practice, a good deal of quillwork was vowed on behalf of men. In the stories discussed below, as a result of being lured away from their quillwork or tricked into exposing their quillwork, women often suffer at the hands of monstrous beings. That danger, however, can only in a narrow sense be portrayed in terms of what Berlo recognizes as displaced objectifications of male fears and wishes. In the Arapaho case, quillwork fits into a larger recurring mythical theme by which many other sacred or medicine objects or practices attract malevolent, curious, and acquisitive beings that are then controlled or transformed by women's power.

Unique to Arapaho mythology, in comparison to most other Plains traditions, is the fact that women's power to effect change, such as through quillwork in particular, is situated at the very center of religious life, intricately related to the most sacred lodges and roles of men in them. Quillwork and women's other powers for generating life movement are, in mythology and ritual alike, necessary and complementary to men's power, rather than framed as a separate, external threatening force to be brought under male control. Quillwork is present in the core series of myths that define the oldest meanings and purposes for ritual practices in several of the most sacred lodges. Indeed, quillwork is probably as old as all the Arapaho lodges and the Arapaho tribe itself (see chapter 6).

Within the plots of the stories, quillwork as an activity or object generates or channels motion and exchange between human and other-than-human realms. In the many stories that follow a similar plot, a woman is tricked or lured into a relationship with an animal or spirit being who appears in some false but attractive form. A break in core relationships follows as a result of marriage, violation, or isolation, but eventually some blessing in the form of knowledge acquired from animals or sacred beings comes back to the people. Quillwork is specifically recognized in several stories as a special power and knowledge acquired from other-than-human beings, or in Arapaho, *ceyotowuneniteeno'* 'false persons', that is, nonhuman persons who can appear as human. Women perform the recurring role as mediators between the camp circle and animals, sacred beings above, or dangerous beings in this world.

Quillwork, then, is one among various activities (such as hunting, war, reproduction, and ceremonies) that, in mythical time, define humans and mainly Arapahos as *3owo3neniteeno'*, "rising from lying down" or "resurrected" people (Dorsey and Kroeber 1903: 6). In the beginning—after the Creator Hihcebe' Nih'oo3oo, also known as Father-Above, had assigned gender to the first two persons and taught them about sleeping and sexual intercourse—the people arose in the morning, at which point Father-Above assigned the tipi and red paint to Arapahos as their markers of culture and identity. After some events, the first gift of quillwork to humans came from Woman-Above (Mother-Earth), or Mother-Above, who was married to Man-Above, or Father-Above.

The story containing these events is the most frequently studied single Arapaho myth; it has come to be called the Star Husband type in early folklore studies. Among the various comparative studies of the myth type throughout North America (Dundes 1964; Knight 1997; Reichard 1921; Rich 1971; Swanson 1976; Thompson 1964; Young 1970, 1978), only Lévi-Strauss (1968) connects the Star Husband myth to quillwork and various other dimensions of women's lives. All other studies focus on reconstructed historical diffusion of the story based on formal, quantitative comparison of discrete elements or deeper structural elements among various stories from diverse cultures across the Plains or North America at large. None of these approaches pays close attention to each cultural context in fine detail. On one extreme, selection of surface elements is distant from or even distorts the facts about what makes a difference within any particular culture. On the other, the formulation of deeper structural themes achieves a level of abstraction that allows its application to any tale or story anywhere while overlooking many themes that would function as meaningful for a listener or reader from inside the culture. For example, Dundes's (1964) sequential model for the Star Husband story of interdiction/violation/consequence/attempted escape is so generic that it applies to many Arapaho stories, including nearly every story in which women are principal actors. What is more, it misses the cultural context of each theme related to women. Quite simply, the theme is that young women should not wander far from home and protagonists in general should not be isolated from their home camp. In all cases, some deception has occurred to make this separation happen.

Despite the standing criticism that his work is synchronic and ahistorical, Lévi-Strauss's study of the Arapaho Star Husband variants introduces more levels and dimensions of time and movement than do any other studies to date. In particular, his analysis interweaves multiple levels of periodicity into the relationships among Arapaho women, the porcupine, celestial beings, and the life trajectory. Equally ironic is the fact that his analysis uses more ethnographic evidence than do other existing interpretations, though that evidence is drawn from an admittedly limited range of sources. Also, only his analysis appreciates that, among all Plains cultural variants, the Arapaho Star Husband version alone intricately links women's quillwork to the origins of culture. The story is one in a continuous series of the most sacred Arapaho myths for chartering ceremonial lodges, nature-culture transitions, and social morality. The Arapaho Star Husband myth is the foundation for the practice and symbolism of the Offerings-Lodge, now commonly called the Sun Dance (see Lévi-Strauss 1968: 210–14). As with most stories in that series, quillwork plays a significant role in the plot sequence, primarily through women protagonists.

For Arapahos, in contrast to other groups, the Star Husband myth is most intricately tied to self-identification and continuity in time. No researchers of the myth ever mention that *hinono'eino'*, the original Arapaho endonym encompassing both northern and southern bands, derives from the Star Husband story and the action of women. Though this term has been consistently translated, since Virginia Cole Trenholm's work (1970), as "Our People," it does not literally mean that at all. There are two complementary indigenous glosses of the term: "wrongrooters," referring to the act of the woman in digging the root she is instructed not to dig; and "painted or blue sky," referring to the descent of the mother, her son, and cultural knowledge from the sky (Jesse Rowlodge in Michelson 1910: File 1791). In either case, the events of the Arapaho Star Husband myth define Arapaho identity, and in the sequence of events, quillwork was present before that identity emerged.

There are six published versions of the Arapaho Star Husband story: five are titled "The Porcupine and the Woman Who Climbed to the Sky" (Dorsey and Kroeber 1903: 321–41) and one is titled "Little-Star" (Dorsey 1903: 212–28). One unpublished version, titled "The Girl and the Porcupine," appears in Michelson's field notes (1910). Warden observes that these and other events of the story of Little Star are the basis for the Sun Dance (Dorsey 1903: 224–28). The following summary of the basic story places emphasis on the role of quillwork in it.

Sun and Moon are brothers living with their parents, Father-Above and Mother-Above. (In one version, the original father and mother are designated Sky and Earth, respectively.) In the "Little-Star" variation, the family is described as generous, innocent, and industrious, serving as the chief family of a large camp circle and living in the prototypical tipi "formed of daylight, and the entrance (door) was the sun" and "fastened by means of short-wing feathers from next to the shoulder." The Black Lodge style, described in chapter 2, is thus in a way a microcosm of the sky, or firmament, as well as the center of the cosmos. The young men decide to seek marriage partners from the earth below: Sun chooses a frog wife and Moon a human wife. To entice her to the sky, Moon changes into a porcupine and descends to earth down a cottonwood tree. Several women out collecting wood see the porcupine. Desiring its quills to give to her mother for quillwork projects, one woman climbs the tree and is lured higher and higher into the sky. When she reaches the above, Moon has changed from a porcupine into a handsome young man. His beauty attracts the human woman, who then marries him. In one version, quillwork enhanced his charm: "The young man was clothed in fine skins, and had a handsome buffalo robe which was nicely quilled and ornamented. His complexion was very fair, and he had long black hair. His footsteps were firm and persevering, and his hands bold and grasping" (Dorsey 1903: 216). Moon's brother Sun marries Frog because she, contrary to proper behavior for human women, has big eyes that can stare directly at him without squinting and wrinkling her face. As discussed in chapter 5, young women were socialized to avoid eye contact and maintain a quiet disposition. Each of the new wives receives the traditional tipi with furnishings, including quillwork, from their mother-in-law. In one version, each wife receives a buffalo robe with forty parallel rows at the bottom (Dorsey 1903: 217). Frog proves to be the disgusting and unproductive wife, a fact made evident by her inability to chew in a contest with the human wife. Out of spite over his repugnance for her, Frog jumps into her brother-in-law's chest, becoming a permanent mark on the surface of the moon and, in one interpretation, changing him into a female form called Old Woman Night (Warden-Dorsey 1903–1906: Box 1, Folder 1: 11). This event explains why Moon is spoken of as male in some contexts but as the female counterpart to the masculine Sun in others. Moon's wife then gives birth to a boy, and the family prospers on the buffalo they have retrieved from the earth, leaving humans to starve below. Mother-Above instructs her daughter-in-law not to dig up a particular kind of root called *hi'oceiin,* but the young woman disobeys by digging it up anyway and thus sees her family's camp below through a hole in the sky. Collecting sinew, like that used for sewing and quillwork, the woman makes a rope so that she and her child can escape to the human world below. Moon discovers the escape in progress and throws a stone down to kill his wife, hanging on the too-short line, while the boy drops safely from the sky, "like geese dropping birds." There he is adopted by an old woman, who names him Little Star in most versions but Moon-Child in one version. He then grows up fast to become a beautiful man with powers to hunt buffalo, defeat monsters, and live a long life. One version concludes, "He became chief of the people; his tent was very large and full of robes and [quill-] embroidered work. He lived a hundred years [i.e., the ideal length of life] remaining strong and vigorous. When he died the moon took him up to the sky to live there" (Dorsey and Kroeber 1903: 339). In the above version, he becomes the morning star and serves perpetually as a messenger to humans from the beings above and the harbinger of the sun at each dawn. In one version he becomes Found-In-Grass, thus providing a transition to one of the other Arapaho charter myths. (Recall that Little Star, or Morning Star, is one of the most pervasive symbolic forms in quillwork and other Arapaho art forms.)

The Arapaho Star Husband story demands a full study for all meanings well beyond what can be provided here, but connections among women, quillwork, and time deserve elaboration. One key dimension that only Lévi-Strauss identifies is that the myth establishes regular paths of motion, such as for Sun, Moon, Morning Star, and human beings, and synchronizes different types of time, including cycles of day-night, menstrual-lunar, seasons, gestation, the ceremonial calendar, the life cycle, and processes of gift exchange (1968: 225–27). In short, all periodicities in time are set in motion; however, Lévi-Strauss overstates the role of male-imposed periodicity through appropriation of feminine periodicity as the break from nature to culture. Exchanges of value and gifts involving women are the prime mover. The driving force in the story for listeners is that at the outset, time and space in the story are chaotic and out of sync with normal processes: that is, "crazy," in Arapaho terms. The gift of quilled items from Mother-Above to her daughters-in-law is the first exchange of quillwork, but the order of things is reversed, as is often the case in myth. At marriage, Arapaho gifts associated with the tipi and quillwork normally flowed from the wife's family to the new couple. The difference in the story is attributable to the facts that Mother-Above is the mother of all humans and that the woman was a "stolen" wife in a marriage by elopement. In a traditional marriage, the typical arrangement negotiated by senior relatives of both families, the couple resided matrilocally, the husband's family provided gifts of horses and goods to the wife's family, and the woman's female kin supplied the tipi and furnishings, including pendants and other quilled items. In turn, the husband became a servant for a time to his parents-in-law as reciprocation for the gifts and other support they provided. In the story, the woman becomes a servant of sorts to her husband's family. As an alternative to the negotiated marriage and exchange between families, a couple could elope and run off to stay in the husband's relatives' camp, but there was generally an expectation that in time some relationship with the wife's family would be reestablished and proper exchanges would be completed. After an appropriate time for the wife's family to accept the marriage elapsed, the necessary exchanges could be arranged, and the woman could return home, at least to visit (Kroeber 1983: 12). To prereservation Arapahos hearing this story, then, the plot maintains tension as it anticipates the possibility of an eventual exchange and renewed connection with the wife's family. There were thus several social forces pulling the woman back home. One was the need motivated by pity and respect to share the gifts and success acquired in the marriage with her family suffering below. The other was the matricentric bond of women to family. As Michelson's notes (1910: MS3087) summarize from Arapaho informants, "Arapahoes prefer daughters to sons because the former stick to their parents better. They have more sympathy for them."

The bonds of women to their home camp and to their male kin, especially brothers, are a moving force in all of the core myths involving quillwork. In several other stories, a woman is left alone in the camp. By sitting still and doing quillwork, she tries to allay loneliness. She is usually then distracted from her quillwork, often over time, by a menacing being or group and either invites the being in or follows the being or group out of the tipi. In some stories, a woman character is able to recover and reunite with her kin, usually with some new knowledge or ability to share with the people. As in many other Arapaho stories, a man or woman who is left alone in camp or becomes separated from the camp circle meets a challenge with some other-than-human beings and returns to the camp circle with a life-giving blessing to share with the people. While men are generally banished, fasting, adopted, or hunting, most women are cut off by elopement or deception for sexual encounters or marriage. This mythical tension is the very dialectic (as mentioned in the introduction to this volume) that is transvalued through quillwork exchanges. Women have strong ties to family but also must in later stages of life form connections to the social world beyond through production and exchange of valuable things and blessings in general.

In terms of movement in life-cyclical time, the Arapaho Star Husband story charts the transition of a young woman through the second and into the third stage (or hill) of life, marked by marriage and child rearing. As with life transitions in many cultures, whether through ritual passage or informal social processes, life-cyclical time is phased by homology with other cycles of time, often established in myth. The Little Star story here establishes natural and cultural cycles of time and connections among them. In the story, Moon's wife suddenly and unexpectedly gives birth. Though pleased with their grandchild, the parents-in-law confer and then give a blessing to their daughter-in-law and ultimately all women. Mother-Above states that she is not finished giving gifts to her daughter-in-law: "The fact is, I don't like the method of sudden deliveries, and have decided to remedy it. It is not humane for women to give birth unexpectedly" (Dorsey 1903: 220–21). To give women a sign of pregnancy and a sense of their own time as women, she establishes the time of gestation and of menstrual flow, synchronizing both with the disappearance and return of the moon, as when he disappeared from the sky while seeking his bride below. Pregnancy was thus established as nine moons or months, and menstruation was synchronized with a ten-day period between the last and first quarter of the moon. Thus, women's lives are defined by cycles of time bestowed as a special power to them by Mother-Above and synchronized with the cycle of the moon. These cycles begin as a woman moves into the second stage (or hill) of life, which is marked by an introduction to quillwork as gifts she receives at marriage and, in the third stage, as a learned sacred art form. At another level, they establish periodicity for gestation and birth, which also provides a time of preparation for birth as a life transition, including, among other things, time for making a cradle. Life processes in myth that happen suddenly or at an accelerated pace must, when made cultural, be slowed down and periodized. Things that "move too fast" are crazy (*hohookee-*), because there is no time to prepare and plan for proper action (see Anderson 2001: 229).

The full place of quillwork in women's lives and the seasonal cycle is developed in other stories. Just as once women gave birth suddenly, so too did they originally have the power to produce quillwork instantly, without the long process of hide preparation and the many days required to complete vows. In several stories, a woman acquires the miraculous power to sit on a pile of green hides to transform them into beautiful quillwork. Again, a power or ability defining human culture and identity requires no time in myth but will require humans to invest effort and time when they acquire it. "Nih'ā^{n}ça^{n} and the Seven Sisters" (Dorsey and Kroeber 1903: 92) relates that seven women snubbed the advances of suitors and, upon the advice of their only brother and to lighten the load on the family, moved off to live alone. The second-oldest sister learns that she is able to kill buffalo instantly with her eyesight alone. Then all the sisters discover that they are able to sit on piles of hides and turn them into quilled or painted robes. The sister with hunt-vision successfully kills an elk, the hide of which the sisters make into a quilled bag.

Parallel to that story, "Splinter-Foot Girl" (Dorsey and Kroeber 1903: 161–78) begins with a war party heading out from camp. Along the way one warrior picks up a splinter in his foot, and an abscess swells from which a girl is born. The men set up camp to raise the child, named Splinter-Foot Girl, themselves. She grows to adulthood very fast and shows special powers. She turns the warriors' brush shelter into a beautiful tipi, and when she sits on hides they are magically marked with quillwork diagrams. While the brothers seek game each day, she spends her time alone in the tipi embroidering quillwork on the hides. Each day as they leave to hunt, the men warn her not to look outside when she hears people playing shinny ball. After three unsuccessful attempts to draw her away from her quillwork, she is finally lured outside and finds herself in the midst of buffalo-beings playing the shinny game, a sport women traditionally played. After scoring a goal herself she is carried away with the herd. Lone Bull, the highest-ranking bull, then takes her under his control, keeping other bulls away from her. Splinter-Foot Girl's fathers wrest her away from Lone Bull and then kill and burn him. In the process, buffalo become prey for humans and lose their original ferocity and human form. Their horns are shortened and skins softened. After Lone Bull is burned, his ashes can be used to paste feathers on arrows and as paint for hides.

Also involving quillwork, "Snake Boy" is told as a true story in the first person. Back in the days of conflict with the first settlers entering Arapaho territory in southern Colorado, a war party ventured out. A wife of one member of the party begins the story: "As I was alone on the hill, doing some quilled work, and at times thinking of my dear husband, wondering whether or not he would come home, a very charming young man came before me" (Dorsey and Kroeber 1903: 147). The man entices her into a relationship with praise, promises, and even a vow to Flat-Pipe and Water-Monster to be faithful to her. As time passes, she finds more and more excuses to leave camp to meet her lover. The woman reflects, "My favorite work, which was with porcupine quills, did not keep me at home." After numerous secret meetings she becomes pregnant, gets progressively sicker, and eventually dies while giving birth to a rattlesnake, which the women midwives burn in the fire. Upon returning, the husband calmly accepts the news that his wife had been deceived by a snake who appeared to her as a man. These things happen. As in other similar stories, the moral is that quillwork should keep adult women in the tipi and focused on moral values but that there are powerful distractions to be resisted that are beyond one's control.

In the story of "The Painted Porcupine" (Dorsey and Kroeber 1903: 230–31), human women learn about the seasonal cycle of porcupine quills, another type of time, and acquire all of the colors for sacred quillwork. The modulation of colors as expressing periodicity thus originates from the seasonal cycle of porcupines. The story begins in autumn in a camp near the timber. While prospering in every other way, the women do not have enough quills at that time of year. Having pity for her mother, who has too few quills to complete a vowed quillwork project, the daughter ventures out and pleads for marriage with Painted Porcupine: "'I have come over to offer myself to you; my dear mother is out of quills at a very important time; it is my sincere desire to marry you so that you may be a help to me and my parents,' said the young woman pitifully." After some time considering the offer, the porcupine-man agrees to her proposal. One sunny day while lounging outside, the husband allows the wife to collect quills from his body: "Now you can go to picking quills (lousing) and deliver them to your mother; at this time of the year I have plenty of quills but late in the summer I have very few, so bear in mind that I cannot furnish many during the hot seasons, but I am ever providing during fall and winter." After collecting them, the woman takes bladder bags (see figure 4.1) of white, red, yellow, and green quills to her grateful mother. Before returning to live in her new camp, she informs her parents of the "ways of her husband," and from this original knowledge "the women still adhere to the various colors of quills for ornamenting wearing apparel."

The woman's action is another crazy act but in a good way, since it is a sacrificial act that brings blessings to others. A woman proposing to a man is diametrically counter to the moral code and even habitus expected of mature women. As I discuss in the *Four Hills of Life* (Anderson 2001a), craziness is not univocally bad. There is good craziness that aims for and generates blessings and life movement for others, and negative craziness that ends in the opposite. The story also emphasizes the sacrifice women make for quillwork, in this case, a marriage that benefits her mother and in turn her family as a whole. Like the woman who climbed the sky to marry Moon, she was motivated out of pity for her mother's poverty of quills and thus made a meritorious sacrifice by setting her own interests aside. A nontraditional marriage to an other-than-human being, then, generates another form of motion and time, which brings knowledge to human beings, in this case, colors to represent that motion and time in quillwork. The relationship between seasonal time and the colors is not just a coincidence. As discussed in chapter 3, the colors in sacred quillwork represent

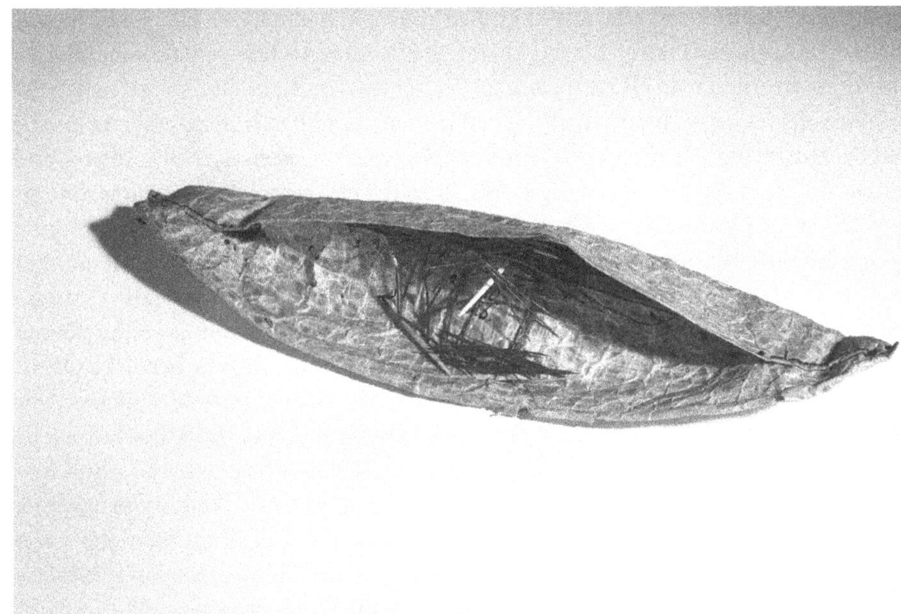

FIGURE 4.1
Bladder bag for quills. Courtesy of the Division of Anthropology, American Museum of Natural History (AMNH 50/126).

different seasons, stages of life, directions, and ages of the earth. The sequence of colors in turn aims toward a long and prosperous life, that is, the desire for the completion of cycles of time for individuals, families, and the tribe. Dorsey's comment to the story relates, "The young woman married Painted-Porcupine in order to be supplied with quills, already prepared—i.e., to a well-to-do man, that had a good home and attractive surroundings." Quillwork is again identified with beauty, prosperity in marriage, and wealth. The Arapaho ideal of beauty and wealth was a tall clean white tipi with quilled pendants on the outside and furnished inside on its western quadrant with quilled tipi liners, bags, robes, backrests, and other items that exuded the uniquely Arapaho red, white, and yellow quills, with added black fibers.

Women quillworkers do not always act appropriately in stories. One version of the Found-In-Grass story (Dorsey and Kroeber 1903: 341–50) begins with a young husband and wife living alone near a river. One morning, as the husband leaves to hunt, he instructs his wife not to look or go outside in response to any voice she might hear. The story relates, "The woman did not even move, and kept to her quill work until her husband returned." On the fourth day, after her husband warns her again, she begins her quillwork but looks out through an awl hole in the side of the lodge. It was the traditional custom that visitors would speak or knock to request entry but were not welcomed inside unless and until the host spoke or looked outside. Tangled Hair thus enters and sits on the west side, the place of prominence reserved for the most senior or important visitors. In the traditional way of welcoming a guest, the woman cooks and offers him food.

Violating norms of politeness, Tangled Hair rejects a series of increasingly valuable food receptacles the woman presents to please him. In one version, after he rejects the bowl, the woman offers in turn a buffalo robe, a white buffalo robe, her best buckskin dress (which she was wearing), and finally her own body. In another version, following the bowl, she presents, in order (Dorsey and Kroeber 1903: 361–63), an eagle tail-feather set, a beautiful quilled robe she had been working on, moon-shells, a beautiful war bonnet, a red kit-fox skin, a sacred white-buffalo robe, an elk-hide dress adorned with elk teeth, and finally her own body. In all versions, when the woman offers food on her body, Tangled Hair cuts her open to release the twins she had been carrying. He tosses one twin outside, where he then lives by a spring, and throws the other by the door of the lodge. Thus, the first twin takes the name Spring-Boy, the latter By-the-Door. When the father returns, By-the-Door helps him lure Spring-Boy back. Then father and sons put up a sweat lodge to bring the mother back to life, a revitalizing practice used in other stories. Against their father's warning not to wander too far away, the crazy twins do not listen and thus venture out to defeat the monster Tangled Hair and smash open his skull. Thus he becomes Open-Brains, identified as the first murderer in history. The twins continue to ignore their father's warning to stay away from dangerous places and act crazily but bravely by going forth to kill more monster beings, including Water-Monster, Buffalo-Bull, and Thunderbird. Punishment finally befalls them, though. While the boys play with a wheel in one version, a whirlwind carries them away. Thus, the rotation of the wheel stirs up the spinning air. In another version, the whirlwind blows them away because one twin violates an Arapaho taboo against using the same arrow more than once to shoot at the same prey, which, in this case, is a bird called Scaly-Foot. What becomes of one twin is not known, but an old woman finds the other and adopts him, naming him Found-In-Grass for the place where she discovers him.

Found-In-Grass grows up quickly. As he approaches marriageable age, the chief of the camp offers his oldest daughter in marriage to the first man who can kill a kit fox and deliver it to him. Found-In-Grass cleverly sets a trap and easily catches a kit fox, but Crow steals his quarry and claims the first daughter for his wife. After explaining the trick to the chief, Found-In-Grass is allowed to marry the younger daughter. Each man receives a beautiful quill-ornamented tipi from his mother-in-law.

As time goes on, his sister-in-law Crow-Woman ridicules Found-In-Grass because he is dirty and ugly, but the hero miraculously becomes handsome and uses a special power to kill many buffalo. In time, Crow-Woman's aversion gives way to a strong attraction for him. With Gopher's help she traps her brother-in-law in a pit up to his waist. He remains there for all time as a stone monument (*3i'eyoo* 'it is standing up'), a place for travelers to leave offerings for his mercy. Stone monuments were found at places along Arapaho trails where tragedy or suffering had been overcome. A traveler could leave a stone, cloth, shell, or other item as a prayer for blessings, such as long life for children or health for those suffering from illness.

The second version of the story ends differently. As in the first version, Found-In-Grass grows from outcast orphan to ideal adult man with superpowers. Among those powers is the ability to release from a bladder bag porcupine quills that metamorphose into warriors who attack and overwhelm enemies. When the battle is over he retrieves the quill-warriors and returns them to the bag. Using this power he goes on the warpath four times, returning victorious each time with many scalps. He thus becomes highly respected and recognized as a chief. His powers, like many such powers, attract the acquisitive trickster Nih'oo3oo, who comes to the camp to request that the bag and its power be transferred to his ownership. After much thought, Found-In-Grass agrees. The trickster turns his life around by leading three successful war parties, but the fourth time, as in many similar other trickster stories, Nih'oo3oo uses the special power to excess, marked by the "fourth time," with bad results. In this case, Nih'oo3oo recklessly drops the bag without being able to open it and is killed at the edge of the enemy camp. A curious and foolish enemy warrior shoots at the bag, upon which the quill-warriors burst out, defeat the enemy warriors, and destroy the entire camp. The party returns to camp in victory for the scalp dance. After the celebration, the warriors retreat to Found-In-Grass, who places them back inside the bag for safekeeping, after which he resurrects Nih'oo3oo. The trickster dies and recovers many times in other stories when he lets a power get out of his control, especially by using it too many times.

This story reveals the strong connection between women's quillwork and male success in battle, as well as the strong metaphorical relationship between quills and warriors. One of the main reasons women vowed to make quilled robes was to protect and empower male kin away on war parties. As warriors set off, sisters or other female kin made vows and arranged for the Seven Old Women to open their sacred bags and release the quills for robe making. As quills in the story can change into reinforcements for human combatants, so too did the quills women used form a connection with their kin on war parties. In Arapaho tradition, any powerful object for making or taking life had to be carefully bundled and released only under the ritual authority of elders. Traditionally, women quillworkers stored their quills in a special bag made from buffalo intestines or a bladder and bundled in another layer or two. The quills could be released only when a ceremony had been performed under the authority of the Seven Old Women. Quills are also known to penetrate other materials and, if entering human skin, travel farther inward, even attacking vital organs. Their lethal potential is like the ideal power of warriors to penetrate an enemy camp and return. As discussed in chapter 5, because of this danger, women's counts of quillwork objects made were analogous to the counts of male deeds in war. In both cases, control of powerful, crazy motion requires moderation and skill.

Women's power through quillwork to create beauty and wealth serves as a force for attracting dangerous beings in other stories, as well. The several versions of "White Dog and the Woman" (Dorsey and Kroeber 1903: 205–25) begin with an unmarried woman alone in her lodge doing quillwork, including robes, bags, and furnishings. Attracted to her beautiful lodge, men constantly approach her, but she refuses their advances with the rebuff, "I am too busy." One night a man sneaks in wearing a white robe that is so beautiful the young woman cannot resist. They sleep together. To identify him later, she leaves a handprint of red paint on the man's robe. By daylight she discovers outside a white dog with a red hand-shaped spot on his back. Soon the woman gives birth to two dogs, which the man then comes to retrieve. Oddly, the story ends without resolution, save for the realization that the dog was the sun.

In "Origin of the Buffalo Lodge" (Dorsey and Kroeber 1903: 31–41), a woman leaves all her belongings and elopes with an attractive young man who is really a buffalo. When the couple nears his camp, her father-in-law, Scabby Bull, asks the woman to close her eyes while he vomits up beautiful provisions as gifts for her, including "a well-fringed buckskin dress, with copper pendants, a pair of leggings and moccasins nicely made, a beautiful robe well quilled and ornamented with pendants, a gorgeous belt covered with round plates and many other articles of wearing apparel." The woman's husband is the jealous sort, so he does not allow his new wife to go out of the tipi. With help from Gopher, the woman's mother and father steal her back. The buffalo herd chases them, but the family takes refuge in seven cottonwood trees. The buffalo tire enough from trying to knock down each tree that the people are able to escape with Gopher's guidance. Upon returning to her camp circle, the woman announces that she has acquired and now wishes to share "the foundation upon which we all must live." Until that time the old men and women "had no knowledge of the laws of nature," so her first act was to appoint seven old men and seven old women to whom she gave "intellects to understand and reason with her" and knowledge of their duties in all the ceremonies, including the men's age-grade lodges, the women's Buffalo Lodge, and the Sun Dance. Along with that knowledge, the first White-Buffalo Woman supplied the tallow symbolizing the role of old men and women in painting the dancers for all the lodges. She then vowed to hold the first women's Buffalo Lodge for the benefit of the people. In this story, marriage to an animal-being again brings sacred knowledge and art forms, as well as the material needed for both.

Through the Buffalo Lodge, too, the Seven Old Women, owners of the bags for quillwork, received their original authority and knowledge. What role they played in the series of lodges of the *beyoowu'u* (all the lodges) is not clear. Quilled items and clothing were required for the Sun Dance, Buffalo Lodge, and most of the men's age-grade societies (see discussions in chapters 3 and 5). For men, their ceremonial grandfathers and older brothers organized the making of paraphernalia for various ranks within each lodge, but quillwork for most dancers must have been made by women.

The story also reveals more about the seasonal activities related to quillwork. When the buffalo herds gathered together on the plains for birthing in spring and again for rutting in the fall, bands came together in large camp circles for well-organized collective hunting. When those hunts were bountiful, camps were full of meat and women well supplied with hides. As discussed earlier in this chapter, autumn was a time when quills were in short supply, especially if women had completed their vows the years before. This season following the buffalo hunts and also the lodge ceremonies, including the Sun Dance, was the time of year for war parties to venture out to raid other tribes' camps for horses and glory and, thus, when women made vows on behalf of brothers, husbands, and other men in their lives at that time to ensure the men's return.

Porcupines were part of a duality and oscillation of time in Arapaho seasonal life. As Lévi-Strauss (1968: 247) recognized, tribes in which the porcupine was central to mythology saw the animal as the "harbinger of winter," because at that time the animals began to produce more quills and climb trees where they could subsist on bark during the cold months. As Sherman Sage states (Hilger 1952: 86), Arapahos formerly recognized only two seasons of winter and summer. The porcupine also marked the transition to night, because it is generally nocturnal. For Arapahos, in some instances the Four Old Men at the corners of the world are the homologous axes of seasons and the daily cycle: winter-summer as northwest-southwest and night-day as northeast-southeast (Dorsey 1903: 14, 96, 124).

Quillwork was also a way to secure spatial boundaries, such as the wearer's body or the lodge, as protective both through the activity of making it and in its finished products. That shielding power frames the story titled "Big Owl, Owner-of-Bag"

(Dorsey and Kroeber 1903: 239–46). Specifically, it sheds light on the power of quillwork designs to confound and deter dangerous beings or forces that threaten humans. In the beginning, a mother, father, and their young son are living well together, but the boy becomes crazy. After several threats to do so, the frustrated mother throws her son out of the tipi door to Owner-of-Bag (Big Owl), who captures and adopts him. Out of profound remorse for her transgression, the mother vows to make a sequence of quilled items to bring her son home:

> 2 pairs of moccasins
> 1 pair of women's leggings with moccasins attached
> 1 short shirt quilled from shoulder to the sides of chest and shoulder to hands
> 1 scalp-lock shirt with breast disc pendants
> 1 buffalo robe well quilled
> 1 image or shadow robe (hard to make)
> 1 robe with eagle design (pictures of eagles at four corners)
> 1 one-hundredth robe (parallel lines from end to end)

Upon completing her vow, she heads off alone with the bundle of articles into the dense forest in search of her son. She finds him, but he has become Little Owl, the adopted son of Big Owl. In Arapaho tradition, owls are embodiments of ghosts of some humans who have died but not yet left for the afterlife above and thus have potential life-threatening power (Kroeber 1983: 317). In this story, as in all its sacred uses, quillwork has the power to neutralize death. As the mother escapes with her child, she leaves articles one at a time to confound Big Owl. First, she leaves the moccasins at his lodge. As he stops to count quills on them, he is distracted and delayed enough to give mother and child a head start for their escape. Repeating the same trick in sequence, she then leaves the leggings, short shirt, scalp-lock shirt, stake-pin robe, eagle robe, shadow robe, and one-hundredth robe. Each time, Big Owl must count more quills and lines, becoming increasingly confused and delayed by each. Finally, upon trying to count the quills in the one-hundredth robe (the highest ranking and most complex of all quillwork), he collapses in exhaustion. Taking advantage of his vulnerability, the mother dashes Big Owl's fontanels with his own club. The story concludes by explaining that this is why people crush the bones of the dead they encounter protruding from or lying on top of the ground.

The Big Owl story, according to Dorsey and Warden, is the charter for quillwork vows. A woman makes a vow to do each project and must follow a sequence as she moves through life from the lower- to higher-ranked items, as listed in the story. As for all Arapaho vows to sacrifice, fast, or enter a ceremony, the aim is to "throw away," or discard, hardship. Warden's rough notes state, "By making this vow drives away or vanishes the sic[k]ness or trouble from the person or persons" (Warden-Dorsey 1903–1906: Box 3, Folder 46: 22 [1905]). The discarding or giving of the quilled piece thus follows the practice of throwing away hardship that pervades all Arapaho ritual (see Anderson 2001a: 130). The designs and patterns in quillwork, then, have the power to drive away life-threatening beings or forces or leave them behind as humans move across the land, as well as to draw loved ones back home from dangerous, distant places. Simply put, blessings are drawn in and life-negating things forced out. As a woman becomes more advanced in the projects she vows, the designs carry more power to protect the person for whom the vow is made.

In the story "Skull Acts as Food-Getter" (Dorsey and Kroeber 1903: 278–82), quillwork likewise drives away a dangerous being. A father, mother, and daughter are living alone. Skull, another ghostly form, tries to attract the daughter as a wife by secretly leaving meat for the family, but she remains safe inside the tipi doing quillwork. The family finally tries to escape. The girl makes four pairs of moccasins, then leaves them inside the tipi to confuse Skull by speaking to him and provoking him to return to the tipi. Eventually he pursues the family anyway, but the woman tricks Skull by making him fall into a deep canyon. The conclusion states that this is why humans bury their dead.

Once again quillwork is central to the ceremonial process of sustaining boundaries between the living and dead. Quillwork confuses a dangerous being enough to allow the victimized family to escape. In turn, a form of the dead caught betwixt and between two worlds finds proper final placement. Quillwork designs, like Whirlwind Woman and her incarnations, have the power to daze and confuse any attacker. A mythical contest of power between the trickster Nih'oo3oo and Whirlwind Woman ends with the former losing his senses and places a whorl on his head (Dorsey and Kroeber 1903: 97–101). In Arapaho, the word for whirlwind, *neyóoóxet,* also applies to caterpillars and the whorl of hair on a person's head. Thus, the story concludes with the message that the result of a direct visual encounter with whirlwinds is that the victim's "senses are lessened,—he may lose his hearing or be nervous the rest of his life." Also, whirlwinds, like owls, can carry the spirits of the dead. According to Left Hand, a famous Southern Arapaho chief, "Sometimes when there is a sick person in a lodge and whirlwind strikes the lodge the sick person dies and the spirit goes out of the body with the whirlwind. When we see a whirlwind coming down the road, raising a vortex of dust, we get out of the way—it is a dead man's spirit" (Scott 1907: 559 in Hilger 1952: 161). Yet even the crazy power of owls or whirlwinds can be controlled by humans for life movement. The power of owls was used, for example, in the Crazy Men's Lodge, and the power of the whirlwind is carried in some quillwork designs. Just as Whirlwind Woman stuns opponents and moves on, so too was the mother in the story of Big Owl able to use the same sort of mesmerizing power embodied in the quillwork designs to outpace her pursuer. While for humans who make or wear quillwork the designs can provide focus and a straight direction in life, for nonhumans or "false humans" the same designs are distracting and disorienting. That is quillwork's protective power. It extends, straightens, and focuses human life but has the opposite effect on other-than-human beings.

Curiously, the power of sight or vision is a creative or destructive force in almost all narratives involving quillwork. Normally prohibited ways of seeing often lead to encounters with danger, death, or monstrous beings, but as a result, humans usually acquire new abilities or cultural knowledge. Sun selects Frog for a wife because, among other reasons, she could stare at him constantly without blinking, the antithesis of what would become the desirable modesty for Arapaho adult women. The Woman Who Climbed to the Sky looked down to earth through the hole left by digging the wrong root and died as a result, though her sacrifice brought knowledge to humans through her son. The blind Deceived Man (below), who regains sight through the gift of the eyes from the owl, a representative of death and contrariness, becomes crazy in his vengeance against his family, who tricked him. The mother of twins was murdered by Tangled Hair because she violated the Arapaho taboo against looking out of a hole in a lodge other than the door and the general norm of letting her eyes wander in a way inappropriate for women. Also with disastrous but ultimately beneficial results, Splinter-Foot Girl, who can sit on hides to mark them with quillwork designs, looks outside through the lodge to see the buffalo-persons playing shinny. As a result, humans acquire the ability to kill buffalo. One of the seven sisters acquired the power to kill animals with her vision. Quillwork ideally keeps women's vision focused and the family or camp thus healthy and prosperous. Conversely, quillwork can confuse the vision of dangerous beings, such as Big Owl, slowed in his pursuit of mother and child.

Quillwork in myth involves motifs of revenge and justice, as well. In "The Deceived Man and the Deserted Children" (Dorsey and Kroeber 1903: 286–93), an old man, his wife, son, and daughter live alone outside of the camp circle. The man goes blind but tries to kill game with his wife's help in aiming the bow. She deceives him several times by pretending that his arrows missed the game and hoarding the meat of the animals he actually kills. Out of pity, the owl gives the man his eyes. The man discovers his wife's trick, kills her, and then stakes out his children for the wolves to devour. The chiefs of the wolves pity the children, though, and provide them with bounty and blessings, including a gift to the girl of the power to make all of the types of beautiful quillwork. With the help of the panther and the bear, she kills her father and goes to the above, like Little Star, to live with Man-Above, or Our Father, where her embroidery lives on forever.

Throughout Arapaho oral traditions a man or woman wronged or wrongfully abandoned by relatives is pitied and then receives a special power from animals or sacred beings. In this case, the girl who became a woman was given the power to make a series of quilled items: a bird-ornament robe (the eagle robe); a painted robe made of cow's hide; a robe made from a middle-aged buffalo hide and adorned with round embroidery at the four corners (a quilled style, with a name translated as Painted Robe), eight lines of embroidery along the length, and black charcoal lines between them; a pillow (actually the yellow type of leanback cover) made from the wooly front half of the buffalo hide and decorated with an "eye" of black *hotohinee* fibers surrounded by yellow quills (including one hundred yellow bars on the throat), an ear with a yellow cross, a round yellow head, an embroidered tail, and four quilled loops, two on the front and two on the back; a white pillow (white-style leanback cover) with an eye dark in the center and white and black around it, a black cross on the ear with white around it, a throat with one hundred bars of white and black, a quilled tail, loops in four places, and black and white bars following the edge all around; a calf hide of yellow and red quills with an eye red inside and surrounded by yellow, plus a throat with fifty quilled bars; a shirt with an embroidered circle of quills on the front and another on the back, strips over the shoulders and down the back, and on the seams fringes of alternating weasel skins and long tufts of hair attached to quill embroidery; leggings and moccasins with the bird design; a woman's dress covered with cross design embroidery, fringed with four rows at the breast, waist, hips, and bottom, and with a yellow sun on the left shoulder contrasted with a yellow half-moon at the right shoulder.

In various stories, quillwork is an expression of the prosperity of the family. Quillwork, prosperity, and life are linked in the families of Mother-Above and Father-Above, the children left to the wolves, Found-In-Grass's adopted family, and others whose fortunes are often reversed by a turn from poverty to success through quillwork. As in other myths, though, prosperity is an expression not of accumulated wealth but of the ability to share knowledge, goods, and artistic forms with relatives and the people at large.

In mythical time, quillwork sheltered women inside the tipi; focused them in mind, vision, and body; and temporarily protected them from nonhuman beings or monsters that tried to and at times did lure them away from their families. In each case, the woman and her family lived apart from the main camp circle, so that during the day she was left alone, without contact with other women. This contrasts with the way most Arapaho women actually lived. In most cases, the heart of each tipi was a group of women related as mother to daughter, sister to sister, or grandmother to granddaughter. Older women looked after younger women, and sisters found their closest social bonds with each other. The dialectic resolved is that women who were left alone doing quillwork, disconnected from their families or camps, drew the attention of other-than-human beings but in the long run were able to return with blessings to the camp circle.

Quillwork in myth was also associated with the ideal of the quiet life, which is especially emphasized for young women, who were taught not to respond to noises and movements around them but to remain quiet while sitting still. Recall that women's sitting has power in several stories. A part of this is that their eyes should not be overly curious by looking about in public or peeking outside the tipi when they hear noises or voices. Quietness, though, was not a repressive requirement for women but rather an expression of the ideal person in Arapaho terms, ultimately achieved by both men and women who reach the fourth stage of life (Anderson 2001a: 73–79). While men developed the quiet life by moving through the age-grade sequence, women acquired its ultimate expression through quillwork. Quillwork as quieting work also implies sitting still rather than moving about, an ideal young women learned under the constant watchful eye of mothers and grandmothers and to be carried over into married life. In all cases where quillwork was a quieting activity in stories, women characters were always eventually distracted and either drawn outside or coaxed into allowing the entry of a dangerous outsider. In Arapaho terms, loss of focus and leaping into a dangerous situation of this sort is "crazy" (*hohookee-* or, for women, *hoheis-* as the stem form). Though craziness is negative in some contexts as a sign of immaturity, it can also have a positive side or outcome in myth by leading to new blessings of knowledge or goods.

Women's agency through quillwork to connect with both other-than-human and human beings is thus realized in myth, but often in contrary or "crazy" types of motion. Quillwork was present in the mythical establishment of proper relations between humans and buffalo, as well as Sun, Moon, Morning Star, and sacred beings in the above. As chartered through myth, quillwork has a dual power. Its beauty attracts and forms social bonds, but it can also repel or even destroy ugly, impure, or life-negating beings and forces. Quillwork is also connected to redemptive justice, though for users of quills it can be very dangerous. In the Big Owl story, for example, the mother is able to reverse the wrong she had committed, but in the

Found-In-Grass story, quills in the crazy hands of Nih'oo3oo become life-negating. To some extent, mythical episodes involving quillwork charter the perfectibility of a woman's adult status through personal vows, sacrifice, focus, and generosity, which are similar to fasting, war, and pledging in all the men's ceremonial lodges. Quillwork is tied to women's heroic feats in ancient times. Lévi-Strauss concludes that quillwork on the plains was "the noblest expression of human culture" (1968: 250). In his analysis, it is a mediating and transformative practice in the opposition between nature and culture. Myth establishes quillwork as the highest and most powerful form of beauty, in contrast to the ugliness of monsters, death, and human moral weaknesses. Quillwork for women was also the preferred "clean" work, as contrasted with the dirty work around the tipi, often assigned to younger women who had not yet learned quillwork. While quillwork, like hunting and other human work, was once easy in myth, stories emphasize that for humans it will thereafter require great practice, focused dedication, and endurance of suffering. In other words, makers must endure difficulty so that they can lighten the burden of life in times of crisis that their relatives experience. Quillwork also created regularity to and homology among different cycles of time, including lunar changes, female physiology, seasons, women's social life trajectory, ritual exchanges, and mythical time itself. In particular, it defined women's identity as intricately inseparable from Arapaho identity, not just as complementary to or supportive of male roles or lodges. As is evident in various sacred narratives, quillwork positioned women in the center of space and time in a way and to an extent unique among Plains cultures.

Through pathways established in myth, women generated designs connected with various kinds of motion associated with the principal sacred beings whose power for generating life was actualized through them. Each sacred being was associated with forms iconically representing his or her particular place or path in the cosmos, shape of motion, and type of energy. To make a sacred shape of motion in ritual walking, dancing, gestures, and art production allowed humans to communicate with the being(s) associated with it. In the beginning almost all sacred beings were human-like actors in mythical events resulting in their proper placements in distinctive positions and paths in the cosmos.

Kroeber notes, "The beings addressed in certain prayers are, in order, first our father, second the sun, third hiiteni [the Four Old Men], fourth hitaxusa^{n} (or last child, equivalent to hiincäbiit 'water-monster' or 'owner of water'), fifth the thunder, sixth the whirlwind, and seventh, the earth" (1983: 313). In other prayers Moon and Morning Star are also included, along with all creatures on or in the earth. In modern orthography, the principal beings are Heisonoonin (Our Father), Hiisiis (Sun), Biikousiis 'night sun' (Moon), Hiiteeni (the Four Old Men), Neyóoóxetusei (Whirlwind Woman), Hiincebiit (Water-Monster), Biito'oowu' (Earth), Boh'óoó (Thunderbird), and Nookoox 'cross' (Morning Star). Depending on the lodge, ritual, or one's stage of life, one could pray to or graphically represent one or several of those beings. Man-Above, or Our Father, is the only being who does not move but sits directly above (*hihcebe'*) in the sky and is often identified with it. As I discuss earlier in this chapter, the oldest and most sacred persons and things become in Arapaho time the least mobile and thus most "quiet." The younger or newer things are deemed more "crazy"—that is, foolish, lacking sense, and so on—the more they move. At one time in the mythical past, Man-Above, or Heisonoonin, was a youthful "crazy" trickster (named Nih'oo3oo) who constantly wandered about getting into trouble but creating many things in his wake. As the oldest being and father of all things, he was married to Woman-Above (who becomes the earth or Woman-Night in some way not described in available sources). The sacred couple were the first parents of Sun and Moon, and grandparents of Nookoox, who was also adopted by grandmother Old-Woman-Night. Heisonoonin was a distant figure in the mythology associated with quillwork and is symbolized nowhere in quillwork or other art forms, though prayers were directed to him in quillwork ceremonies. Direct prayers and appeals to him were reserved for the oldest men's lodges and women's quill society, both most strongly associated with him.

In the various lodges of the Sun Dance, men's age grades, Women's Buffalo, and women's quillwork ceremonies, different beings were emphasized more than others in paraphernalia, designs, and origin stories. The sacred being most associated with quillwork is Whirlwind Woman (Neyóoóxetusei), about which more should be elaborated here. Although no narrative survives about her role in the creation of quillwork and the earth, Kroeber's postscript to another story about her notes, "Whirlwind Woman was several times mentioned as having brought the earth to its present size by spinning around it, while it was still small after having been made from the mud brought by the turtle from the bottom of the primeval water. Her circular course and her stops to rest are represented in decorative symbolism. She is also said to have been the originator of quill-embroidery, at which she worked as she circled the earth, and of decorative designs painted on rawhide bags" (Dorsey and Kroeber 1903: 97–98n). There is a deep connection, then, between women's artwork in paint and quillwork, and the original formation of the earth's surface. Whirlwind Woman's motion overlaps with other actors in myth, too. Comparable in one way to the male trickster Nih'oo3oo, she is a contrary of sorts, in this case, to the proper character and motion for adult human women, for she never stays in one place very long and is constantly on the move. The most obvious dimension of her motion is the radiating outward of creative power. This motion is the earthly complement to that of Sun in the sky, a convergence mentioned in chapter 2 in the context of the Painted Circle Robe. It also is homologous with the generative radiant power of both making quilled disks and women's agency in the human world to radiate blessings and make social connections outward from the lodge. Referring to what Warden classifies as the Day, or Yellow Lodge, design, Kroeber notes, "The black and yellow concentric rings represent the whirlwind, or perhaps more exactly the course of Whirlwind Woman."

On the body, Whirlwind Woman is associated with the motion of head or brain, like Sun again, specifically, through the whorl of hair on the back of some people's heads, which is likewise called *neyóoóxet*. At the end of the story of the contest of power between Whirlwind Woman and Nih'oo3oo, the latter, who loses the battle, acquires a whorl of hair on the side of his head. Kroeber adds, "Whenever a person has the whorl on the side of his head, he is considered dull, lazy, and talkative" (Dorsey and Kroeber 1903: 101). As with all such things, though, there is both a positive and a negative power associated with whirling motion. Warden notes that the line of ten dewclaw pendants on the top of the head of most quilled cradles represents the "whirlwind of the baby," which is associated with mental motion of "thought and activity" (Warden-Dorsey 1903–1906: Box 2, Folder 13: 10–25). There is a connection, then, among Whirlwind Woman, mind, and the spiraling motion.

On the earthly plane, her circular motion is also modulated by stops and breaks: "When the earth was first made (and was still small), Nāyāa^{n}xäti'sei (Whirlwind-Woman) did not know where to stop to rest, and went from place to place. As she circled, the earth grew until it reached its present extent. When she stopped, she had gone over the whole earth. It was she who first made this tent-ornament, which represents what she did" (Kroeber 1983: 60–61).[1]

Her motion is comparable to that of women artists in both myth and history who stopped to sit in order to create quillwork. Whirlwind Woman is also associated in this motion with Hiiteeni, since her four stops also created the four ridges upon which the Four Old Men sit at the four directions, respectively. As she did so she also created two very old, sacred designs Kroeber identifies in several painted parfleches: "This design (*häneisa*^{n} *biitaawu* 'ends of the earth' [or *heneisee' biito'oowu'* in modern orthography]), as well as that called *wasixta* ('bear-foot'), was first made by the mythic cosmological character Whirlwind-Woman" (1983: 109). The former is a set of four squares at the four corners of a parfleche design, the latter any narrow triangular image culminating in claws, each often with a small bulb or dot representing the claw itself. The bear-foot design is a uniquely Arapaho form of a series of sloped promontories, each with a dot at the tip representing a person sitting, just as the Four Old Men are stationed on the four hills. Though sacred in paint designs, the bear-foot symbolism is rare in quillwork; however, it is a focal symbolic form in the Spotted Cradle style (Warden-Dorsey 1903–1906: Box 2, Folder 13: 18–19). Though the design eludes precise interpretation, it is strongly associated with the old age and the sacred bundles of both the Seven Old Men of the sweat lodge and the Seven Bundles of the old women quillworkers (discussed in the next chapter).

Wind is a creative power that also connects Whirlwind Woman with the Four Old Men, but whereas her power expanded the earth outward, the latter send life-giving breath to the people in the center from different directions associated with the changing seasons. The power of a whirlwind can also take breath away: "If a whirlwind happens to travel toward a person, he must squat down and cover his face and wait until it passes" (Dorsey and Kroeber 1903: 101). If one fails to do so, one's "senses are lessened,—he may lose his hearing or be nervous the rest of his life." She can thus generate motion but also stun or stop the motion of others who gaze at her. Thus, ambivalent power is like that of Owl and others in Arapaho medicine, such as that once used by men in the Crazy Lodge to stun animals or other people using the crazy-root medicine. Nothing is known about the medicine power of the Seven Old Women, but this was perhaps a power controlled by them.

In summary, the power, styles, and exchange of quillwork were chartered in myth, and the designs themselves represented sacred beings but were not statically mapped in space, for the designs contained the various types of motion and directionality they both follow and can engender for human beings. Quillwork was a gift from above to humans, and powers of sacred beings were generated with each new quillwork creation in turn given as a gift from women to their relatives. The spiraling outward motion of Whirlwind Woman, the linear path of Sun each day, the mediating movement and cross-like radiance of Little Star, and the time-extending power of the Four Old Men were inscribed in quillwork designs and attachments. The wearer or owner of quillwork absorbed those powers into his or her body and life path but also radiated them outward to others. Through these connections, quillwork related past to present in time while serving as a materialized prayer for a good and long future. It also protected the boundaries of the body for the person and the tipi for a family while radiating beauty, life, and blessings outward to the social space beyond. In all, quillwork generated sacred relationships of life movement among humans, animals, and other-than-human beings. Creativity through quillwork was thus not about simply replicating form or essence in some closed system of thinking or acting, then, but about channeling unpredictable forces arising from the vicissitudes of history into life-giving types of motion and keeping life-threatening forces at bay. In experienced reality, the life-giving or negating power of anything is never pre-given but must be enacted in prescribed ritual actions. Meanings and functions are never permanently attached to forms or movements but must continually be re-embroidered through women's motion in quillwork and the movement of their creations into the world when the quillwork items leave their hands. The irony is that only recently have Western scholars, proclaiming some new discovery that breaks from the past, realized that maybe this is how creativity and meaning work in many spheres.

CHAPTER FIVE

Quillwork and the Four Hills of Life

Many social and cultural dimensions of quillwork have never before been fully examined, because of a tendency to focus only on the objects themselves, the individual makers, or isolated meanings. Quillwork was a social product, and the social world was shaped by it in a life-cyclical process. Culture, personhood, and habitus are never simply acquired in childhood, remaining static throughout the life course. Every society must actively reshape each generation's motion, demeanor, and dispositions to fit each life stage. It is not simply a mechanical relationship between an individual and society writ large but a social process involving concerted social action and a complex web of relationships on multiple levels. Agency in this temporal process always already engages both self and others. The isolated individual passing through a "system" is a modern Western model. Through quillwork, women served as agents for socioculturally constituting the life development of others while simultaneously giving direction and change to their own life development. Until the early reservation period when it began to disappear from cultural life, quillwork played a major part in almost all Arapaho life transitions for both men and women, as well as most of the lodges in the *beyoowu'u* series. Women vowed quillwork projects so that relatives could make life changes and overcome challenges and thus be blessed with long, straight lives extending through all the four hills of life: childhood, youth, adulthood, and old age. Through the creation of quillwork, women's life paths found direction as family, band, and tribe received and recognized their achievements in quillwork. Neither the life trajectory nor the quillwork career was a mechanical system of social reproduction or isolable life biography. The four hills of life was neither a single road for all to follow nor the modern Western path to individual self-realization, but many roads that eventually converge, perhaps at the place where Old Woman Night lives. Women chose to do various quillwork projects to give shape and meaning to their lived worlds but not in terms framed by Western notions of creativity. Quillwork was a social product because it activated relationships of exchange and cooperation among individual relatives, within and between families, and between women of different age ranks. As both makers and recipients of quillwork moved through life changes, the meanings and functions of the art form also changed, along with women's social relations and habitus. As women quillwork artists moved through their careers by completing ever more complex, demanding, and higher-ranked projects, their knowledge of the materials, medicines, designs, ceremonies, and relevant stories moved them closer to the center of Arapaho religion where all elders sat. The practice of quillwork also functioned to reproduce an age hierarchy among women based on the acquisition of increasingly sacred knowledge throughout adulthood. Women's age structure shaped by quillwork in adulthood paralleled the age-grade system of men's societies but with unique aspects of its own. Quillwork was an object of meaning, value, and exchange that shaped, along with many other things, the temporality of the human life cycle and connected its progression to larger orders of mythical time.

In my previous, more detailed study of the Arapaho life trajectory and historical changes it experienced (Anderson 2001a), I emphasize that both the definition of personhood and the type of ritual agency changed as male and female individuals and age sets moved through the four stages of life. In anthropological terms, agency, habitus, and social space-time changed with movement through the life trajectory. Life stages were associated with different types of personal motion and capacities to control the motion of others. At birth and during childhood, through ritual actions and forms such as cradles, parents and grandparents aimed to promote the acquisition of human capacities for movement of various kinds, including speech, thought, and walking. Parents, aunts, uncles, grandparents, and the entire camp were oriented toward generating the life movement of the child. In the second stage of life, emphasis turned to being useful, and thus ceremonies emphasized motion related to endurance and quickness as men's warrior and hunting pursuits and for women in the work of being useful and productive for the camp, the culmination of which was the acquisition of quillwork skills. Although merged in the first hill of life, young men's and women's lives were segregated at the outset of the second by a generalized brother-sister avoidance and the formation of separate peer groups. While men's agency opened out to a larger space beyond the lodge and camp circle, women's movements were kept close to the camp. For both genders, this was the time, too, when young people's movements were brought under the ritual control of older age groups, as expressed in the junior men's age-grade societies and the women's Buffalo Lodge ceremony. For women, quillwork was confined to them in a ritualized space of the tipi, but the tendency to assume diminution or restriction of such women's space as "domestic" must be avoided here. Quillwork sustained domestic space as social and cosmic space writ large.

By the end of the second stage of life, men's and women's roles converged through marriage and the cooperation needed for both secular and sacred activities. As they moved through the third stage of life, women and men experienced decreasing mobility but greater agency and recognition in a larger social space, as well as increasing indirect and spiritual responsibility for others' movement. In other words, adults in this stage turned their efforts more to actions for generating the life movement of others as their own personal movements began to retreat from wider spaces into the center of the camp. Sitting quietly, that is, without movement and contact with public space outside the lodge, women created quillwork to ensure the life movement of their kin, whether through cradles for infants, tipi ornaments for newlyweds, or robes for brothers off on war parties. During the same life stage, men entered the Dog Lodge and, with both literal and symbolic "leashes," became the last to move unless compelled by others in battle or camp movements.

In all, in the third stage of life, one's personal agency became subservient to collective concerns. Thus, no longer was agency, and quillwork by inclusion, a matter of extending expression of a public social self for recognition, achievement, and prestige, all of which are appropriate only to the second stage of life. A woman who wished to pledge increasingly complex quillwork projects had to demonstrate to elders that she was not motivated by this kind of self-oriented agency. In the fourth stage of life, the person withdrew from a social world of wider movement and public expression in social space into the quietude and social centeredness of old age, but with the greatest agency to control the lives of others from his or her stationary position. Elders directed younger generations with gestures, markings, and other quiet means of communication. The separation of genders at the outset of the second stage of life was mirrored by an increasing convergence in the third and fourth stages of life in ceremonial contexts. One striking exception in the Arapaho case was ceremonial quillwork, which remained exclusively of and for women. Quillwork was the only ceremony, according to the available evidence, at which the most senior old men were not present. Furthermore, young women were introduced through quillwork to the quietude and stillness anticipating the habitus of old age much earlier than men were in the life trajectory.

In terms of creative expression and work, women's lives would have moved from play in childhood, to the freer media of paint and beadwork in the second stage of life along with an introduction to simple quillwork projects (accompanied by daily routinized domestic work in the camp, such as gathering wood and water), to ritualized work in the third stage and more advanced quillwork, followed by increasing supervisory roles over work and quillwork in the fourth stage of life, culminating perhaps in ownership of one of the sacred bundles required for quillwork ceremonies. In the third stage of life, both men and women took on increasing sponsorship roles, by providing the feasts and the bulk of gifts exchanged in various rituals, that is, giving much more than was received. For example, as described below, a woman who pledged a quillwork project would provide all the materials, the feast, and gifts to the old women needed for holding the ceremony to initiate the project. The work and resources she contributed to the project would have far exceeded any gift received in return.

Existing evidence either varies or is vague, though, about the sequence of quillwork projects in a woman's career. According to old stories, women began formal quillwork with moccasins and leggings and then advanced to men's shirts, followed by robes of increasing difficulty (Dorsey and Kroeber 1903: 239–46). As discussed in the previous chapter, in myth there is no evidence of the place of cradles, tipis, and various other quilled objects (such as pillows, possible bags, awl cases, navel amulet bags, and lodge society paraphernalia) in the sequenced order of projects. However, the Black Lodge style is positioned in mythical time as the oldest of all quillwork, since it replicates the lodge that Woman-Above gave to the wives of her sons Moon and Sun (Dorsey 1903: 212–28; Dorsey and Kroeber 1903: 321–41). While decisions about robes seem to have been left to the women pledging to complete them, the Seven Old Women appear to have had control over the assignment of some other types. According to Alfred L. Kroeber's notes, for example, the decision about what style or type of cradle a woman was to make was left to the old women bundle owners, who marked out the designs on the hide (1916–20: Notebook 7: 43).

In the beginning of life, before a child was born, women relatives would have already been making quillwork to promote and protect his or her life. An aunt or grandmother usually made a cradle in advance of a child's arrival and stored it away safely until needed. At some point she would invite one or several of the old women quill bag owners, along with their female relatives, to a feast in her lodge. After eating, she asked the old women to mark out the designs. All elders present then prayed for the child in turn to close the small ceremony. When the baby was born and preparations for a feast were made ready, the women of the camp held a ceremony described here by Sister M. Inez Hilger from information given to her by Northern Arapaho quillwork artists Agnes Yellow Plume and Ann Wolf:

> After the child was born the maker invited many old women to her own large tipi or to a borrowed one, if she owned no large one. Younger women relatives were invited, but these stayed outside the tipi. The mother of the baby for whom the cradle had been made brought the baby into the tipi and gave it to the maker of the cradle. Before the baby was tied into the cradle, the hood of the cradle was incensed by being held over a smudge. If the baby was a boy the smudge was made of sweet smelling grass, called *nēyāā'hū* [*ni'oxu'* 'sweetgrass']; if a girl, of a turnip-shaped root of a plant, called *niădā'* [*nii'eetee'* 'biscuit root'] found in the mountains. While the hood was being incensed, the maker prayed that everything would go well with the child. The maker then tied the baby in the cradle and prayed to God "to spare the child, to have it grow up to be a strong man (or woman), to let no sickness come upon it, and to let it be good." One of those for whom I [Ann Wolf] made a cradle and for whom I said this prayer is a successful man now with a good-sized family. A similar prayer was said by the woman who took the cradle apart after the baby outgrew it. Only one of the women prayed; the others bowed their heads and listened. Holding the baby in an upright position, the maker next walked toward the four corners of the earth within the tipi: first, to the door, the east; then towards the south; next, west; then north. Then the mother was called in and the cradle with the baby in it was given to her. Then all ate: the old women, within the tipi: the mother and the younger women, outside the tipi. I [Wolf] made four cradles and cooked four times for the old women who helped to make the cradle and for as many old women as could get into the tipi. The daughters and daughters-in-law of these old women waited outside and the food was taken out to them. I usually cooked a pot of coffee, made tea, prepared meat I had bought in town, served water melon, rice, gravy, grease bread, doughnuts, and cinnamon rolls. When we built a tipi, the same thing was done. (quoted in Hilger 1952: 37)

One striking aspect of this description is that whereas other childhood ceremonies (such as naming and ear-piercing) involved men, preferably warriors, Arapaho cradle ceremonies drew only women of the camp together to celebrate the new life. Only grandmothers of the quillwork society, the maker, and the child's mother were allowed inside the tipi, though women related to participants joined the feast outside.

Infant girls and boys first experienced quillwork from inside the cradle, their first home, which was in a sense their first social skin. The cradle conferred blessings on the child and, as Candace Greene notes, "was also the first symbolic link in the complex web of social relationships into which a child was born" (1992: 95). Though a child's paternal aunt typically made the cradle, other women relatives could do so if no aunt had the training or time required. Through the father's sister, the cradle activated the bonds of mutual support and the Arapaho value of respect between mother's and father's relatives. Exchanges along such paths originated at the child's parents' marriage (or even earlier), also involving gifts of quillwork. Throughout life, father's sisters and mother's brothers were responsible for ritual and even disciplinary roles in each other's children's lives. Out of respect, until they became much older they avoided being together in the same social situations; if that was unavoidable, they did not joke or appear "crazy" (*hohookee-*) in each other's presence. The other side of the respect relationship involved gifts, often initiated by quilled items that passed from sister to brother to ensure his own well-being or were vowed for his children, in the case of objects such as cradles. Brothers often directly or indirectly reciprocated with gifts of horses to their sisters. Gifts between brother and sister were thus part of a long-term process of narrowing the distance between them so that as their lives moved on through the four hills of life they could perhaps eventually speak to each other. Respect in Arapaho kinship and age-graded relations requires distance in everyday life but also obligations to give gifts that bridge that distance in ceremonial contexts. It is therefore somewhat misleading to refer to the relationship with the traditional anthropological term "avoidance," since that was only one dimension and applied only during the second and third hills of life (Eggan 1937: 91). Kinship relationships were dynamic and evolving throughout the life trajectory, and quillwork, among many other things, played a significant role in that process.

The connection to a mother was the most direct in a child's first experiences of the cradle. Within the cradle a mother placed a small pillow behind the head and wrapped her baby into one or several of the softest fetal or young calf hides. As with the larger buffalo robes worn by adults, the hairy side was worn near the body. In winter, a cradled baby was often clothed in a fur-lined wildcat-hide bag with his or her head covered by a cap of the cat's head and the baby's legs placed into the sewn-up legs of the animal (Hilger 1952: 42–43). The mother also tied a baby's navel amulet bag to the outside of the cradle at about shoulder level on either side. When the umbilical cord fell off, the new mother let it dry, then placed it, along with a filler of sage or soil, in an amulet bag she made in the shape of an insect, a rodent, or a reptile's body and embroidered it with quillwork in early times, later with beadwork.

Generally the quillwork design on navel bags is simpler than the sacred designs on ceremonial quillwork, such as cradles, robes, and tipi items. One striking example at the National Museum of the American Indian (NMAI 023227) was collected from Northern Arapahos by the German-born artist Emil W. Lenders, known for his paintings of buffalo and travels with Cody's Wild West show. The amulet is about eight inches long and shaped like a long lizard, with quilled legs and tail. Perpendicular to the line of the body, each side has twenty-one quilled stripes, each approximately one-quarter to one-half inch (or four to five thick quills) wide. One side alternates red and blue stripes across the body, the other white and black. On the head of each side are two red eyes. The feet for both sides are wrapped in three more white and black stripes, the tail in four. At the tip of each foot and the tail is a pair of metal cones. Another quilled navel bag at the National Museum of the American Indian (NMAI 232963) is shaped like a turtle or horned toad, with a more intricate red and black design and four feet, each with paired cones. The quilled design is trimmed with light blue beads. The outer quilled row alternates between black and red, as does a row along the length down the middle of the turtle's back. The field between the outer and transverse rows is solid red.

When a child grew out of the cradle, a mother kept the navel amulet bag for her son or daughter until adulthood, when each person would begin to keep his or her own. Many families still make beaded navel bags. If a navel bag is lost, Arapahos believe that the owner will wander, crazily searching for it by means such as snooping in or even stealing other people's belongings (Hilger 1952: 22–23; Kroeber 1983: 54–56). In Arapaho terms, the navel amulet bag, like all ceremonial quillwork objects, aimed to give the recipient a straight path to walk in life and thus avoid a crooked path associated with the concept of "craziness" (*hohookee-*), attributed to childish, foolish, rash, inquisitive, or acquisitive types of behavior.

There were no differences between the navel bags, clothing, or cradles of infant boys and girls. Gender differences in clothing began only when the infant learned to walk, talk, and listen, that is, acquiring the primary abilities of a real human being. Mothers, paternal aunts, or grandmothers made cradles so that their children would acquire these abilities, live long lives, develop a good mind and senses, and grow straight and strong bodies. During the day, cradles were set up in a vertical pose, anticipating and encouraging infants' transition to standing and walking straight, an important aspect of becoming human in Arapaho culture. The bottom pair of cradle straps holding a child symbolized legs and the desire for him or her to stand and walk. The category of *3owo3neniteeno'* once referred to humans generally and now only includes Indians; the term means "standing up persons" (Dorsey and Kroeber 1903: 321–40). Inside the cradle, babies were usually placed so that they could see what was going on in the social world. Carl Sweezy describes this: "Strapped in his cradle, he learned to look and listen to everything that went on around him, and he grew straight and strong" (quoted in Bass 1966: 31). The cradle suited the Arapaho emphasis on ways of learning by observing and living quietly but with direction (see Anderson 2001a). When a mother was busy, the cradle was set up against a tree or tied to a tipi pole. When she walked about during the day, the mother strapped the cradle to her back; while riding, she tied to it the side of horse; and when the entire camp was moving, she secured the cradle inside the willow basket on the horse-drawn travois (Hilger 1952: 38).

When the child was ready to move about on his or her own, the cradle was ceremonially dismantled, as Ann Wolf describes:

> My brother had a cradle that he outgrew. My oldest grandmother called together as many old women as she could get to come. Then she herself prayed that my brother to whom the cradle had belonged would grow up to be a man. She chewed roots, drew some water into her mouth, and then blew the mouthful on the cradle. Then she said some more prayers and took the quill work off the cover. She rolled the quill work into a little bundle and kept it as a souvenir. It was not again used. The canvas cover she tore to pieces. Whenever I tore up a cradle, I prayed. I prayed to God and the old ladies who started the making of the cradles and to all to whom the old Indians used to pray, like the sun and stars that gave us light and to the moon, telling them that the baby was big now and didn't need the cradle any more; that we were thankful that the cradle had done its service. Then I tore the cradle apart and saved the quill work as a keepsake. (quoted in Hilger 1952: 37–38)

After this a toddler wore only a simple buckskin shirt or nothing at all if the weather allowed, and would be wrapped in a robe or blanket when carried on a mother's back. By the time the child began to walk, he or she wore moccasins and clothes more like adult dress. When an infant made its first walk, the family often held a feast to honor their child's acquisition of that human ability (Hilger 1952: 41).

As they moved farther over the first hill of life, children swam, raced, rode horses, and played games together. Out of these playgroups, boys and girls usually paired up with chums of the same gender and age who would be their closest friends throughout life. In and around the tipi, as time went on, girl partners stayed and played closer to their mothers and grandmothers, watching the work and creativity that would become theirs on the second hill of life when they would marry and begin a family. To prepare them for tipi life, girls played with toys, including small cradles, robes, and saddlebags like those mature women decorated with quillwork. In 1932, a Southern Arapaho woman born in 1855 described her childhood toys to Truman Michelson:

> My chum and I each had doll cradles which were beaded and also beaded saddle bags. Mother made us buffalo-calf hide robes to play with. These were tanned with hair on, just like real robes. Some were decorated with porcupine quills and some were painted. We also had play-tepees and poles. Whenever the camp broke for a move we were made to care for our playthings, that is, to bundle them up and to see that they were properly packed on the travois; and when camp was pitched it was our duty to unpack them and place them in our tepees where they ought to be. (quoted in Michelson 1933: 598)

Mothers and grandmothers thus made toys, including some embroidered with quillwork, which girls used to imitate adult life. Toy tipis and doll cradles even contained small versions of quilled lines and pendants. A surviving doll and doll cradle (see figure 5.1) are in the National Museum of the American Indian collections (NMAI 214833.000, 214833.001).

Toy cradles had the ribs, bar strips, rosettes, and pendants of the full-size cradles. At least one example (AMNH 50/641) of a child's blanket survives, though whether this type was used as a toy or as a child's actual blanket is unclear. It is a Hereford calf's hide with hair on one side and eighteen straight rows of red quills along the line of the body. Each red line has white segments as dividers for five sections, each also marked by red tufts of wool. At one end of each break are pairs of dangling pendants, one capped with a bell and the other with an antelope dewclaw.

According to the famous Southern Arapaho artist Carl Sweezy, toys were objects of beauty to which mothers devoted as much craft and care as to the full-size versions: "For their little girls, Arapaho mothers made dolls dressed in perfect buckskin costumes, beaded and fringed just as our costumes were. The tiny moccasins these dolls wore were made as carefully as moccasins for people, top sewed to bottom with deerskin string that came together in a kind of tassel at the heel. Such perfect little things made even a great chief smile, and pleased everyone that saw them" (quoted in Bass 1966: 35).

From play with toys, girls learned to see and share the feelings for form that surrounded women's art. They learned the touch of materials and shapes of designs for quillwork and beadwork as embodied knowledge, as well as the places and uses of objects in the space and daily cycle of camp life. In time such items became so much a part of their experience that they began to dream designs and stories to go with them. By the time they were ready to become young women, they had acquired the basic motor and cognitive skills to learn and make the sacred designs in quillwork for cradles, robes, and tipi decorations.

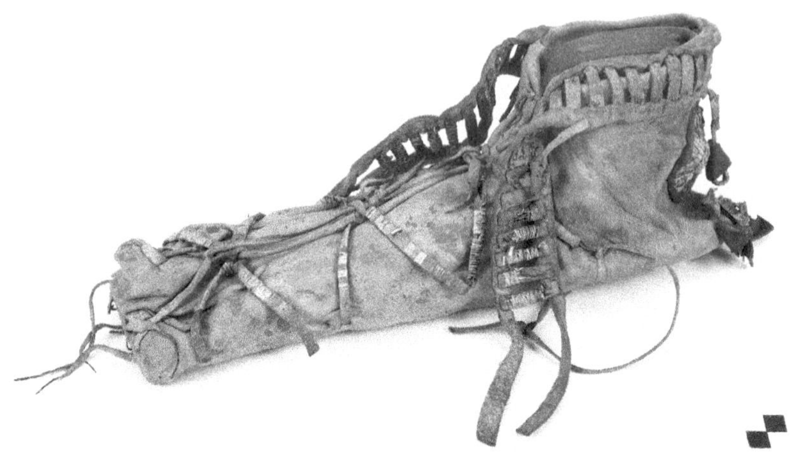

FIGURE 5.1
Toy cradle. Courtesy of the National Museum of the American Indian, cat. no. 214833.

Before taking on larger projects, though, young women probably began quilling smaller things not requiring a vow or ceremony, such as hair ornaments, moccasins, spoon handles, navel amulet bags, knife scabbards, pipe bags, game wheels, necklaces, armbands, pipe stems, and myriad other items now in museum collections or about which no evidence remains. With the introduction of beads by the early 1800s, young women also could learn basic sewing and design skills through beadwork on common items. By painting on parfleches, storage boxes, and other rawhide forms, young women also learned and experimented with Arapaho geometric designs inspired by their individual imagination, experiences, and dreams. Through many genres' graphic artistry, young women acquired the embodied, perceptual knowledge of materials, forms, and storytelling. When and if they showed proficiency, younger women would be introduced by older women to more complex and sacred quillwork projects. At first a young woman was bound to make mistakes and experience frustration as older women tried to correct her:

> When an inexperienced person tries for the first time to do quill-embroidery, failure ensues. The points of the quills stick out, and the whole embroidery becomes loose. When she was young, she once helped other women to embroider a robe. She had never done this before. The line of embroidery which she was working was spoiled, the quills would not stay fast, and the other women refused to work with her. She arose and prayed that she might be able to work successfully, and said that she would make a whole robe in this style of embroidery. An old woman who was present said that this was good. After this the quills remained fast, and she was able to embroider. (Kroeber 1983: 29)

Quillwork was thus a struggle requiring much fortitude, prayer, and practice for young women. They also learned to respect the knowledge, teaching, and oversight of older women, as well as the values conveyed by quillwork gifts.

Young women began quillwork early in the second hill of life at about the time they reached puberty and before they married. Cleaver Warden, the Arapaho ethnographer, interviewed one of the most prolific artists in 1904–1905 and recorded this account in his notebook: "Fire-Wood, an old woman of the Northern Arapaho, Wyoming began to quill cradles, tepees, robes and various other articles when she was fifteen (15) years old. This inducement to work was encouraged by her own parents to keep her home surroundings and honor her kindred. All the old women began to notice her skill and good memory, that they would invited [*sic*] her over to notable gatherings of old women" (Warden-Dorsey 1903–1906: Box 2, Folder 8: 4–5).

In 1932, a Southern Arapaho woman narrated the story of her seventy-seven-year life to Jesse Rowlodge, another Arapaho ethnographer: "By the time I was fourteen years old, I learned to do good bead-work, tan hides, and make almost anything. I also learned to do porcupine quillwork" (quoted in Michelson 1933: 599). She also states that she learned to braid lariats for various functions, though young women were not allowed to haul wood, which was a job reserved for older women.

When girls reached puberty at about age twelve to fourteen, they were expected to become useful, but their mothers also became more watchful of their daughters' movements by minimizing the time they spent out at night, around young men, or engaged in the public world. A girl at this stage was expected to withdraw her eyes, body, and voice from others' attention. Mother and grandmothers took control over girls' daily lives and encouraged them to focus on learning and doing various chores and arts, including quillwork:

> Although she could still play with boys, she had to be in when the sun went down; she could play only in daytime; there was no playing at night. She had to come to where her mother, her aunt, or whoever was guarding her, lived. She had to learn now also to attend to duties similar to those of her mother, aunt, or whoever the person might be with whom she lived. She had to take lessons in caring for and preparing food, tanning hides, making moccasins, and porcupine-quill decorations. Porcupine quills were used in decorations on buckskin shirts, tobacco pouches, moccasins and other wearing apparel, and on the end of feathers used for decorating the head. From now on she had to make the decorations for her own clothes. When a girl reached puberty she gave care and attention to her hair. She wore a wrapping about her body called tŏ'jēhet [informant's translation, "apron"], wore a blanket about her body and head so it covered her eyes to some extent. The apron and blanket were to conceal the direct form of her body. Dresses had to be longer, and arms were not to show. Especially was a girl not to throw her arms around so as to show them. The apron was decorated. The belt which she now discarded was one that had been decorated with silver decorations or beadwork. She commenced now to obey all the orders of her mother or whoever cared for her. She did not cast careless glances around, nor giggle when she was among people. She was continually reminded not to be quick in her actions; not to be silly in order to draw attention upon herself. She also avoided noticing the movement of people around her. From now on she respected her brother. She talked to him only when it was necessary. . . . A boy was really no different than before in his exterior appearance, but a girl had to wear a shawl. (Hilger 1952: 73)

In the second stage of life, a woman's demeanor and disposition were directed away from engagement in the social world outside the lodge. From a modern Euro-American perspective, such restricted seeing, moving, and speaking tends to be seen as oppressive, especially with respect to women, but many studies of Native American traditional communication reveal that maintaining such composure or "shame" is considered a positive expression of self.

In Arapaho language and culture, there were also different stages distinguished within the first two hills of life, but little evidence of these remains. These were classified by different abilities and marked by changes in clothing. Jesse Rowlodge provided Hilger (1936–40) with a list of these distinctions for young women. From birth to the time of walking, an infant was called *tei'yoonehe'* 'little child' regardless of gender. A girl was referred to as *hiseihihi'* 'little woman' from the time of walking to wearing her first belt; from that point until puberty, when a young woman began wearing an apron, she was known as *hiseihitei'yoo* 'woman-child'. During the time between her first apron and marriage, she was called *hiseinit* 'she is a woman'.

At the time girls began to wear aprons, their lives followed different paths from those of their brothers. Whereas teenaged women's lives were shaped by the authority of other women in the space and time of tipi life, the lives of male youths of the same age moved out of the tipi into peer groups that would eventually enter the men's age-grade system at about age sixteen or seventeen. At this time of life, both genders entered the second of the Arapaho four hills of life. The second hill of youth was defined by learning to be useful and showing respect toward others. Brothers and sisters were now obligated to show great mutual respect, which required them to avoid being together in the same tipi or other dwelling if possible and, if their mutual presence was unavoidable, avoid laughing or joking in any ribald way around each other. Because the category of brother and sister extended to all parallel cousins (that is, mother's sister's and father's sister's sons and daughters) and given that families tended to live matrilocally (with the wife's parents' band), brother-sister respect could very well extend to most of the young people in one's camp.

By puberty, the everyday lives of boys and girls took diverging paths that came together only later through marriage. Thus, during the time between puberty and marriage, women's and men's lives began to be socially segregated. Arnold Woolworth mentions, "As soon as a boy's voice has changed . . . he is considered a full grown young man and is turned loose" (quoted in Hilger 1936–40). While young men were on the "loose," they were gradually brought under the authority of older men through the age-grade societies. As young men in their mid-teens entered the first two age grades of Kit-Foxes and Stars, respectively, they began to serve older men and age grades as messengers and runners for ceremonies and day-to-day chores. Both genders, then, were entering the second stage of life of learning to be "useful," but this occurred in different ways and social spaces.

While young men were becoming useful by movements in horse care, hunting, and carrying messages, women were being drawn inside the tipi. Devotion to quillwork within the lodge kindled the quiet, respectful, focused, and family-centered ideal dispositions for young women. Other art forms could be done in the flow of women's social lives, but quillwork was done alone, inside, and in silence. It was not done while chatting, eating, joking, or cooking. Among all roles and tasks, quillwork became the one most associated with personal qualities of persistence, intelligence, and focus, as well as with the power of beauty that women would extend to their surroundings for the remainder of their lives. As a woman's quillwork became known in the camp and band, she became known as a potential wife to many young men and their families. Greene summarizes these values for Plains quillwork in general: "Productivity was taken as an indicator not only of industry and hard work but also of high moral character, particularly sexual chastity. Prestigious craft associations accepted as members only women of acknowledged virtue. Young girls were exhorted to stay home and do beadwork as the alternative to running around with young men" (2001: 1049–50). One of the paradoxes surrounding quillwork, then, was the fact that the more a young woman remained out of the public eye and succeeded in quillwork, the more attractive she became to young men and their families (see Schneider 1983).

As established in the mythical past, quillwork was valued for its power to keep young women inside, close to home, and quiet in their relationship to the world outside. Various facets of the "quiet life" were considered among the highest Arapaho virtues for men and women alike. Children were taught to remain quiet and to listen and observe in adult social spaces. In the same way, all ceremonial times required respectful silence, and all life aimed toward the ultimate quietude of old age (Anderson 2001a: 73–79).

There were only a few times when young marriageable women could leave the tipi on their own: "The custom of the Arapaho mothers was to watch their daughters strictly at all times. They would even accompany us girls to the brush when we went there to attend to nature's demands, for fear some young men might be ambushed, watching their chance to have even an opportunity to talk to us girls. At nights my mother would go out with my chum and myself to see that no young man would molest us" (quoted in Michelson 1933: 599).

Young men and women could see each other only occasionally. Each morning, young women could leave the camp to haul water from the river or stream. Because camps were never located on the water's edge, there was often a path a mile or so in length extending from the camp to the water. Young men could hide along this path to attract the attention of young women fetching water. In the evening, a young woman might be allowed to go outside when the wind changed, to adjust the ears of the tipi for smoke to escape more fluidly. Sometimes young men adjusted the ears themselves so that a young woman would have to come outside, though they would never use such a trick if medicine was stored inside (Michelson 1933: 600). From a distance, too, young men played flutes to serenade their sweethearts.

For a time a young man and woman had to be very clever to court secretly. When they wished to marry, the young man held a meeting with his family, who then deliberated on the matter while they ate a feast. After reviewing the young woman's character, they made a decision. If they decided against it, the couple could, if they desired, pursue another marriage path by eloping and living away from both families long enough for any real or potential bad feelings among kin to die down.

For the arranged-style wedding, if the young man's family determined that the marriage was acceptable, they selected an old woman with respectful manners and a quiet voice to approach and propose the marriage to the young woman's family. Other relatives were called in while the family and old woman ate a meal together. They in turn made a decision, based largely on the word of the woman's brothers, especially the eldest. If the young woman's family accepted the proposal, the old woman returned home to inform her family in another meeting-feast. Then women began gathering presents of food, goods, and robes (though whether quillwork was involved at that stage is not clear), while male relatives contributed horses. Once the presents were delivered and accepted, the young man began serving his parents-in-law by caring for their horses and bringing them meat he had acquired in hunting. The first contribution of meat was marked by a feast, attended by the family, the young man himself, and all the headmen and elders in the camp.

Allowing for time to make and prepare presents, the husband's family gathered together an even larger amount of presents and horses, then delivered them as a group to the prospective wife's family, which then convened to decide how the gifts should be divided among themselves and what date should be planned for the actual wedding. Since the first decision to allow the marriage, the woman's female relatives would have been engaged in many quillwork projects, while men were also making some goods. On the day of the wedding, the woman's mother erected the tipi and arranged the wealth of gifts inside: "For the husband there were one leanback, a warbonnet, bow case and quiver, with contents, a well-made buffalo robe in porcupine quills, shirts, leggings, several pairs of moccasins in various style, and a good pipe, with a well-quilled tobacco pouch. . . . For the wife there were double bags, with contents (of clothing), toilet bags, parfleches filled with dry meat, bags well quilled to keep small articles in, willow leanbacks, willow mattresses, a painted buffalo robe, cooking utensils, a good bucket for water, with a goat horn dipper" (Warden-Dorsey 1903–1906: Box 2, Folder 4: 8–9).

Ponies packed with gifts were set outside, and a feast was prepared. An old woman then informed the new husband and his family that all was ready, upon which they traveled together to the wife's camp. When the couple sat together on a bed at the west side of the tipi and were greeted, prayed for, and lectured by relatives present, they were considered married. After a feast, the new wife gave all the remaining food away and the young man distributed gifts to relatives and friends from his camp, who then returned home. To the sister who had done the most for him, he perhaps even gave the tipi itself to show his respect. According to Warden, the mother-in-law then erected a temporary brush shelter for the couple and arranged for another tipi, usually provided by her brothers. This tipi, too, might then be taken by or given to the young man's age peers or relatives who contributed gifts to his wife. In the end, it is not clear how much of the wealth given, including the quilled robes, tipi, and receptacles, was actually kept by the couple themselves. While many gifts passed through them to their relatives, they began married life with little wealth of their own. From the point of marriage on, a couple in turn would become providers for themselves and others. As young men and women entered marriage and moved through the second and into the third hill of life, they took on increasing and more constant obligations in redistributive gift exchanges of many kinds, for which quillwork played a significant role.

Most published works on Arapaho marriage tend to emphasize the exchange of horses and are confined to the time of the wedding itself, thus offering scant mention or only passing treatment of the complex production and flow of goods involving women. Warden's more comprehensive account includes mention that, among the gifts exchanged, the most valuable were quilled robes, leanback covers, various bags, moccasins, pipe bags, and tipi ornaments. In all, senior women would have been engaged in the largest collective quillwork production for any life transition. A wedding tipi was a major quillwork project, requiring a considerable number of buffalo hides (which had to be scraped ahead of time), many days of work, and considerable provisions for a ceremony or several under the authority of the Seven Old Women. There were expenses men had to bear, too, such as in providing horses and making such items as arrows and quivers (a task often assigned to specialists among them), but the bulk of productive and creative work for marital exchanges fell upon women.

The flow of the most valuable quilled items passed through the couple from women in one family to women in the other, while between men on each side other gifts flowed, such as horses and a few male-manufactured goods such as pipes, bows and quivers, and the like. Determining which side contributed the most value to the exchange is difficult; this was perhaps relative to the time of the marital process. For some years after the marriage, the husband engaged in bride-service to the wife's parents in part to reciprocate for the greater investment they had made in the marriage exchange.

While the public ceremony of the prereservation wedding was one of the least elaborate in Arapaho religious practice, the production and exchange of wealth was greater and more elaborate than in most other ceremonies. The major share of the work fell to senior quillworkers among the sisters, aunts, mothers, and grandmothers of both the husband and the wife. Each wedding held in the proper way would also have involved at least several weeks if not months of quillwork and other arts, as well as at least one or likely several quillwork rituals for producing the tipi ornaments, robes, and leanback covers. These would have required the makers to bear considerable expense in gifts and feasts for the older women involved. As women married and entered the stage of making ceremonial quillwork, they in turn expressed their Arapaho identity and status through the goods they made and gave away across lines of gender and family boundaries. As a woman's quillwork moved across camp boundaries, it carried her name and family's reputation into other camps.

Through quillwork, women also formed age-structured relationships among themselves in ways that were similar to yet different from those that men formed in the age-grade lodges. Also, both practices formed enduring ceremonial kinship between older and younger age groups, though for women the nature of these relationships is less clear in the existing evidence. They were perhaps less formalized than among men and more continuous with actual kinship, because women could learn quillwork from actual mothers or grandmothers.

Women counted their quillwork projects as being central to their life histories, including memories of the kin involved and other stories associated with them. A Southern artist named Mrs. One-Eye Left Hand kept a stick that in 1899 had thirty notches, one for each robe she had made in her life. By that time she had made three robes for one relative and a robe for all but one person in her family (Kroeber 1916–20: Notebook 12: 24–25). About Firewood, the prominent Northern Arapaho quillwork artist, Warden noted, "After she had married her occupation continued until she had reached the mark of sixty assorted baby cradles, fourteen buffalo robes, five ornamental tipis, ten calf robes and one buffalo leanback. Of course she had made five tipis of the standard degree" (Warden-Dorsey 1903–1906: Box 2, Folder 1: 8).

To count the different items they made in their lives, women etched dots in different lines on a stick or personal hide scraper, made of elk horn. Two very good examples are at the American Museum of Natural History (AMNH 50/946, 50/586).

On some scrapers, including those two, you can identify different lines representing different items made, including, for all women, the number of hides they had scraped.

Interestingly enough, women marked the ages of their children in the same way. Each winter, a mother or grandmother notched or punctured a hole on a stick or even her hide scraper, running from the open end to the handle, for each child's added year, since age was always counted by snows or winters, not by each person's birth. At the head of each row a symbol was often etched, representing a child's name, which had been added shortly after birth (Hilger 1952: 87). When children became adults, they were charged with keeping their own ages. Usually the youngest daughter inherited a mother's hide scraper and would keep the count going. That children's ages and women's quillwork projects vowed to promote life movement were marked in this way shows the strong focus women's lives placed on extending life for others, especially children.

Counting quillwork achievements paralleled the counting of men's deeds in war, as well. At one level this is based on a mythical metaphor connecting quills to warriors. In a narrative discussed in chapter 4, the culture-hero Found-In-Grass owns a powerful bladder bag from which he can release the quills as warriors to defeat enemies. Nih'oo3oo cajoles him into teaching him to use the bag, but (as in all such stories) the trickster uses the power inappropriately, with destructive results (Dorsey and Kroeber 1903: 375–78). George Grinnell describes the same valorization for the cognate Cheyenne quillwork practice: "This work [is] considered of highest importance, and when properly performed, quite as creditable as bravery and success in war among the men" (1924: 159–60).

At a practical level, porcupine quills can indeed harm the body. A shooting quill can injure the eyes, and quills not extracted can penetrate the body of an animal or human, traveling in time deeper into vital organs. Anyone who has tried quillwork for the first time knows that the quills indeed jump around. Arapaho ritual logic of life movement, as I discuss elsewhere (Anderson 2001a: 255–59), also associates ceremonial leadership and use of powerful medicines with sacrifice through increased risk to self and family. Each quillwork project required a vow and different sorts of sacrifice, including fasting before the ceremony, gifts to the old women involved, the risk of doing quillwork, and a time commitment of one to several months depending on the rank of the vow.

Significant amounts of work and movement of resources went into quillwork besides the application of quills. Among one of the most arduous tasks was the preparation of hides, which involved staking, pounding, scraping, soaking, drying, and softening. Warden describes the process:

> The hide is prepared by women when the hide is yet green. It is staked out on the ground by means of stake pins, the women take a meat scraper and scrape the meat off the face of the hide cleans. The hide is staked out in the sun until it is perfectly dry, it is then taken out of the ground and turned over, it is then beaten with a stone club to take the hair off, and then it is thinned out or scraped on the hairy side with the hide scraper until it is at the proper thickness. The liver is then secured and roasted in the fire and mixed with tallow until it is like lard. The women then take this mixture and paste it on both sides of the rawhide and hangs it out on a tree to dry. After the rawhide is perfectly dry, it is then soaked in water wrenched out and stretched, it is then hung out and the water scraped off with a

> bone scraper, which is a flat bone notched at one edge, it is then dried. The women then select a leaning branch of a tree and tie a sinew from this "branch" to a trunk of a tree making it like a bow. The hide is then rubbed to and fro by women on a bright day until it becomes soft and pliable, it is then ready for use. The hides are usually complete, that is the heads, limbs or tails still appear on the hides. (Warden-Dorsey 1903–1906: Box 3, Folder 46: 21)

Women would have had many hides to scrape at specific times of the year. Carefully coordinated communal hunts were timed to the gathering buffalo herds for birthing in the late spring and again for the rutting season in the fall. In late spring, small groups of Arapahos left their winter camps in the shelter of the mountain foothills to come together for buffalo hunts, summer ceremonies, and intertribal trade encampments. At the height of summer's heat and the depth of winter's cold, herds dispersed, though men hunted occasional buffalo, elk, deer, antelope, and other game individually at other times. Buffalo hides gathered in the large fall hunts were best for robes because the animals had grown their new winter coats. Hides from spring and early summer when buffalo were shedding their winter coats were generally better used as hides with hair removed.

To prepare for quillwork, women also had to collect quills, dye them, and, for sewing, extract and prepare sinew from butchered game animals. For pendants and other decorative features on quillwork projects, they also had to collect, make, or prepare dewclaws from deer or elk legs, hair strands from buffalo, fringe or thongs from tanned hides, feathers and wool for tufts, rawhide strips for loops and bars, and various other items. They would need to acquire some trade goods as a complement to quillwork, such as bells, metal cones, cloth, and beads. For holding a quillwork ceremony, the sponsor also had to supply gifts, feast foods, medicines, and various other ceremonial goods. In all, as women moved from the second into the third hill of life, the burden on them to provide for others increased, and quillwork came to involve much more by way of obligations than merely the supplies for the project itself. By the end of third hill of life, some women who excelled in all these ways were chosen by their elders to become the new keepers of the sacred bundles and thus the leaders of all quillwork ceremonies.

Cedar-Woman, who was one of the last Southern Arapaho quillwork bundle owners, left most of the descriptions of quillwork ceremonies documented by Kroeber and Warden. Ceremonies were held when a bag was transferred to a new owner or when a woman vowed to make a robe, tipi ornament set, cradle, leanback cover, tipi door, or tipi liner. Women vowed quillwork projects for various troubles or life transitions relatives faced, such as to ensure an easy childbirth, to enable a relative to recover from illness, to secure a safe return from a war party, to contribute to a wedding gift exchange, to maintain the well-being of relatives while traveling away from them, or just to honor a relative.

Once the vow was made, the pledger required some time to acquire the materials, accumulate gifts, prepare foods, and set up a tipi. As in all Arapaho traditions, the woman's relatives would share her burden by contributing to the provisions for the ceremony. All of the Seven Old Women sacred bag owners were invited to a ceremony, though only one of them acted as the principal director, who sat at the western side of the tipi, the place of greatest honor. The director applied the medicines, prayed, blessed the food, burned incense, painted the quillworker, marked out the design on hides, and instructed the pledger. The markers the grandmothers used were made from buffalo knee joints and stored in their sacred bundles when not in use. Kroeber (1983: 209–10) collected a set of three such markers, which are now stored at the American Museum of Natural History (AMNH 50/713DEF).

When necessary, larger projects required dividing some of the work among the other sacred bag owners. Only the pledger and the old women were allowed in the tipi set up for the ceremony, while younger female relatives of the pledger sat outside. Each type of ceremony roughly followed a similar sequence: (1) food and gift preparation by the sponsor; (2) purification of the sponsor with dog-root medicine; (3) presentation of the food to the four directions; (4) feasting; (5) incense purification of the lodge and object made; (6) final preparation of the object; and (7) giving. Though the ceremonies were not considered part of the main ritual complex of the *beyoowu'u,* which included the Sun Dance, age-grade lodges, and the women's Buffalo Lodge, the quillwork ceremonies included many of the same sacred elements, prayers, practices, and medicines and are often mentioned in association with the other lodges (see Dorsey 1903). All quillwork ceremonies took place in a large tipi owned by the sponsoring woman or borrowed from a relative or another family in the camp. Men were excluded from all quillwork ceremonies, save for the final stage, when a male recipient was invited to receive a robe. Kroeber and Warden, however, were allowed to attend and observe a tipi-making ceremony:

> The owner of the tent that was to be ornamented sent a wagon to bring Cedar-Woman. She, however, was not ready, and remained in her tent, painting herself and putting on a good dress. Finally she came on foot, followed by another old woman who possessed a sacred bag, and by a third elderly woman. The food, which is a requisite of the ceremony, was already in the tent, set on the ground around the fireplace. There was now a delay in order that more elderly women might be secured. At last enough were found. With the last comers the writer entered the tent, from which men are ordinarily supposed to be excluded. Cedar-Woman, the head of the ceremony, sat at the back of the tent (i.e., opposite the door, which, as always, faced east). At each side of the tent sat four women, the owner of the tent sitting next to the door. The women were cutting the red cloth into strips and attaching it to the ends of the pendants. The entirely yellow pendants were being worked upon on one side of the tent, the four-colored ones by the women on the other side. Cedar-Woman had the piece of hide on which the large circular beaded ornament was embroidered, and was cutting out the ornament from it. Later she fastened the thin pendants to the cow-tails. While at work putting the ornaments together, all the women seemed to speak and laugh freely. The owner of the tent once went out to get an awl.
>
> The owner of the tent now arose from her place by the door and kneeled before Cedar-Woman, who took medicine from her sacred bag and began to chew it. The kneeling woman held out her two palms together. Cedar-Woman touched her finger to the ground, and then placed it five times on the other woman's joined palms, in four spots forming a circle and then in the middle. The course of her finger was from right to left, contrary to the usual ceremonial order. Then she spit a minute quantity of medicine on the same places on the woman's two hands; the latter then rubbed herself all over with her hands. Cedar-Woman spit on her two cheeks, and then on her own hand, which she placed on the kneeling woman's breast and then on the top of her head. She also took some of the medicine

from her own mouth and put it into the other's. The woman then rose and walked around past the fire and the dishes (which occupied the centre of the tent) to the door. Then she took up a dish of food that stood towards the southeast (i.e., not far from the door), and, holding it just above the ground, walked around the fireplace from left to right. Then she gave it to the woman before whom it had stood. Going to the southwest quarter of the tent, she took up a dish there, and, after having made a complete circuit with it, gave it to the woman nearest whom it had stood. Then she did the same at the northwest and northeast. The rest of the food, other than these four dishes, was not moved. The women all produced plates or kettles, and the owner of the tent ladled out food to them from one dish. The remaining dishes she set before Cedar-Woman. Cedar-Woman took five crumbs from one of the dishes and laid them on the tent-owner's palm. This woman then went around the tent, laying one crumb on the ground at each of the four ends or sides (southeast, etc.) of the tent. The fifth she placed on the fire in the middle. Then she came back to Cedar-Woman, who placed five pieces from another dish on her palm. The woman then rubbed her hands together, and, going around the fire, stood before a tent-pole on the southeast side of the tent. She moved her hands down in front of it with a motion as if she held it and were letting her hands glide down along it. She went successively to the southwest, northwest, and northeast of the tent, and made the same motion before the tent-poles there. The fifth motion she made in the same way before the door. Then, going to Cedar-Woman a third time, she received five grains of corn on her hand, and placed them on the ground and on the fire, just as she had placed the first food given her by Cedar-Woman. The fourth time, Cedar-Woman put pieces of a soft food on her hands, which she "fed" to the poles as previously. Then she brought Cedar-Woman a pot of food standing northeast of the centre (i.e., to the left of the door, viewed from inside the tent), and, having had a little of the contents placed on her hands, made the same motions in front of the four tent-poles and the door as before. From a dish at the southeast (to the right of the door), she then again "fed" the ground. Occasionally she mistook the place or made a wrong motion, whereupon all the other women laughed at her. After she had sat down, a young woman, apparently her daughter, entered the tent and kneeled before Cedar-Woman. She also had her palms touched by the old woman's finger after it had been placed on the ground, and she also had chewed medicine spit upon her. Then Cedar-Woman fed her with a spoon; she passed her hand lightly down over Cedar-Woman's arm several times, apparently as a sign of thanks. Rising, she carried several dishes of food to the door; then took a dish from Cedar-Woman to the other old woman who possessed a sacred bag. Leaving the tent, the young woman returned with plates on which the food in the dish last mentioned was distributed. She went out for more plates, and all the food was dished out. Then she sat down against the door. All now ate. The second old woman with the sacred bag once held up a piece of food and said a short prayer, and one of the other women did the same. When they had nearly finished eating, the young woman left the tent, taking several dishes with her. Several women were now called in from outside, and food was given to them to carry away. At last all the food had been removed from the tent.

Then the owner of the tent, who had again been sitting near the door, went out and brought in live coals, which she put on the fireplace. (As it was summer, there was no fire in the tent.) Cedar-Woman took out from her bag a root which looked like that called niäätä and sliced pieces from it. The owner of the tent now took two forked sticks and with them picked up two live coals from the heap which she had brought in; she laid them on the bare ground before Cedar-Woman, and kneeled before her. With her arm guided by Cedar-Woman, she slowly took a small amount of the finely-cut root from Cedar-Woman's other, outspread hand. Still guided by Cedar-Woman, she moved her arm up and down four times, then four times made a motion as if dropping the root on the two coals, and with the last of these motions dropped it. Then she returned to her seat by the door. Cedar-Woman put the remainder of the finely-cut root on the two coals, and, as the smoke rose, began to pray. She prayed a long time. All the women in the tent bowed their heads, and some covered their eyes. Most of them wept a little. The owner of the tent, then replaced the two coals in the fireplace.

This done, she brought in the cover of her tent. It was laid on the ground, to the south of the fireplace, folded so that it was about a foot wide and perhaps twelve feet long. The head was next to Cedar-Woman, the other end near the door. Cedar-Woman rose, and, followed closely by the owner of the tent, walked around the fire, touching the canvas with the two forked sticks that had been used to pick up the coals. Again she circled around the fire, followed by the woman owning the tent, who carried the ornaments that were to be attached. This time, in walking around the fire, they stepped over the tent four times. . . . Then the top of the tent was spread out. The owner of the tent stood up, motioned four times with the bundle of ornaments, and threw them on the canvas. Cedar-Woman gathered them together, and holding them up, spoke a short prayer. Then she handed the four smaller circular ornaments to four women. All now gathered around the canvas, which was rolled out somewhat, though not fully spread. All the participants were now on the south side of the fire, where the canvas lay, except Cedar-Woman, who kept her place at the middle of the back of the tent, west of the fire, and one woman who remained idle on the other side of the tent, north of the fire. The five circular ornaments were now sewed on the canvas. The large one at the top of the tent was attached under Cedar-Woman's direct supervision, but neither she nor the other old woman possessing a bag sewed. The owner of the tent also did not sew. As one woman remained idle, there thus were five who were sewing on five ornaments. While they worked, they conversed freely. Cedar-Woman never exposed her bag plainly, but kept it covered and wrapped even while taking something from it. This caution may have been due to the presence of the writer. When the circular ornaments had all been sewed to the canvas, Cedar-Woman took two of the cow-tails, and directed one of the women how to attach them to the large ornament. When this had been done, the part of the canvas that would be at the front of the top of the tent was spread out and held flat on the ground. Then seven of the yellow pendants were laid in a row upon it, and their places in a row upon it, and their places marked with a bit of charcoal. In these places holes were then made in the canvas with an awl. The tent had been folded so that it was pierced twice, which made two rows of seven holes. By means of strings of buckskin and small squares of hide, the fourteen yellow pendants were then attached in these places. Then the four-colored pendants were attached in the same manner, below the others, and just above the door; they formed two vertical rows of eight each. The tent was now bundled together and taken out by the woman who owned it. Together with her daughter, she at once began to put it up on the poles that were already standing. This was done, as usual, by taking out the pole at the middle of the back (called hinana'kaya^{n}), laying it on the ground, and tying the canvas to it near its top, so that by raising the pole the canvas was elevated to the proper height. The other women now all came out from the tent in which they had been. Cedar-Woman took the pole that was lying on the canvas and partially raised it four times. Then

> the owner of the tent, unassisted, raised it altogether, put it in its place, and spread the canvas around the framework of poles, though without fastening it either in front, over the door, or at the bottom edge; so that it sagged and hung loosely.
>
> Cedar-Woman now took the four tails which had had embroidered pendants attached to them, and which were to be fastened to the four small circular ornaments that were a few feet above the ground on the southeast, southwest, northwest, and northeast sides of the tent. Starting from before the door and followed by the owner of the tent, she took a complex course that finally brought her before the northeast side of the tent, where one of the tails was to be attached to the beaded ornament. . . . Altogether she walked past every part of the circumference of the tent three times (excepting the distance between the place where she stopped and the door from which she started); crossed the tent four times from north to south or south to north, lifting up the canvas once at each of the places where the ornaments were, going under it, and emerging under the ornament directly to the north or south; and in all her course kept turning from left to right, making five complete revolutions. When the two women had stopped on the northeast of the tent, the owner pierced the ornament with an awl, and Cedar-Woman fastened the tail to it. The remaining participants in the ceremony, together with several other persons who had been watching outside, looked on from a distance, sitting on the ground. The two women then went to the ornament on the southeast side of the tent, and, having fastened a tail to it in the same manner, did the same at the southwest and then at the northwest. Then Cedar-Woman sat down with the others; and the owner of the tent, assisted by her daughter, took down the now completely ornamented tent.
>
> Ordinarily this would have ended the ceremony; but the same woman had another tent to be ornamented. Accordingly the women re-entered the tent in which they had been, and the owner brought in to them a second canvas. Presumably this was decorated and set up like the first, although without another meal preceding.
>
> This ends the account of the tribal decoration of the Arapaho. (Kroeber 1983: 71–77)

Many remarkable facts are described in this account. First of all, Cedar-Woman and the other old women are slow and methodical in preparing and arriving. As I discuss in *The Four Hills of Life* (Anderson 2001a), Arapahos in the fourth hill of life, or *beesneniteeno'* 'big people' (now called "elders"), had moved toward quietness in their ways of speaking and acting and thus were slow to move. They arrived for ceremonies or initiated actions in them only when it was the right time and after all preparations had been completed. As one moved through the four hills of life, one's tempo slowed into more respectful, quieter, and increasing straightness of bearing. As such, elders were the social clock for proper actions in all ceremonies and all things important to the tribe. They made sure that things were done with due preparation, with methodical care, and in the right sequence. However, the social atmosphere of the ceremony was, as Kroeber notes, lighthearted and cordial. When the senior woman made mistakes in the ceremony, laughter from the other senior women redirected her, and, as Warden describes below, the director could purify with incense any younger women who made a mistake.

Another dimension of the ceremony present in all Arapaho ritual is the proper placement or orientation of paint, prayers, medicine, food, and ornaments in the four-directional sequence that recurs in quillwork designs. All four directional movements with a return to the fifth point in the center represent appeals to the Four Old Men to watch over all present and desires for a long life to extend through all the four stages, or hills, as in the concept of *hiiteeni*. Furthermore, movements and ritual speech often require four circuits around the periphery. In all these ways, movement in space was a way of constituting ritual time, as governed by the knowledge and power channeled through the old people and, for quillwork, through the old women specifically.

Warden's notes offer the following account of a similar ritual for the making of a tipi liner with quilled lines:

> A married woman prepares a feast and invites the older women to her lodge for directions and instructions for lines and quill work on the lining. The women must reach the age and have a knowledge of [the] tepee ritual in order to conduct any work of this kind. This class of women own what is called the sacred bags about a foot long and five inches wide[;] they are made just like the clothes bags of the women and contain medicine roots such as main root, dog root, sweet grass and spruce needles. These bags also contain a cup shaped stone called incense stone, black and red paint and a piece of tallow for the woman[']s ritual. Before the lines are drawn and quilled, one of these owners of [a] sacred bag take a bit of dog root[,] chews it and spits on both palms of the hands in five places[;] this signifies consecration. She runs this spittal [*sic*] on her head, heart and parts of the body, then directs the scholar to do the same thing. This scholar draws with black paint lines away from her. The food is placed by the old women and eaten. Most of the food is again taken out of the tepee by [a] relative of the old lady and also friends of those participating in the ritual. Events of this character are being told during the assemblage to correct any mistake which may have been made by other women. Women who have made blunders on the lines and discs may be purified by the older women. Women have hints or jokes exchanged during the ritual.
>
> The maker of this lining asks the permission of the director of the meeting to have the disposal of this lining made [and then gestures to the] assistants to put the insense [*sic*] on the live charcoal on the stove for purification. She passes this lining over the smoke of the insense [*sic*] five times and gives it to the person[.] [T]he maker of this lining then relates . . . her vow. (Warden-Dorsey 1903–1906: Box 3, Folder 46: 21 [1905])

Seven of the oldest women in each of the two Arapaho tribes owned the sacred quillwork bags. Ordinarily men were not allowed to see the bags, though both Warden and Kroeber were permitted to see them and observe the ceremonies. Kroeber was able to purchase one of the women's sacred bags from a daughter of Backward, who had made it to replace the bag she transferred to Cedar-Woman in the description below. The bag is currently housed in the American Museum of Natural History (AMNH 50/713A–J), but none of the relevant medicines are stored in it.

The bag is tanned red with four red-, blue-, and white-beaded rectangular designs, two on the side and two on the rim. It contains six cloth wrappings (perhaps for the bag itself), two small bowl-shaped stones used for paint mixing, three bone pieces for marking designs on quillwork, and a red-painted hide bag about eleven centimeters long and eight centimeters wide with four round separate sections for storing natural red paint. The bag as a whole was likely stored carefully in the owner's tipi, wrapped in several pieces of calico, as is the practice for all sacred bundles or bags. The bags containing women's quills were stored in a bag made of (buffalo) intestine and shaped like a long enclosed canoe (see figure 4.1). Several of these bags are stored in various museums, suggesting that all women quillwork artists owned one or more of these. Each color of quills was stored in a separate gut bag, and these were stored in women's work bags, containing all their instruments and materials for quillwork, including "awls, sinew, quills, needles, bones for quill-flattening and for painting, incense, paint, medicine, and similar miscellaneous articles" (Kroeber 1983: 28–29). The work bags are similar to those used by women throughout the plains, though with variations of quillwork or beadwork designs on them.

Two Arapaho bags at the Museum of Natural History (AMNH 50/1002; 50/1006) are described and illustrated by Kroeber (1983: 99–100. Several others are stored in the museum (AMNH 50/29, 50/725, 50/726, 50/744). Made of buffalo or cattle hide with the hair retained, they are all rectangular flat envelope-form bags from twenty-two to thirty-three centimeters long and fifteen to twenty-five centimeters wide. The hair on several examples is completely worn off from use. One is very old, with signs of wear, and has no beadwork on it (AMNH 50/726), suggesting much use over a long career. Another work bag (AMNH 50/1006) is worn but newer and made from Hereford calf or steer hide. Several (AMNH 50/29, 50/725, 50/1006, 50/1002) have a beadwork strip along the flap at the top, narrower beadwork lines along each lateral side seam, and a short segment in each corner of the bottom, either separate from the lines on the side or continuous with them. A smaller, old work bag made of buffalo hide (22 by 15 centimeters) is also stored at the museum (AMNH 50/29). On the lip of the flap on the worn bag is a single line of quillwork that has almost worn off. Symbolism includes simple common beadwork and paint designs for tipis, elk hooves, mountains, paths, trails, and springs (Kroeber 1983: 100). They are thus the common designs of nonritualized women's art that allow individual creativity.

Warden's description of Firewood's sacred bag also includes the same items, with the addition of four cupped incense stones, dog root, sweetgrass, main root, natural red paint, and tallow (Warden-Dorsey 1903–1906: Box 2, Folder 8: 3). Medicines and paints were usually stored in each of the Seven Old Women's quillwork bags, as well. Red paint made by combining ochre and tallow seemed to be the only color used in quillwork ceremonies. Charcoal was used for marking out designs for quillwork projects. Incense stones were found in mountains or on hills, partially embedded in the ground. Main root, dog root, and four different types of incense were contained in smaller bags.

Succession of the bundle owner followed the pattern of all Arapaho ceremonial leadership. One never asked for or lobbied for such a role outwardly. Rather, elders selected as successors those whose personal demeanor and disposition were appropriate, based on personal observation of the candidates throughout their entire lives. All succession ceremonies also involved the transfer of sacred objects associated with the position. Cedar-Woman describes the ceremony through which her sacred bag was passed on to her from Backward, mother of a famous Southern Arapaho chief:

> Backward, the mother of Little-Raven, was the owner of my bag before it was transferred to me. This bag was owned successively by Night-Killer, Bihiihä ('Female Deer'?), Backward, and myself. When I was about to obtain this bag, I provided

food, clothing, and horses (to be given away), and called all the old women who then had bags. There were seven. They were River-Woman, Large-Head, Thread-Woman, Sore-Legs, Flying-Woman, another Thread-Woman, and Backward. A tent was put up. The clothing was laid all around the inside of the tent, the food was set near the fire. I also provided four knives and some fat. The Seven Old Women sat around the tent, each with her bag. I went to each in turn, putting my hand on the top of her head, and prayed. I said that I wished to get a bag in the straight way. Before they opened their bags they spit hëçawaanaxu [*he3owoonoxu'* 'dog medicine'] on them (this is a root which is chewed fine, and usually spit on sacred objects before they are handled). Then incense was burned. One of the women took fat and rubbed it with paint; then, holding her hands palm to palm, and turning them from side to side, she painted four spots on my face, and a fifth (in the centre) on the nose; then she painted five spots in similar position (that of a quincunx) on the top of my head. The food had been placed southwest, northwest, northeast, and southeast of the fire (the tent always faces east, the fire being in the centre). The food towards the southwest was taken up, carried around the tent, and set down in the same place as before, in front of one of the old women. This woman then carried the other food around the tent in the same way, replacing it all. Then she took hëçawaanaxu, chewed it, and rubbed it over her body (a very frequent act in rituals). Then she took food from four dishes and placed it on her hand in five spots. Two of these pieces or heaps of food she placed on the ground, southwest and northwest of the fire; two she raised and laid on the ground, northeast and southeast of the fire; and the fifth she put into [the] fire. Then she took (a dish of) blood-soup or pudding (bëëk^{u}) [*be'eek*]. She touched it with a finger, touched this finger on the palm of her hand, and rubbed her hands together. Then she moved her hands downward four times towards the southeast of the tent, representing the planting in the ground of a tent-pole there. Then she touched the pudding in three other places, after each time rubbing her hands, and successively motioning towards the southwest, northwest, and northeast. The fifth time she made a scoop in the middle of the pudding; this she followed by motioning lower down, towards the pegs holding the edge of the tent. While she was doing this, the others looked down, holding their left hand on the top of the head, the right hand on the ground. A small dog had been cooked whole. Backward took the dog by the head, and I took its hind-end, and we walked around the tent. We walked around again, stopping on the southeast side and making a turn there, and then the same successively at the southwest, northwest, and northeast (i.e., going in a circle with the sun). Then we made a turn before the door (inside the tent), and held the dog outside the door, moving its head, and telling it to look about at the people, the clothing, the food, the water, and so on. Then we took pieces of meat from its four paws, its nose, the top of its head, and its tail, and put them on the ground four times, and a fifth time into the fire. Then Backward who performed this took the dog's tongue, and, holding it at the tip, touched one side of it, and then the other, to the ground at the southeast, southwest, northwest, and northeast successively; and at last, with a downward movement, touched the tongue against the wooden pins fastening the front of the tent above the door. Then the food was eaten. A dish standing southeast from the fire was first taken and passed to each in the tent, travelling in a circle; then the food at the southwest was taken; and so on around the fire until all the food had been passed around. Then friends were called, and the remnants given to them. After the dishes and plates had been taken out of the tent, incense was again burned inside. Then she told me to give her the

> four knives, and a board on which she cut medicine. I took niibaa^{n}tou (hemlock-leaves) and niisêna^{n} (part of a beaver) and cut them fine. Backward took biihtcei-hina^{n} (yellow composita) and niäätä^{n} (a greasy carrot-like root), the rest cut up and mixed ni'ôx with niisêna^{n}, and niäätä^{n} with niisêna^{n}. This made four kinds of incense. Then Backward, with a spoon of mountain-sheep horn, took up the several incenses and put them into the small bags into which they belonged. Again she put incense on the coals. Then they all painted themselves with red paint and tallow. After that they painted their bags: they touched them with their palms in four places, and then in a spot in the middle of these four, and thereupon rubbed the whole bag with paint. They also painted the stones (used for holding coals for incense) and the pieces of bone (used for marking designs on robes) that were in the bags. The latter two incenses are used when a tent is decorated; the former two, with the stones and bones, when a robe is to be made. They replaced all these things in their bags and closed them. Then Backward told me to give her the cloth goods I had provided. I gave them to her. She touched the ground and put her finger to her tongue; then she rubbed me over with medicine from her mouth. She spit medicine on a piece of the goods, and put it under my dress from below, and, passing it under the dress to my other side, took it out there and laid it down. Then she passed another piece under my dress in the opposite direction. She repeated this three times more, so that at the end there were four pieces of goods lying on each side of me (those on one side having been interchanged with those on the other by passing them under the dress). Then she pushed two pieces under my dress on my stomach, and successively placed them below my shoulder, over the heart, and on my stomach again. There she left them. The other goods were given away. Backward told me to leave the pieces of cloth on my stomach for four days, while I fasted; then to prepare food and invite all the old women in again. I fasted and cried for four days, on the fourth, food was prepared, and the old women came again. After they had eaten, I received the bag, with instructions how to use it. Backward made a motion four times to give it to me; then, at a fifth motion with it from her heart, she gave it to me. (quoted in Kroeber 1983: 29–33)

The ceremony follows the same pattern of the tipi and robe ceremonies and includes a sequence of ritual action and some elements commonly found in other Arapaho sacred ceremonies. As in many Arapaho ceremonies, there are four incomplete motions before any important act of transfer or construction is completed on the fifth. Further, all medicines in the new bag had to be resupplied for the new owner. The four incense mixtures were made from combinations of (1) *niisenoo,* beaver castor gland; (2) *nii'iboootou'u,* pine or fir needles (*Abies lasiocarpa,* Rocky Mountain fir); (3) *biihceyeinoo'oo'* 'it turns pink' or *biihce'einoo'* 'it has a pink head', a yellow Compositae, probably of a species of the genus *Erigeron,* commonly called daisy or fleabane, with a flower with a yellow center that turns from white to pink; (4) *nii'eetee',* called greasy carrot root, classified as *Lomatium dissectum* and commonly known as biscuit root, fernleaf, or carrotleaf and related to various types of wild parsley; and (5) *ni'oxu',* sweetgrass, a common Native American incense of the plant *Hierochloe hirta.*

In the ceremony, Cedar-Woman mixed the fir needles and beaver castor gland while Backward cut and mixed biscuit root and the yellow daisy. The other women made two other incenses by mixing beaver castor gland with sweetgrass and biscuit root with beaver castor, respectively. The former two were used for robe ceremonies, the latter for tipi ornament making. As in other ceremonies, these types of incense were most often used to prepare people or ceremonial objects for the next stage of painting.

As mentioned above, dog root and main root were the two medicines used in quillwork ceremonies. The dog-root medicine used, also called bear medicine, is said to represent "purity, protection, and expectation" (Dorsey 1903: 66) and the "future seeds, [or] livelihood of the race" (Warden-Dorsey 1903–1906: Box 2, Folder 5: 3 [1905]). Main root, associated with peace and quietness, was used in the Sun Dance and men's Dog Lodge, as well (Dorsey 1903: 68). It was especially associated with older people and the quieting phase of core ceremonies they directed. Dog root was also used in all the age-grade lodges, in the Sun Dance, and in the women's Buffalo Lodge. Dog root was apparently not used in the sweat lodge of the very old men. Main root and dog root are thus complementary but age related. Main root was burned as incense in many ceremonies. As a purifier prior to all other actions, dog root is applied with spittle after chewing to sacred objects and participants' bodies before painting, preparing objects, or doing quillwork (Kroeber 1983: 30).

All Arapaho medicines and the homes of their owners were highly respected. They were kept apart from expectant women, birth itself, illness, children, and menstruating women. It is thus highly likely that women in any of these states would not have been allowed to participate in quillwork ceremonies and that only women beyond childbearing years could become bag owners. This explains why all of the younger women attending the ceremonies remained outside. A quillwork bag owner and her lodge were thus as respected as any male-owned medicines. The seven sacred quillwork bags were considered parallel to the seven bags owned by the seven most senior old men of the sweat lodge. Children were taught to avoid playing or making noise near such lodges. Lodges with medicines also had to be kept immaculately clean, and when cleaned the medicines had to be removed to a stand at a distance from the lodge.

The bag transfer ceremony also involved painting to renew the bags, stones, and bones used for marking robes, and the owners themselves. Warden observes of the common quincunx order of face-painting that "[i]t represents [the] creator's distribution of parcels of clay at the four corners and in the center of the horizon. The painting upon [the] head also typifies the same purpose. Hands are tinted the same way" (Warden-Dorsey 1903–1906: Box 2, Folder 18). During the creation, turtle as earth-diver returned to the surface of the global deluge with red dirt he had recovered from the muddy bottom below. Taking the earth from his claws, Man-Above, or Our Father, placed the earth on the Flat-Pipe and then radiated the earth outward to create land. While other colors of paint were used in younger age-grade ceremonies, for both men and women, red paint was the only color associated with the fourth hill of life. As a person matures, he or she thus moves closer to the center and becomes increasingly "human," thus more and more Arapaho. As women became quillwork bag owners, they entered the center of Arapaho life, personhood, and religiosity. Along with fellow male elders, they also became directors of all the lodges and all things crucial to the tribe.

The first project Cedar-Woman supervised as an owner of the quillwork bag was a twenty-line robe (*niisoòuht*) vowed by Yellow-Woman for a male relative:

A few days later, Yellow-Woman called me to make a buffalo-robe. The hide was already dressed and prepared. I entered the tent. At the back of the tent lay the buffalo-skin, folded and laid like a buffalo. Its head was toward the door. By it lay five pieces of goods as payment. I sat down at the middle of the back of the tent, behind the buffalo-skin. I told Yellow-Woman to call the other women. After they came, food was taken around (and sacrificed), as at the time when I received my bag. Then we ate, and the remainder was taken out for friends and the children. Then I burned incense. Then two of the women motioned toward the buffalo-skin with sticks, whipping it as if to make a buffalo rise. Then I spread the robe (the hair-side to the ground). I put a burning coal on the ground and placed incense upon it. I spit medicine on one of the marking-bones five times. I held the bone successively on four sides of the coal, near the ground; the fifth time I drew the bone across above the coal, to signify the marking (which is done by drawing the edge of the bone along the hide). Then all came close around the buffalo-robe and held it. Yellow-Woman with the marking-bone drew lines across it, which were to be embroidered with porcupine-quills. In her mouth she had hëçawaanaxu [dog root], and she wet the end of the bone with saliva. When she had drawn the lines, she raised her right arm. I took the robe and four times I made a motion as if to give it to her; the fifth time I gave it to her, putting it under her arm. Then Yellow-Woman held out her hands, and I spit medicine on them four times. Then I laid on her hands four quills tied together, one each being red, yellow, white, and black; and with them I gave her sinew (thread) and needles. Yellow Woman passed the quills between her lips, and then held them in her mouth. Then she began to embroider one line, beginning nearest the head of the skin. I watched her and gave her directions. When she had completely embroidered this line, she stopped. After this, one line was embroidered a day. It took a month to complete the robe. A line of embroidery must not be left unfinished over night. When the robe was completed, Yellow-Woman notified me. She invited me to come the next day to eat. The next day there was a feast like that given when the robe was begun. The robe was set up again to resemble a buffalo, and after being perfumed with incense, was touched as if to make it rise. Then it was spread out and five feathers laid upon it,—one at each corner and one in the centre. Then the women sewed the feathers in those places. Then Yellow-Woman announced the man for whom she had made the robe, and he was sent for. He was Bird-in-Tree. He came in, and sat down in front of me, looking toward the door. Yellow-Woman spit on the blanket four times, moved it toward him several times, then gave it to him. Then both he and the robe were perfumed with incense. Then he gave Yellow Woman his best horse; she kissed him for it. Then he went out with his new robe. (quoted in Kroeber 1983: 33–34)

In the traditional Arapaho way, she had to prepare her mind and heart in the right way. Throughout completion of the vow, the pledger apparently was not allowed to do any other kind of work but quillwork and, in the traditional way, thus focus her mind on that exclusively. A woman's quillwork pledge or bag transfer required the cooperation of other women in the camp, mainly married and unmarried daughters, sisters, and perhaps co-wives. A one-hundredth robe, for example, required the regular time of preparation and at least three months between the opening and final ceremony, because the quillworker completed one row each day. A bag transfer ceremony required more gifts, a larger feast, and fasting for four days in the same way men and women fasted for the lodges. As in other ceremonies, all objects involved were treated as living beings associated with life forces of animals, sacred beings, and humans. Throughout all ceremonies, goods and intangible values were exchanged. As in other Arapaho ritual practices, a vow not only activated cooperation and exchange among kin but also required others to focus their minds on the woman's completion of her vow. Others in camp took up the slack for daily chores, such as gathering wood, fetching water, cooking, and carrying out the other daily and seasonal work. It also required men, whether husbands or sons-in-law, to provide meat for feasts and the raw materials for the project. Some ceremonies required more cooperation and support than others, for some were more prolonged and thus involved more serious vows. A woman pledger in each case did indeed increase her status, as so many others have emphasized, but not solely because of the completed project or vow or the value inherent to it, for the gifts, feast, and the transfer of ownership of the object were public expressions of her and her family's respect, generosity, and sacrifice toward those of all ages. As in other contexts of giveaways and feasts, women were the primary organizers. The difference for quillwork ceremonies is that all feasts and giveaways therein were for and by women.

Because quillwork ceremonies were sacred, many details are not documented, including those about the involvement of women quillworkers in other ceremonial contexts. The least is known about sacred roles in the fourth hill of life, even less for women than for men. For example, the oldest women could also own another kind of sacred bag believed to hold all the laws of the other lodges and used in the old men's sweat lodge. The bag was called *wox(u)sox* 'bear bag' or *wox(u)sihto* 'bear's foot'. One such bag and some of its traditional contents, but not the medicines, reside in the American Museum of Natural History collections (AMNH 50/714–720). Kroeber purchased it, along with Backward's sacred quillwork bag, in 1899 for twenty-six dollars. The large outer bag was made by a man named Curly, who passed it on to Backward, who in turn handed it down to Cedar-Woman. As for all sacred bags or bundles, younger people kept a respectful distance from it and the owner's tipi where it was stored. Children were taught to avoid making loud noises, running, or playing nearby. At particular times, people made presents of cloth to wrap it, much as they did to other sacred bundles and objects, as prayers for their family members' well-being, and thus they were able to see the bag opened (Kroeber 1916–20: Notebook 11: 22–24). Sitting at the west end of the tipi, the woman owner carefully opened the bag, leaving the large outer bag closest to her with food inside, the somewhat smaller bundle in front of it, and then spread out the grizzly bear claws stored within it. A figure called the "man" (*hinenitee*) was set up nearest the fire in the center, and beside it a stick representing a horse. She then put a piece of incense from the bag associated with the woman and another for the man. In mythical time the sacred bear bag was acquired with knowledge of the women's Buffalo Lodge, which was in turn acquired from the buffalo beings. In the story about this transfer, a poor family with only one pony is left behind by the camp, which thus had shown no mercy or pity to them in the way humans should. The man of the family encounters Buffalo Cow, who does pity him and then allows herself and her calf to be killed to provide food for human beings. With this sacrifice, buffalo humanize the people through their gift of all the knowledge for all the old people about all the ceremonial dances. This knowledge gave humans the ability to pity each other and follow a moral code:

> In the camp, there were old men and women, but they were ignorant of the natural law which had just been given to the race through this man; in fact the people at that time were ignorant of things and to a certain extent wicked. They were without tribal law and had no feeling of sympathy one toward another, and for that reason, this man who had rescued the people from starvation was left behind with such a heavy burden. This man gave the old people wisdom and knowledge of the various natural laws. He gave them certain degrees with the right to conduct ceremonial dances. (Dorsey and Kroeber 1903: 48)

The origin of the Buffalo Lodge was thus also the beginning of hunting buffalo, the source of knowledge for all the lodges, and the origin of the sacred bear bag of the Old Man's Lodge, perhaps more aptly called the Old People's Lodge, since both men and women seem have been involved. Before the first Buffalo Lodge could be held, the bag was made, under the direction of both the old men and the old women, to contain "bear claws, buffalo horns, rattles, buffalo tails, paint, tallow (incense), and stones" (Dorsey and Kroeber 1903: 48). Very little is known about the Old Men's Lodge or the sweat lodge of the Seven Old Men, but several references place both old men and women in these most sacred ceremonies and in association with the seven sacred bear bags. By the final stage or winter of life, men's and women's sacred roles were shared and merged with less distinction of gender than in younger stages of life.

As ceremonial leaders sitting beside the oldest men, quillwork bag owners obviously participated in the entire series of sacred lodges in the *beyoowu'u* series, "all the lodges." Quillwork once adorned the paraphernalia and outfits of dancers in all lodges with a public ceremony, including the Offerings-Lodge, women's Buffalo Lodge, and the middle sequence of men's age-grade lodges. The men's age grades included, from youngest to oldest, the Kit-Foxes, Stars, Clubboard Men (also called Tomahawk), Spear Men, Crazy Men, Dog Men, Old Men, and Seven Old Men, but neither the last two nor the first two performed public lodge ceremonies or had quillwork associated with them. By their mid-teens, young men formed age sets that passed through the sequence of societies together. Concurrently, young women began to participate in the Buffalo Lodge at about the same time they began to do quillwork. Men in the second and third hills of life could pledge the Offerings-Lodge, now the only extant Arapaho lodge (and commonly known as the Sun Dance). Prior to every lodge ceremony for the middle men's age grades (that is, Clubboard, Spear, Crazy, and Dog) and Buffalo Lodge was a preparation phase in which the dancer's ceremonial grandfathers and elder brothers passed on paraphernalia or had it remade, most likely by women quillworkers.

Aprons worn in the Spear Lodge ceremony had four short tabs of quillwork similar to the pair at the top of disk cradle styles. The quilled slats of one apron example (AMNH 50/875) have the typical central red section and two outer yellow sections, divided by black fiber lines. Various other items for the lodge have quilled thongs or loops that are very similar to tipi and cradle ornaments. Kroeber's field notes include mention of one case in which some quilled pendants for the women's Buffalo Lodge were used later for tipi ornaments, so some ornaments may have moved back and forth between the lodges and other uses. The rectangular Morning Star design on a yellow background is also found on Spear Lodge arm bands. In the men's Crazy Lodge, dancers wore quillwork on their anklets, headbands, and eagle-bone whistle strap. All examples are wrapped quillwork on thongs in the predominant color of white for the lodge. Some examples appear to share a yellow background with red for the design, which is framed on each line of quillwork by a short black section of fibers. Dog Lodge rattles had quillwork in three sets of three, each forming the rectangular Morning Star design, similar in form to that of the red and white oblong cradle styles. A sash of the second-degree dancer in the Dog Lodge had four sections of four parallel quilled lines. Each line had six sections broken by black dividers alternating between white and yellow.

An extraordinary sash in the National Museum of Natural History (see plate 14) was collected by Emile Granier and once owned by the Northern Arapaho Chief Sharp Nose (NMNH 200788). Made of red wool trade cloth, it has five embroidered quill rosettes and five rectangular Morning Star formations along its length. Both quillwork forms have red designs on white backgrounds. The rosettes have four rings and four red tipi forms in a cross.

The Sharp Nose sash has a series of hair ornaments on the top edge and an array of seven eagle-feather ornaments. Each rectangular section runs the width of the sash and includes four flat quill-wrapped thongs with two longer red sections in the central pair and two shorter ones in the outer pair. Each red section is, as is typical for quillwork, set off by black fiber dividers. The sash is similar in form to the third-degree dancer's sash (AMNH 50/698), which has five smaller white and black rosettes along its shorter length, along with the same feather formation, though lacking the rectangular Morning Star formations. Given its length and red color scheme, this may have been a first-degree Dog Dancer's sash, for which a description is missing in Kroeber's *The Arapaho* (1983: 201)

Surviving regalia for the women's Buffalo Lodge have even more quillwork than any of the men's lodges, though limited to small designs and wrappings. There were five ranks of dancers in the lodge: (1) one highest dancer called White Woman; (2) a second rank called Owner-of-Tent-Poles; (3) a third rank named White Stand; (4) a fourth rank called Red Stand; (4) two young girl dancers called "Calves"; and (5) lowest-degree dancers (Kroeber 1983: 210–25). Similar to patterns on some men's lodge regalia, the most consistent forms are the Morning Star cross and the line or rectangle with five white or yellow sections of equal length separated by black dividers and borders. The latter generally symbolize the four hills of life. An apron for the lodge (AMNH 50/865) has four such designs, each two quill lines wide, arranged vertically across the front among five alternating simple Morning Star crosses of narrow twisted quill lines. All wavy bottom edges on aprons are quilled with a trim line. The apron for the White Stand dancer is the same, with the addition of two pendants in the center, each with three bars of the same design, two loop ornaments on the bottom, and a buffalo hair piece hanging down a few inches below the apron's bottom; two ornament sets of five quill- or fiber-wrapped strings with buffalo hair hanging beneath each; and two hoops, one on each end of a quilled thong belt along the top. As for other Buffalo Lodge rings, each has four white quadrants divided by black marks. One of the rings has a cross of white and black in the middle. A similar alternating five-cross/four-bar design is on the White Stand headdress, except that the five-sectioned lines are arranged vertically among the crosses (AMNH 50/385). The hoops at the ends of the apron symbolize Sun, and the four black marks the ends of the earth, or places of the Four Old Men. The same divided white line is found in a three-lined rectangular form on the forehead of the headdresses (AMNH 50/864) for the first and second ranks. Variations of these patterns are on aprons for the third-degree dancer and lowest-degree dancers. The bar design for the Red Stand feather headdress is the same alternating bar and Morning Star sequence. The buffalo-horn headdress for the lowest-ranked dancers has the same pattern along the front rim and on the apron, rings, and ornaments. The Red Stand belt has slightly different vertical quilled slats forming a rectangular Morning Star design. This pattern compares, according to Kroeber, to the red-yellow-white-black sequence on various ceremonial quillwork for cradles, tipis, robes, and other objects (1983: 220–21). The symbolic meaning of the four quilled strips on each belt is the four hills of life (Kroeber 1983: 214). The bands for the White Stand and Red Stand feathered headdresses represent snakes. Black marks on hanging thongs represent *hiiteeni,* the life principle. All cross forms are, of course, Morning Star. The four marks on rings carried or worn also represent the four ends of the earth (Kroeber 1983: 219). As on other quillwork, loops represent eyes. The embroidered piece of hide on the lowest-ranked dancers' buffalo headdress represents eyes and brain, paralleling the head disk symbolism on cradles.

There are remarkable similarities among many core symbolic associations in both lodge regalia and quillwork projects. The most frequent in the lodge designs are the Morning Star and four hills designs, found also on cradles, tipis, and robes. The rosette designs on Buffalo and Spear Lodge regalia are different from rosettes elsewhere but do resemble those on the Painted Circle Robe. Also, the color scheme is generally dual in lodge quillwork, involving only white and black, yellow and black, or red and white as the primary contrasts, depending on rank and ceremonial lodge.

Given that quillwork is simpler in form and smaller in extent on lodge regalia than on pledged projects, an experienced artist, who could have produced a forty-inch row of quillwork in one day, could have easily embroidered a set of lodge regalia in the three-day preparation phase. The objects themselves were considered more sacred, though, than the pledged forms of quillwork. For the Dog, Crazy, and Buffalo Lodge, much of the regalia appears to have been stored and reused for each performance. Stored regalia had to be treated as "medicine" with shadows or spirits and thus required great care. They were not allowed to touch the ground; children were barred from making noise around them; and no ashes could be removed while the owner or the regalia were inside the tipi. Like other sacred objects, they could be opened and prayed to ceremonially from time to time to keep them in good condition. They could also be transferred from one owner to another in successive generations. Regalia for the Buffalo Lodge, at least, also required a much larger reciprocal gift than for the quillwork projects women pledged. Kroeber notes that one new owner paid her ceremonial grandmother four horses, two cattle, and other property for her Buffalo Lodge regalia (Kroeber 1983: 220).

Descriptions of the lodge ceremonies do not include details about how the quillwork on lodge paraphernalia was applied. Although Kroeber (1983: 160) observes that ceremonial grandfathers made their grandsons' respective regalia in the age-grade lodges, it is highly unlikely that those men produced the quillwork. There are a number of possibilities to consider. One is that a grandfather's wife applied the quillwork for the dancer, given that the two were commonly linked in the ritual process. In either case, the Seven Old Women probably supervised or marked out the designs, as in all other ceremonial quillwork. Another possibility is that the Seven Old Women produced the quillwork during the preparation phase of each ceremony, though there is no mention of that.

Despite the many dangling strands of knowledge left untied about quillwork, when all of the evidence is brought forth, it is clear that quillwork was present and instrumental in almost all life transitions and ceremonial lodges. Quillwork artists were indeed primary actors in all childhood rituals and major, often inconspicuous agents for all adult ceremonies. While ethnographic attention tends to focus on the public side of ritual performances, clearly women were involved at least as much in the space and time mislabeled "behind the scenes" by a Western gaze. In any present or past ceremonial context, one must always try to find out where all of the objects originated. By the fourth hill of life, men's and women's roles, dispositions, and authority converged into authority over all religious life. The bundle owners, in particular, were instrumental to ceremonial life well beyond the sphere of supervising the gifts women pledged for kin. Their ties to medicines and creative power have long been overlooked.

CHAPTER SIX

The Movement of Quillwork in History

As stated at the outset, one aim here is to follow quillwork objects, practices, and ways of seeing them through different paths of history. To move in that direction, we must reconsider the evidence and findings of past research in light of a rigorous concern for the place of quillwork in Arapaho history. The actual path of quillwork through Arapaho history is difficult to trace with precision in several ways, but there are numerous direct and indirect lines to follow to appreciate the depth of quillwork in Arapaho religious history, the factors that contributed to the decline of the art form, and how the meanings and values of quillwork have changed as it became a commodity and object of research.

First of all, determining exactly how and when Arapaho peoples arrived in the plains area is difficult. For the period prior to the eighteenth century, no substantial archaeological evidence is available, and there has been little research into connections between the plains prehistoric record and Arapaho peoples. Moreover, the legacy of early speculative theories has clouded much accepted wisdom today about Arapaho origins and movements on the plains. To the exclusion of other theories, all or part of James Mooney's theory has shaped academic, popular, and some contemporary Arapaho views of origins on the plains. By mere allusion to "their oldest traditions," Mooney (1896: 954, 1907: 72–74) holds that Arapahos were latecomers, traveling westward in the mid-1700s with the Cheyenne people onto the plains from the Red River region of Minnesota. Countering this, other early researchers (Kroeber 1939; Michelson 1912; Trenholm 1970) held that Arapaho and related Gros Ventre bands lived on the northern plains before the horse arrived and before other groups (such as the Cheyennes, Crows, Lakotas, Shoshones, and Utes) entered the area from the north, east, and west. Based on Truman Michelson's (1912) comparative study of Algonquian languages, Alfred L. Kroeber (1916: 73) estimates a thousand years of separation between Arapaho–Gros Ventre and Great Lakes Algonquian languages. This view supports precontact presence of Arapaho peoples on the plains, though not necessarily in the Rockies, and is based on the assumption that the Great Lakes was the center of Algonquian dispersal, which is still held as a historical fact by many scholars in various fields, even though Algonquian linguistic and cultural history may have actually had several centers of development, including one among the Blackfeet, Arapahos, and Gros Ventres that lasted for several centuries on the plains. The prevailing view in ethnohistory today (Swagerty 2001: 256) holds that Caddoan and Siouan-speaking agricultural peoples are among the oldest traditions on the plains. That theory is supported by archaeological evidence connecting those groups to prehistoric settlements. The view further holds that Arapahos, Blackfeet, and Gros Ventres were part of a second wave of Algonquian-speaking groups that entered the plains from the Eastern Woodlands by 1700, a date that must be framed as the latest possible and does not exclude a much earlier one. All theories about the historical movement of Arapaho peoples are based on indirect evidence because there is neither archaeological nor documentary evidence to support any conclusions about the direction and time of the Algonquian arrival on the plains.

The prevailing view of early nineteenth-century history, as formulated by Virginia Cole Trenholm (1970) and followed as accepted wisdom today, is that Arapaho and Gros Ventre bands were once one tribal or ethnic group living in what is now eastern Montana. Out of this large prototribe, the theory proceeds, the Arapaho bands split by the 1820s, moving south into Wyoming, South Dakota, and Colorado. Then, by the 1840s, another split occurred, between northern and southern bands that eventually became the two Arapaho tribes designated by treaty beginning in 1851. While there is some supporting oral history about both splits, the attribution of a single unified tribe sharing a well-bounded territory is a construct that itself assumes social fission rather than fusion as the only possibility in history. Other Arapaho oral history, for example, describes the merging of separate subtribes, such as the Be(e)sowunenno' (Wood Lodge People) and the Arapaho proper. Derivation from a single prototribe is further challengeable by linguistic and oral historical evidence suggesting multiple dialects and subtribes prior to contact (Kroeber 1983: 5–7). Before contact and treaty making, the basic social units were likely small bands that traveled great distances, even before horses were adopted for transport, and came together for collective ceremonies at certain times of the year and maintained a sense of common identity.

Some oral historical evidence places Arapahos in Colorado prior to the acquisition of the horse in the first half of the seventeenth century. On the Toll expedition of 1914, Sherman Sage and Gunn Griswold related that Arapaho bands once used dogs as beasts of burden to travel into and out of the parks region, even extending three hundred to four hundred years into the past (Toll 1914: 68). The importance of this for the present discussion is that the Front Range would have been a reliable source of porcupine quills not found in abundance on the prairies. If indeed Arapahos were camping in the Rocky Mountains in the early 1700s or even earlier, then women would have had access to abundant porcupine quills.

Establishing the origins of ritualized quillwork in Plains history is even more difficult to determine from direct evidence, but separate bodies of indirect evidence can be combined to suggest several viable conclusions and exclusions. Indigenous peoples throughout the northern half of North America were probably doing quillwork for centuries. It thrived and still thrives as a secular art form among almost all Algonquian-speaking groups of the eastern subarctic, Great Lakes, and Eastern Woodlands areas, as well as many Athabaskan peoples throughout the western subarctic and some Siouan groups bordering the inclusive region to the south. Archaeological evidence for quillwork in the northern plains dates to the sixth century A.D. (Greene 2001: 1039). Quillwork is thus very old on the northern plains, though that depth cannot be reliably associated with historical Plains peoples. There are many unanswered questions and only a thin body of evidence to rely on.

Unfortunately, no intensive comparative study of quillwork on the plains or in North America in general has ever been done. And there has been no study to date of the historical and cultural connections of women's quillwork with other Plains religious traditions. It was not a topic, for example, taken up by the early comparative, diffusionist ethnology of the 1920s–50s, addressed below. This owes much to the tendency of research in that tradition to focus on men's rituals and societies, as well as male issues in folklore, and thus see women's traditions as peripheral or invisible to comparison.

Accepted anthropological ways of seeing change tend to hold that ritualized quillwork derived from the wider distributed secular quillwork forms of subarctic groups, since the former is more localized on the plains in the southern geographic edge of North American quillwork distribution. In short, the tendency is again to see the particular case as necessarily derived from the general. Claude Lévi-Strauss (1968: 270) holds to this view of quillwork, speculating that there was an ecologically based shift of value and meaning as Algonquian and Siouan groups moved from the northeast onto the plains. He theorizes that because the porcupine was scarcer on the plains, it took on an exotic nature and thus became a central Arapaho mythical and ritual figure, while cultures that remained in northern regions retained the porcupine as a "real animal" and the art as a secular form. This explanation is questionable if indeed Arapaho, Gros Ventre, and Blackfoot bands had ready and consistent access to the Rocky Mountains and other smaller ranges early in their history on the plains. Lévi-Strauss actually borrows several maps of the ranges for *Erethizon dorsatum,* a couple of which include the Rocky Mountains as far south as Mexico (1968: 268). He simply did not realize that Arapaho territory, along with that of the Blackfeet, included the Rockies. Gros Ventre peoples would also have had access to various smaller ranges. For early Plains groups, the issue of general scarcity was less a factor perhaps than the change to access to porcupines only during specific times in a nomadic seasonal cycle on the plains. As Lévi-Strauss does realize, the porcupine became associated with periodicities, including that between winter and summer. Such associations in Arapaho culture became part of the core of religious belief and practice, including and in addition to quillwork.

Though there is no direct evidence about Arapaho quillwork for the period before the first encounters with Europeans and, later, Euro-Americans, beginning in the late 1700s, a comparative study of quillwork art and its relationship to myth and other rituals on the plains supports great historical depth. In Arapaho–Gros Ventre cultural history there is a strong association of both the Sun Dance and quillwork with the charter myths "Little-Star" and "The Porcupine and the Woman Who Climbed to the Sky." As discussed in chapter 4, these stories are variations of the more widespread Star Husband myth, in which a woman marries a celestial being. Stith Thompson calls this Plains variation the Porcupine Redaction tale, because porcupine figures as the animal form taken by a celestial being to draw a woman upward into the sky to marry him. The porcupine and the woman's desire for quills figure in Porcupine Redaction stories from the Arapahos, Gros Ventres, Crows, Hidatsas, Crees, Arikaras, Kiowas, and Cheyennes, though another subvariation extends to the Blackfeet and Sarsi (Reichard 1921: 270; Thompson 1965: 451). It is curious that no early comparative folklore studies of the Star Husband story follow the connection to women's quillwork. Most are preoccupied with the motif of male competition between the suitors Sun and Moon (deeming this the distinctive feature of the tale), which in the Arapaho case is not particularly significant. Lévi-Strauss alone has emphasized the significance of the story for synchronizing women's roles with various reproductive and seasonal periodicities and thus the perfectibility of culture through the creation of quillwork. While his analysis in *The Origin of Table Manners* informs the discussion in chapter 4 on the mythology of quillwork, some comparative, historical implications can be derived from it, as well. Admittedly, there are serious methodological concerns about claims for geographical origins or distribution in diffusionist studies of Plains myth and ritual, but when their results are combined and then reinforced with the connections Lévi-Strauss draws to quillwork, several curious interconnections distinct to Arapaho–Gros Ventre peoples emerge.

Comparative studies of Plains Indian religious forms have likewise ignored ritual quillwork. Cultural diffusionist studies of the 1910s–20s era focused on the Sun Dance (Spier 1921) and men's societies (Lowie 1916), but there has been no comparative study to date of the connections between those forms and women's ritualized quillwork. Given the very strong interconnections among the Sun Dance, age grades, several core myths (including the Porcupine Redaction tale), and women's ritualized quillwork documented for the Arapaho context, it makes sense to consider the strong association of these traditions with the groups who entered the plains prior to 1700 and the place of Arapaho traditions among them.

Among the cultures with the Porcupine Redaction version of the Star Husband tale, connections to the Sun Dance or other core ceremonies are found only among the Arapahos, Gros Ventres, Hidatsas, Blackfeet, and Kiowas (Lévi-Strauss 1968: 214). Leslie Spier (1921: 495) concluded in his comparative study of the Sun Dance that it probably originated on the plains among the Cheyennes and Arapahos, with "priority slightly in favor of the latter." Coincident with that connection, Thompson concludes his historic-geographic study of the Star Husband myth throughout North America with the statement, "The Central Plains would seem the most reasonable place of origin for the simple tale or basic type" (1964: 455–56). He locates the center of development of the Porcupine Redaction variation in the present state of Wyoming within the range roughly coinciding with the Plains peoples who attach sacredness to quillwork traditions. In the Arapaho case, the association is the most explicit and strongest among all Plains oral traditions, at least given the available evidence. Many components of the Arapaho Sun Dance lodge re-create elements of the story itself, such as the center pole as the tree the woman climbed, topped by her digging stick (Dorsey 1903: 54). Clark Wissler (1921: vi) further remarks that Spier's study of the Sun Dance distribution suggests a strong cultural historical interconnection among the Arapahos–Gros Ventres, Cheyennes, Mandans, and Hidatsas.

As a third connection, ritually structured quillwork organization is documented for the Arapahos, Gros Ventres, Blackfeet, and Cheyennes, that is, the Algonquian Plains groups (Greene 2001: 1051). There is no evidence in the Blackfoot case for a deep connection between the Porcupine Redaction myth and ceremonial quillwork. Further, although Arapaho quillwork designs and practices are similar to the Cheyenne tradition, the latter is not associated with any explicitly deep connections to the Sun Dance or its charter in a Porcupine Redaction story. What remains is a deep interconnection in religious history among the Sun Dance, Porcupine Redaction story, and ceremonial quillwork in only the Arapaho–Gros Ventre culture. Unfortunately, evidence for Gros Ventre ceremonial quillwork is much thinner than for that of the Arapahos, owing largely to the more detailed ethnographic studies and artifact collecting carried out by Alfred L. Kroeber, Cleaver Warden, and George Dorsey.

As outlined in chapter 5, Arapaho women's quillwork was also tied to the age-grade system in ways unanalyzed yet clearly present in the ethnographic evidence provided by Kroeber, Dorsey, and Warden. As Robert H. Lowie recognized, the age-graded system of men's societies applied to the Mandans, Hidatsas, Blackfeet, Gros Ventres, and Arapahos, while other Plains groups had similar societies but in ungraded ritual systems. He concluded that the more general, ungraded pattern was older and that the graded system derived from it, but this does not readily fit the historical fact that the groups with graded systems are among the oldest occupants of the plains compared to most, though not all, of those with ungraded systems. For Lowie's theory to hold, all five groups listed above would have had to adopt the various societies from groups that arrived in the 1700s and then arranged them in an age-graded sequence, somewhat independently. It thus makes more sense to see the graded systems as existing on the plains prior to or independent of the ungraded variations.

As discussed in earlier chapters, women's quillwork figured significantly in sacred paraphernalia for the Sun Dance, the women's Buffalo Lodge, and most of the men's age-grade lodges. Only among the Arapahos–Gros Ventres was the society of the Seven Old Women quill bundle owners so closely and prominently associated with the authority of the most senior male authority, in this case, that of the Seven Old Men. The Seven Old Women and several other women ritual leaders were as essential to the lodges as were the old men, although ethnographic descriptions of their roles are often faded or thin compared to the roles of men. It is highly unlikely, in any case, that the authority of the Seven Old Women evolved late in Arapaho history.

The cultural history of how all of these elements fit together is impossible to reconstruct with chronological or even sequential precision, but there are strong and multiple correlations that place all of them deep in the prehorse, precontact past of the plains with Arapaho–Gros Ventre peoples at the center. Combining comparisons of the place of quillwork in Plains Indian religious history reveals that although the art form was sacred among other peoples, in no other group but the Arapaho and Gros Ventre peoples with a deep time of occupancy on the plains does it appear so often and centrally in core myths, most sacred ceremonies, and ceremonial life trajectory. Partial interconnections of ritualized quillwork, the Sun Dance, the Porcupine Redaction tale, and an age-grade system are all associated with groups identified as the first and second waves of entry to the plains. Combining contextual analysis with insights from existing comparative studies makes a convincing case for the conclusion that Arapaho–Gros Ventre peoples were—along with the Hidatsas, Mandans, and Blackfeet—among a group of cultures on the plains prior to 1700 that shared cultural development of ceremonial quillwork, the Porcupine Redaction story, the Sun Dance, and the age-grade lodge system. The case thus seems very strong that sacred quillwork developed on the plains and that it has been central to Arapaho culture for a time deeper in the prehorse era than for other groups.

There are, of course, several qualifications to consider. First of all, there is a much greater wealth of ethnographic evidence about Arapaho quillwork, as well as ritual and mythical traditions in general, than for almost all other Plains groups.

Quillwork may have been equally or more central to other groups for whom such evidence did not enter the record. Second, though this possibility is highly improbable, Arapaho and Gros Ventre peoples (along with the Mandans, Hidatsas, and Blackfeet) could have acquired the sacred quillwork tradition and Porcupine Redaction story in the eighteenth century from a newly arrived people. This hypothesis, though, would require Arapahos and Gros Ventres to have adopted quillwork or to have transformed a former secular tradition within half a century's time and then placed it in the core of their religion. Plains peoples did in fact acquire ceremonies from each other through ritualized exchange into the historic period, but those sorts of traditions acquired by Arapahos and Gros Ventres have always been placed on the periphery, set apart from the Sun Dance, other core rituals, and their supporting myths. As Loretta Kay Fowler's (1982) work clearly establishes, throughout the historical period Arapaho culture has been one of the most culturally conservative on the plains. That Arapahos would have been inventive and innovative in the eighteenth century and then became quite conservative in the nineteenth seems unlikely, though a very slight possibility.

During the early nineteenth century, Arapaho quillwork entered into European and American travel accounts and associated collecting of culture for scientific or private aims. Through that century and into the early twentieth century, hundreds of examples of quillwork were acquired by naturalists, military officers, government officials, traders, tycoon collectors, tourists, and amateur ethnographers. Two of the earliest travelers on the plains documented the distinctive Arapaho–Gros Ventre quillwork style. During his western travels of 1832–34, Prince Maximilian of Wied observed among the Gros Ventres a "unique" quillwork tradition: "They ornament their large buffalo robes in a peculiar manner, with narrow parallel transverse stripes of porcupine quills, and many little pieces of scarlet cloth fastened to them in rows. This way of adorning their robes is said to be likewise usual among the Arrapahos [*sic*]" (1904: 75). Even though lined quilled robes became part of other tribes' traditions by the end of the nineteenth century, this style is, remarkably, associated only with the Gros Ventres and Arapahos in Maximilian's account. By that time in his journey he had encountered Mandan, Hidatsa, and other Siouan peoples on the Upper Missouri, but nowhere does he mention lined quillwork traditions for them. Images produced by Karl Bodmer, the expedition illustrator (Hunt et al. 1984), show only the painted robe style and the familiar form characterized by a beaded or quilled central belt with intermittent disks, typical of Siouan robes and atypical for early Arapaho–Gros Ventre quillwork. At this time, then, there seemed to be at least two Plains quillwork variations.

The oldest written record of Euro-American contact with Arapaho quillwork is the journal of the English naturalist John Bradbury (Hilger 1952: 185). His entry for June 17, 1810, while camped near an Arikara village on the Missouri River, describes an Arapaho robe the party acquired from a visiting Cheyenne delegation:

> After devoting the greatest part of the day to the increasing of my collection, I went into the village, and found that some Indians had arrived from the Chayenne [*sic*] nation, where they had been sent to inform the Aricaras [*sic*] of their intention to visit them in fifteen days. One of these Indians was covered with a buffalo robe, curiously ornamented with figures worked with split quills, stained red and yellow, intermixed with much taste, and the border of the robe entirely hung round with

> the hoofs of young fawns, which at every movement made a noise much resembling that of the rattlesnake when that animal is irritated. I understood that this robe had been purchased from the Arapahoes, or Big Bead Indians, a remote tribe, who frequent the Rocky Mountains. I wished much to purchase the robe, and offered him such articles in exchange as I thought most likely to induce him to part with it; but he refused. The day following it was purchased by Mr. M'Clellan, who gave it to me for silver ornaments and other articles, which amounted to about ten dollars. (1904: 139)

This small passage evinces many remarkable points. First, Arapahos are placed in the Rocky Mountains in 1810 and producing the same lined style of robe. Second, Bradbury, like Maximilian, was struck by the unique beauty of the robe, noting its distinct color and dewclaw pendants. It is unlikely, then, that he had encountered that style of quilled robe among the Mandans, Hidatsas, Arikaras, or Cheyennes to that point along his journey up the Missouri River. Third, after Bradbury's initial failure to secure the robe, a travel companion continued to pursue the trade. Through that exchange we know something of the indigenous exchange value of an Arapaho woman's quilled robe from the Cheyenne owner's reluctance to part with it until a dear price was offered. According to a standard Consumer Price Index conversion rate table, $10 in 1810 is equivalent to approximately $150 at present. It was thus no small amount. In the Missouri River trade at the time, the exchange or use value of the objects offered would also have likely been even greater for a Cheyenne trader when he returned home or deployed them for intertribal trade. What I find remarkable is that the robe was an object of great interest to both explorers, who were men of letters familiar with European arts and sciences.

Also significant is the fact that a quilled robe, one of the most valuable Arapaho personal possessions, had been traded at all, if only in two documented cases. How and under what conditions women's quillwork was traded to other tribes is difficult to reconstruct. First of all, intermarriage among tribes was probably much more frequent than most definitions of tribes as distinct peoples consider. Thus, for robes and other quillwork objects to travel in ritualized exchange along paths of kinship across tribal boundaries would not have been uncommon. Second, by the early 1800s, opportunities for intertribal trade, especially between Arapahos and Cheyennes, were frequent and substantial. Cheyennes in particular served as middlemen for Arapaho trade on the Missouri River (see Jablow 1950). By that time, Mandans and Hidatsas were trading corn, guns, and other British goods to the Cheyennes, who reciprocated with large numbers of buffalo hides and horses. By the late 1700s, Arapahos and Cheyennes were acquiring horses through raids or trade in increasing numbers from Mexican settlements to the southwest. Intertribal economies stimulated by British trade from the north and perhaps equally strong, but less historically documented, connections to Mexicans to the southwest contributed to great encampments in Arapaho and Cheyenne territory such as the occasional one at Cherry Creek in what is now the Denver area (Trenholm 1970: 42).

To reemphasize, women did not make robes for intertribal exchange. The degree to which men who received robes could give or trade them is unclear, but they were apparently free to sell, trade, or give some robes they received. Diversion of a robe from a cherished family possession identified with respect for the maker to a trade good would have been a dishonorable move of sorts. According to Warden's notes, a one-hundredth robe, the highest ranked of all, could not be traded or given away until the owner passed on (Warden-Dorsey 1903–1906: Box 3, Folder 26: 30 [1905]). As men moved into the fourth hill of life, they would no longer have worn ornamented robes but would have kept them as objects of great value. Sister M. Inez Hilger mentions that men were often buried covered in their best robes (1952: 162). The highest-ranked robes were likely kept as articles of wealth and beauty, though they could have been traded for other goods when extreme necessity arose, when desire for other goods demanded it, or perhaps as a gift to honor someone else. Robes themselves also marked the rank of men who wore or owned them, so owners would not readily part with them. There are several references in Kroeber's and Warden's descriptions to men who had received robes and then sold them to non-Indians (Warden-Dorsey 1903–1906: Box 2, Folder 8: 20, 31). The noted quillworker Firewood made a Legged-Rattle Robe so that her family would be well while she traveled to visit the Sioux. Upon her return to Wind River, her mother, Bird-Woman, asked for the robe as a gift for someone in her home tribe in Oklahoma. On the trip down, however, Bird-Woman's husband, "caring little for such an article, apparently sold the robe to white settlers" (Warden-Dorsey 1903–1906: Box 3, Folder 46: 6 [1905]). The suggestion is that robes were highly valued items that should have been kept by recipients but could be converted, however dishonorably, to commodities for intersocietal exchange.

Trade by the late 1700s also introduced new materials and forms for women's artwork, such as beads, cloth, thread, and metal, as well as other changes that affected quillwork creativity. By the time of early contact, Arapahos had acquired many trade goods, thus the name "Big Bead Indians" that Bradbury and other travelers occasionally applied to them. Gauging how these new trade goods affected women's quillwork by the early nineteenth century is difficult, but assuming that the introduction of beads decreased the production and importance of quillwork is perhaps questionable: beads may have actually enhanced individualized creativity while more sharply defining the sacred boundaries and value of quillwork. Decoration on some items, such as moccasins, small bags, and navel bags, shifted from quillwork to beadwork. The introduction of beadwork seems to have been confined to (and even stimulated) individualistic, secular art forms among women. Beadwork was likely carefully compartmentalized from sacred art forms for the lodges and women's quillwork, though beadwork does appear on some quilled forms and quillwork on some predominantly beaded items (such as pipe bags). Only around 1900 in the reservation era, mostly among the Southern Arapahos, did quillworkers transpose quillwork forms into beadwork. Beadwork in small amounts does appear on quillwork items acquired around 1900, including some from Wyoming. Rows of beadwork were specially used for borders and accoutrements. Some beadwork seems to have been added to cradle pendants that women turned into necklace-form pendants for personal wear or trade.

Earlier changes may also have stimulated quillwork production. By the early 1800s, the emerging horse-based economy contributed to more-productive hunting and access to a larger territory, both of which would have provided greater raw materials and provided more time for senior women to do quillwork. On the one hand, the volume of robes and meat to be processed by women would have increased. On the other, successful hunters would have been able to support larger families, including perhaps larger and even more polygamous camps, thus perhaps freeing more senior women from the other chores required of women in camp life. In the camps of successful families that could keep daughters, their husbands, and their children close by, senior women, supported by the work of junior daughters and sons-in-law completing bride service obligations, would have had more time to devote to higher forms of work, such as quillwork. Moreover, more hides would have been available for quillwork as opposed to other, more direct types of use value (such as tipi covers). In turn, quillwork likely became an increasingly conspicuous expression of status differences during the horse and trade era.

The first half of the nineteenth century was therefore probably the high point in the history of Arapaho women's quillwork art production. By the middle of the century, negative effects of Euro-American movement into Arapaho territory, illegal under the terms of the Fort Laramie Treaty of 1851, began to reduce women's access to time and resources for quillwork. Euro-American settlement, overhunting of game, and violence fueled by racism and militarization forced both northern and southern bands out of traditional areas into reduced territories. Access to traditional subsistence and ceremonial resources, such as quills, was increasingly restricted. Epidemic diseases also reduced Arapaho population throughout the nineteenth century and into the twentieth. Smallpox, influenza, measles, and other diseases especially struck children and old people, many of the latter of whom died before passing on traditional knowledge. In the mid-1800s it became increasingly difficult to hold and pass on many ceremonies, including the age-grade lodges, the women's Buffalo Lodge, and quillwork itself. By the 1870s, some of the men's age-grade societies had begun to dissolve and the Sun Dance became increasingly difficult to hold on a regular basis (Hilger 1952: 122).

Reservation life beginning in the 1870s made things even worse. One very tragic side was the deprivation and epidemic diseases that both reservations experienced. In 1890 the government ration for each person was fourteen ounces of beef and eight ounces of flour each week. Fowler notes that at Wind River in that year the actual per capita portion was thus half that amount, given that the agent allowed only half of the Arapaho population rations at all and those who did receive them invariably followed the Arapaho tradition of sharing them with their extended families (1982: 88). In the same year, the new state of Wyoming, with the support of agency regulation, prohibited members of either tribe from hunting off the reservation.

Scarcity of natural materials for quillwork also contributed to the decline. Access to quills in Wyoming was probably less of a factor, given significant porcupine populations in the forested mountain zones of Wyoming, but hides and other materials would have been difficult to acquire by the late 1880s. Among the Northern Arapahos, Superintendent Sanderson Martin reported that only 10 buffalo robes were traded in 1885, compared to 2,400 in 1882 (Report of Agent in Wyoming Territory 1885: 212). Pressures for survival also thus forced trading of hides for food rather than retaining them for local practical or aesthetic uses. Conditions of scarcity among the Southern Arapahos arrived even earlier and more severely. In contrast to the availability of quills for the northern tribe, porcupines would have been scarce that far south. In Indian Territory, hunting was not a substantial source of food at any time after confinement there in the early 1870s; disease was even more devastating; and the loss of the tribal land base to white settlement and grazing proved considerably more devastating than in Wyoming. Paralleling the same effect at Wind River, throughout the 1890s the Southern Arapaho population declined (Fowler 1982: 90–91).

Epidemics compounded the hardship on families and the tribes. A measles epidemic in 1897–98 took primarily children and old people from many families. In 1897, due largely to the epidemic, the agent reported 152 deaths (compared to 73 births) in the Eastern Shoshone and Northern Arapaho tribes combined (Report of Indian Agent in Wyoming 1897: 314–15). For months on end at times, then, women were preoccupied with caring for the sick, funerals, and mourning. After allotment of lands in severalty during the 1890s to early 1900s, most families struggled to succeed at the government's program for transition to farming and gardening, often on inferior soil with inadequate irrigation. Women's roles changed to diverse subsistence activities, gardening, wage labor for some, and the transition to sewing cloth to provide clothing for their families. By the early 1900s, too, many children were attending boarding schools at St. Stephen's, St. Michael's, and Fort Washakie. Girls and young women spent much of the day or even week away from their families. In all, time, materials, and opportunities for instruction became increasingly scarce.

Production of quillwork seemed to persist longer among Northern Arapaho than among Southern Arapaho women. By the late 1890s, Southern Arapaho quillwork was rare, largely because of the scarcity of quills and the greater supply of beads and corn-husk fibers in the area. Furthermore, Arapaho artists to the south were mixing more forms and traditions with those of the Southern Cheyennes, who also appropriated beadwork for a separate guild paralleling their quillwork guild and for objects once strictly quilled (Grinnell 1924: 159–69). At another level, Northern Arapahos have traditionally maintained a stronger cultural conservatism toward all ceremonial practices.

Less than one hundred years after Bradbury's encounter with the art form, ritualized quillwork was fading from Arapaho culture. Ways of treating and exchanging quillwork had changed to adapt to difficult living conditions. Candace Greene states that only the Sioux, Mandans, Hidatsas, and Arikaras carried on quillwork on the plains after the 1870s, but her statement overlooks the fact that Northern Arapaho women related that they were doing some forms of quillwork by 1900. Warden and Kroeber found only one old leanback cover remaining and a scarce supply of robes, though cradles were still abundant, along with various bags and other smaller forms. It seems likely that cradle making was the longest-lived tradition among types of quillwork and that those requiring large hides disappeared first.

In the early reservation period, ways of using and exchanging quillwork changed as well. Hilger learned that during her consultants' lifetimes, cradle ornaments and even whole cradles were recycled in ways that broke from past traditions: "In the early days no parts of a cradle were used for another child; in more recent years the ornaments were again used. This was done because it was difficult to get quill workers, and 'anyway the younger people didn't believe much in the old ways of doing things, or in the blessings of a cradle.' Some informants knew of entire cradles that had been used for several successive children. Some knew of cradles that had been used by several families. But this was not the conventional way of doing" (1952: 35).

Women recycled existing quillwork for both local uses and trade, especially cradle ornaments they had once kept as "souvenirs." As Ann Wolf related to Hilger

(1952: 37–38): "When a child had outgrown a cradle, the mother ceremonially dismantled and discarded the cover and frame, keeping all the quilled ornaments." She noted that in her generation used cradles were often sold intact, though: "When the baby outgrew the cradle, in the old days, the cradle was ceremonially torn apart. ([I]n more recent years) they were sold to the whites" (Hilger 1936–40). Some cradle ornaments were also attached to new covers for sale to collectors or anthropologists. Many of the cradles acquired around 1900 that are now in museum collections are in fact old quillwork elements sewn on the canvas covers of tents or flour-sack cloth. Ornaments were also (as mentioned in chapter 1) transformed into pendants for necklaces or pouches for sale. Some robes were made on cowhides, and in Oklahoma, women substituted beads or corn husks for quills on tipi ornaments. Aside from Warden's efforts to supply materials for and encourage women to produce quilled objects, Arapaho women engaged in no transition to expanded production for commercial sale. Quillwork was also not transformed by either tribe into an enduring secular form in another medium. The very forms of quillwork designs did not survive long into the twentieth century. The freer individualized forms specific to hide painting, beadwork, and other media began to predominate in artistic design. Furthermore, new cultural forms facilitated by increased intertribal exchange began to emerge. By midcentury, the objects and forms would have been unknown and invisible to Arapahos born in the reservation era.

The majority of quilled items in museums were acquired during the most difficult period (1880s–1910s) through many Euro-American collectors with various motives, some that competed with each other. For example, researchers saw themselves in competition with private collectors, though the boundary between these two types of collecting was not always clearly defined. The combined effect was the creation of a small, brief market for Arapaho material culture in general, within which quillwork was just one among the many objects to be acquired. Collectors included ethnographers, missionaries, local or traveling wealthy collectors, military officers, government officials, tourists, and local store owners. Some items were acquired as gifts from Arapaho people, while others were purchased for museum collections, tourism retail sales, or private collections.

Acquisition for research or the tourism trade probably significantly reduced the store of cradles, tipi ornaments, and other quillwork that Arapahos had been keeping as family heirlooms or recycling for use. Cradles and ornaments transformed into medallion necklaces and pouches also entered the market as commodities. Cradles and their components composed the largest share of the items traded, and they are in the majority of quilled objects now in museum collections. Quilled cradles disappeared from Arapaho communities, though, within the next generation. Four decades after Kroeber's and Dorsey's collection, Hilger (1952: 29) observed, "During the period of the present study [1936–40] no Arapaho, either Northern or Southern, or White person closely associated with them knew of a cradle that was either in use or in the possession of an Arapaho." The one-time Northern Arapaho quillwork artist Ann Wolf told Hilger, "We sold the last ones to the Whites quite a while ago. A White man used to come around here and buy up all the old Indian 'stuff.' I made three cradles for White people that live at Jackson Hole [Wyoming] long after we weren't using them any more. They asked me to make them. I used willows for the framework" (Hilger 1952: 29). Given what Ann Wolf tells Hilger about the cradles she made and Warden's observations of Firewood's construction of a yellow tipi, we can conclude that some Arapaho women were still making quillwork from 1900 until at least the 1920s but only in response to the emerging short-lived market for quillwork and other women's art from anthropologists and traders. They were not making quillwork at that time for vows and traditional gifts.

Following the lead provided by Ann Wolf, there were at least two stores in the Jackson Hole area that sold Arapaho and other Indian items in the early 1900s. One was the famous Klamer General Store at Old Faithful built in 1897, and the other the Mammoth Springs General Store built two years earlier. The Klamer family ran the former until 1915, and the Henderson family founded the latter (Goss 2003). The two families became closely related through intermarriage and often traveled to reservations in Wyoming, Montana, and Idaho to collect items for their inventories. One cradle acquired in that manner was donated in 2000 to the San Diego Museum of Man by descendants of Klamer-Henderson former store owners who moved to southern California in 1915 (accession description for SDMM 1958.031.0042).

Missionaries, military officers, ethnographers (both trained and untrained), and private collectors in the period's tradition of wealthy collectors' expeditions also purchased quillwork, along with many other Arapaho items. The self-trained anthropologist James Mooney contributed a few items to the National Museum of Natural History collections that he acquired during his field research in both Arapaho tribes during the early 1890s. George Gustave Heye is known, of course, for having assembled the largest private collections of Native American art. His field collector, William Wildschut, acquired many Arapaho quillwork items in the 1920s that are now in the collections of the National Museum of the American Indian. Heinrich R. Voth (a Mennonite missionary and amateur ethnographer among the Southern Arapahos at Darlington, Oklahoma, during 1882–92) likewise donated rare quilled items to the National Museum of Natural History. Walter C. Roe (a Presbyterian missionary in Oklahoma) also donated a few quilled items to the National Museum of Natural History in 1899. Military officers Colonel Stevens T. Norvell, Colonel Richard H. Wilson, and Lieutenant Clough Overton, all of whom served at Fort Washakie near the turn of the century, added several Arapaho pieces acquired by purchase or as gifts to the Heye collections of the National Museum of the American Indian. Many Northern Arapaho items, including several quilled pieces, came to the National Museum of Natural History from Emile Granier, a French-born mining engineer who came to South Pass City, Wyoming (south of the reservation), in 1884. Driven by the same natural scientific curiosity that motivated Bradbury, he apparently privately purchased many things from both the Northern Arapaho and Eastern Shoshone tribes.

One major source of Arapaho collections at the Carnegie Museum was the Fred Harvey Company, which sold 149 items to the museum in 1904 with George Dorsey acting as the middleman. Dorsey sold the collection on the arguments of salvage, documenting symbolism, and reliable research (Bol 1996). In a letter to the Carnegie's director, Dorsey emphasized that "it will never be possible to make another collection" and "the symbolism of each object is fully described in an exhaustive catalogue" that was "done by the Indian who prepared the symbolism for Dr. Kroeber's paper on symbolism" (Bol 1996: 110). In this case, the "Indian" was, of course, Cleaver Warden. Quilled items in the Carnegie Museum of Natural History, American Museum of Natural History, and Field Museum constitute at least half of what remains for study today; most of those have some connection to Warden's efforts. There is very little in the correspondence between Warden and Dorsey to shed light on the former's motives, aside from a general sense that he was doing a job for wages, as Dorsey directed, of collecting the objects, stories, and interpretations.

Attention to how and under what conditions Arapaho material objects were acquired adds clarity to our understanding of the historical reality of the exchange. The vast majority of items in the Field Museum were purchased by ethnographers Warden and Dorsey in 1899–1905, and almost all in the American Museum of Natural History were purchased by Kroeber during his research of 1899–1900. The research and acquisition for the latter were sponsored by Mrs. Morris K. Jesup, wife of the founding benefactor of the museum and sponsor of the famous Jesup North Pacific Expedition. Cleaver Warden's research was funded by the Field Museum.

Kroeber and Warden entered the Arapaho communities under the direction of Franz Boas and Dorsey, respectively, but at times neither was exactly clear about their directions. Each was provided with a list of specific items or general types of artifacts to purchase, ceremonies to inquire about, and some guidelines for amounts to be paid. Kroeber's inventory for collections at the American Museum of Natural History indicates that he paid from $2.50 to $3.00 for each cradle acquired, $2.50 for each set of tipi ornaments, $3.00 for a quilled child's robe, and $.75 to $1.00 for single cradle or tipi rosettes (1916–20). Elsewhere in his notes he often indicates that he paid $1.00 for each story or interview. (Each dollar in 1899–1900 is equivalent to approximately $27.00 in 2010 [Historical Currency Converter].) The value of quilled articles, along with all Indian artifacts, was low in the Euro-American economy at the turn of the nineteenth century compared to the value today. From the point of view of an Arapaho woman trying to provide for her family in 1900, though, the prices paid were not insignificant. Based on U.S. Census data for prices in general for the time, a woman who sold a cradle for $3.00 could purchase the equivalent of two weeks' rations for a whole family of four.

Kroeber's correspondence with Boas indicates that he grappled with the conflict between his roles as researcher and bargainer for items. First of all, Arapaho sellers were apparently not just accepting Kroeber's asking prices and thus were not entirely hapless economic actors. At the beginning of his field research in Oklahoma, Kroeber remarked in two letters to Boas that he thought the prices demanded were "pretty high," adding in a second letter, "They are generally short of money, of course, but have the handling of a good deal, so that they do not overvalue it" (Kroeber-Boas Correspondence: July 9, 1899). Later that summer Kroeber expressed his confusion between a consumer's sense of value and the ethnographic value of artifacts by asking Boas whether he should prefer items in good condition to older ones: "Many of the best dancing regalia are quite old and worn. Do you attach much importance to neatness and prettiness of specimens? For instance, there is an old buffalo bed-blanket, with typical ornaments, related to the tepee ornaments. It is probably the only one left, and complete, but almost ready to fall to pieces. Would it be advisable to spend seven or eight dollars for this? I mention this as a typical case" (Kroeber-Boas Correspondence: August 6, 1899). Boas responds with what would seem to be anthropological common sense for the time: "For our museum purposes

I would rather have a good old specimen, no matter how dirty or dilapidated it may look, than something new that is not characteristic of the life and mode of thought of the Indian. The buffalo blanket, for instance, to which you refer, you ought to secure, under all circumstances" (Kroeber-Boas Correspondence: August 10, 1899). According to Kroeber's subsequent published work, he was unable to purchase the "buffalo blanket" (that is, leanback cover), though he offers a description from observations of the one he had encountered (1983: 65–66). Kroeber's role conflict between researcher and purchaser of culture is more remarkable perhaps than any of the established concerns with salvage anthropology.

Research itself affected the economy, culture, and ways of exchanging knowledge surrounding quillwork, as well. The temporary economic impact of ethnographic research and artifact collecting on family economies would not have been small, and the effects of both material and intellectual culture as commodities for sale or capital for value conversion linger today. Sales and commissioned artwork (along with informants' fees for stories and information, and even holding ceremonies) supplied a source of income in the dismal local economies in both Oklahoma and Wyoming. Researchers' monetary resources also facilitated the performance of culture, including that associated with quillwork. Kroeber, Dorsey, and Warden often supplied the materials, informants' fees, and other resources needed to hold various ceremonies that would not have been performed otherwise. In 1899, with such support, Southern Arapaho women were able to hold a tipi ceremony (quoted in full in chapter 5) that Kroeber and Warden were allowed to attend and observe (Kroeber 1983: 29–33). In 1905, Warden wrote to Dorsey to report that he had acquired materials so that Arapaho women could make numerous items, including quillwork, but that the porcupine quills Dorsey had sent were inadequate for the proposed items. Because Arapahos had not yet gone to the mountains, they had few quills, but, he adds, beads were substituted (Warden to Dorsey, January 4, 1905, in Bol 1996: 115). In a way, anthropology stimulated the commodification of ethnographic objects (both material and mental), or what Northern Arapaho elders today call the "commercialization" of culture, though other Euro-American imposed traditions (including community celebrations, rodeo shows, private collectors, granting agencies, motion picture production, and educational institutions) also contributed profoundly to this change in the long run. The money-to-culture and culture-to-money conversion is an ongoing contradiction in Arapaho and many other Native American communities today. It is a topic of many discussions and social tensions in contemporary reservation life that deserves deeper critical historical reflection in anthropology in particular than can be offered here.

Measuring the effect during the 1890s–1920s of various types of Euro-American acquisition of Arapaho quillwork objects is difficult. Several thousand objects in total, including roughly several hundred quilled items, moved either directly or indirectly from Arapaho reservation communities into known museum collections. An indeterminate number of other items entered private collections and occasionally circulate in various markets. In time, quillwork items in collections, as well as many other Arapaho artifacts, were simply ignored by popular, anthropological, and museum interests that had moved on to other things.

In popular and amateur art historical spheres, Arapaho quillwork did not develop a significant presence in the art and craft markets, either locally or nationally.

Such interest is generally framed more by fad and fashion than by the cultural value of objects to Native peoples themselves or researchers. Some items that originally required minutes to make and were of transitory interest to the makers now sell for more than Arapaho cradles. Museum collectors, traders, and local casual buyers probably extracted a major share of the quillwork that had survived from the time when quillwork artists were in full production. Ann Wolf's comment above is revealing in that she notes that the sale of quilled cradles outlived Arapaho women's production and use of them for their children.

For several generations after quillwork was no longer produced for local uses or for sale, several older women were known to continue to own quillwork bundles and retain knowledge of the ceremony. The locally produced book *Arapaho Memories* (Spoonhunter 1985: 5) contains a photograph from about 1930 of Singing Underwood in front of her tipi, adorned with either beaded or quilled ornaments. She was one of the last keepers of a sacred quillwork bag who also knew the requisite knowledge to hold ceremonies. During my field research at Wind River, several women who have passed away in the past two decades were known to have possession of the bags (though in the Arapaho tradition, giving their names here would be inappropriate, because I was not able to talk to them myself). Several of these quillwork bags may continue to be held discreetly in family collections in the way sacred objects from other extinct ceremonies are still owned and cared for.

The irony is that at the time Boas's students were gathering Native American art to demonstrate the aesthetic wealth among humankind, tribes were experiencing the worst material conditions they had ever known, and that poverty was sapping energy and resources that could have been devoted to the creation of beauty through quillwork. Arapaho quillwork entered the history of anthropology to support the Boasian principle of the "psychic unity of humankind" and universal creativity. In particular, Arapaho art, including some quillwork, formed part of the evidence for Boas's aim to demonstrate that the "esthetic pleasure is felt by all members of mankind." Beyond the energy and work required for satisfying material needs, he argued, all peoples, whether wealthy or poor in resources, "devote much of their energy to the creation of works of beauty" (Boas [1927] 1955: 9). In turn, the aim of ethnographic museum exhibits was to impress the public with the richness of form, meaning, and color of so-called primitive art and thus somehow engender appreciation for the Boasian principle. In many cases, though, exhibits of art often failed to convey the Boasian mission. Dorsey's review of the Native American exhibits at the American Museum of Natural History, for example, predates similar reactions I have to such exhibits today: "It was evident that the objects on exhibition were neither placed there with the idea of their beauty nor was their arrangement such as to present primarily a beautiful picture" (1907: 585). Exhibits often restrict ways of seeing that beauty or the ethnographic context. The review goes on to remark that the Plains exhibit, which included primarily Arapaho and Blackfoot material at that time, is the most inconsistent of all the Native American sections because it "fails to recognize the actual conditions which exist in that culture" (Dorsey 1907: 587). In the case of the American Museum of Natural History, a change in directorship and policy in the anthropology department appears to have been largely responsible for the loss of context Dorsey describes.

Through anthropologists, the Arapaho researcher Cleaver Warden, and others who assisted in collecting data and objects, quillwork objects became framed by

Euro-American regimes of knowledge about material culture. They became artifacts to be classified and with symbolic meanings interpreted like texts. Objects were also accompanied by knowledge produced for published academic works and unpublished archival files. Despite a wealth of knowledge, few quillwork pieces were displayed in public exhibits, and the vast majority of them have remained in permanent storage with supporting archival data scattered and accessible only to qualified researchers. Along with other artifacts, they became objects with alienated meanings and values sequestered from the context in which they were made, used, exchanged, and empowered with social and cultural functions. The objects and knowledge associated with them moved from Arapaho communities into collections and texts in distant museums or libraries in major American cities. Following the enduring modern contradiction of Western knowledge, quillwork was acquired as knowledge and objects that were intended to be shared and further studied as part of the human stock of knowledge but that became invisible and inaccessible, except to a few very specialized, academic researchers. That, of course, has all been changing dramatically in the last few decades through the Native American Graves Protection and Repatriation Act (NAGPRA) and the Internet databases and digital technology used by many museums.

Anthropology itself involves various kinds of movement, including travel, movement of knowledge and things to and from a place, paths of movement in a field context, conceptual movement in analysis, motion within chronotopes of narrative and history, and many more. The primary motives of anthropological collectors were framed by the ideology of "salvage ethnography," which involved types of movement that were both unique and shared with contemporary anthropology. It was contradictory in its orientations to time and movement in several respects. Denying coevalness, as Johannes Fabian (1983: 25–28) coined it, between present sociocultural realities, such research required moving the thinking of consultants and researchers back to a pristine past culture while excluding attention to the new forms of culture and social conditions in community life going on in the present. In addition, anthropology adopted the popular chronotope that Native American cultures were caught in an irreversible, degenerative flow of historical time without considering the real forces behind it. Accordingly, the loss of quillwork was taken for granted but rarely investigated or explained. Defining genuine indigenous culture as an increasingly scarce source of value for science promulgated a certain urgency to collect as much as possible before it was indeed "too late." The "value" of the objects was defined within the scientific quest to collect and preserve what progress was destroying using the technology and institutions provided by that same progress. Despite all the criticisms of this approach, in the case of quillwork the assumption was correct. It is a form of lost culture. However, its place in history has been shaped by these contradictions.

Published and unpublished comments that Kroeber, Dorsey, and Hilger recorded from older Arapaho informants reveal that they also saw many traditions, including quillwork, as disappearing in the younger generations. Their explanations of loss, as in other past and present contexts (see Anderson 1998), often focus on younger people's lack of interest or initiative. Unfortunately, from early ethnographic accounts our sense of local knowledge is confined to elders' views. We do not gain a sense of what translators or researchers, such as Cleaver Warden, think about these cultural changes. Arapaho elders who participated in research efforts did understand

and embrace the value of the overall project to document disappearing traditions and collect material representations of it, primarily for future generations of their own people. Interestingly enough, at least at Wind River, the objects and associated knowledge have been in recent years of greater interest to local Arapaho scholars than to mainstream anthropology.

While attempting to recover the past, most Western academic ways of knowing ironically continually break from their own pasts. Like the practitioners of every other modern Western way of knowing, which must always be on the move in history toward progress, the anthropologists involved in studying quillwork were making a break from essentialist-evolutionist-ethnocentric views. In time, the discipline made a break from the Boasian school and thus from its own past by caricaturing and then conceptually negating the anthropology that had produced the knowledge and collections of quillwork. Such a break ignores the fact that a conceptual break made in the halls or pages of academia does nothing to address the real knowledge and objects left behind, not to mention the more important connection to the peoples once studied who did not disappear as expected. Anthropology itself has never made a full break from a cosmopolitan specious present. If anything, more recently some sectors of anthropology have embraced the transitory present and flow of historicity as the only valid time frame, such that much of indigenous knowledge and culture is framed as imagined, constructed, and invented for interests serving an agency of short duration. Anthropology—as is true of all colonizing projects of discovery—must always move on to new topics, places, and jargon while reifying the sociocultural world as always already doing the same. While much has been written about positioning anthropological research in space, much less has been done about positioning it in time. For present purposes, quillwork must be understood in terms of the types of time involved in its collection and subsequent history.

Like other fields, anthropology is always on the move, leaving behind vast amounts of accumulated surplus knowledge and objects that never found their way into publications, museum exhibits, academic discourse, or appropriations by other disciplines or fields. Thus, from one very strong anthropological perspective today, discarded objects and knowledge from the past of our discipline have become reversed from their original value as "authentic" to now "inauthentic" or at least low-interest things that should not move in our mental, discursive, or published spaces. That transformation began with the temporal break made by early research. Bol recognizes the irony in the early study of quillwork: "Most of these anthropologists flitted in and out of the field, staying only for a few weeks at a time, often relying heavily on their native collaborators to carry forth" (1996: 117). Some years later, Kroeber observed, "I think that the plan of visiting several new tribes in a short time was not a good one" (Kroeber to Boas 1900, in Bol 1996: 117). As Kroeber and Dorsey moved on to other interests, anthropology never fully completed research on Arapaho art and material culture to the extent required of later ethnographic study; as a result, the evidence was left discarded by anthropological interests that had moved on to other things with the assumption that the topic had already been covered. While the tradition of both Dorsey and Boas aimed to place traditions in the permanent human cultural record, understand all cultural elements in holistic context, and raise appreciation for primitive art to something comparable to that for Western art, anthropologists and museums tended, after a period of initial interest, to more or less neglect many art forms as topics of study and set aside many collections themselves. Fortunately, in a way, most of these Native art forms (including Arapaho quillwork) were never actually appropriated for any subsequent missions to exoticize, valorize, romanticize, or modernize "primitive art" or Native American art. In reality, the vast majority of what was collected from the Native American cultures has been left unattended in books, archives, and collections.

Throughout the history of anthropology and even with some lingering momentum today, conducting original fieldwork and forming a personal relationship with consultants have become the identity markers of the "authentic anthropologist." The priority has always been on acquiring fresh knowledge connected to current theoretical or social issues, rather than (re)analyzing old knowledge. As I witnessed in my own "fieldwork" at Wind River, streams of researchers arrive in Native American communities to do something original without previously acquiring a background in what has already been done on the topic at hand. What is more, many arrive wanting to learn all they can about a vast topic in a short period of time. On numerous occasions, folks visited our center with the aim to learn all they could about Arapaho religion over the next week or even weekend. Researchers who came to the North American Indian Heritage Center often seemed disappointed when we, other local scholars, or even elders directed them to published works or archives rather than offering them a meaningful interview. In the community, too, there is often a resistance to texts as sources in favor of face-to-face consulting about the topic at hand. Thus, accumulations of tapes, notes, and publications from past projects in the community end up in storage rooms, unused and discarded by researchers who see no utility in them for a more current interest. Arapaho elders today do have a vast amount of knowledge to share, but in many cases local and visiting researchers ask them about things that had already been covered, even by the same consultants, or that did not match with the consultants' life experiences. Commenting on this problem, Vine Deloria, Jr., recognized the ironic disjuncture in the aim to get close to Native communities: "After several centuries of investigation and publication of an immense body of information, what further needs to be done? We can, I would suppose, synthesize existing studies and offer a corrective in the emphasis placed on certain kinds of interpretations previously given to Indian materials. But the need for any profound or prolonged study of an Indian community by people from the outside seems to be artificial and fruitless" (1991: 461).

The aims of this study are, I hope, in keeping with that synthesis and corrective, though this sort of work does not gain as much anthropological interest and support as does fresh face-to-face fieldwork experience. Some prepublication reviews of this work, for example, on general principle naively assumed that I had overlooked a vast amount of evidence to be gained from new field research on quillwork and that that evidence would lend my work greater authenticity.

After the initial flurry, anthropological, museum, and art historical interests in Arapaho quillwork between 1900 and the 1970s, with the exception of a few pages contributed by Hilger (1952) and Michelson, were confined to occasional references to Kroeber's work, passing study of the collections for general research aims, or inclusion in publications or exhibits of broad scope. By the 1980s–90s this began to change somewhat through the several investigations by Greene, Bol, Santina, Coleman, and myself (mentioned earlier in the chapter), of which only one besides myself is trained as an anthropologist. As mentioned at the outset, interest at Wind River among several Northern Arapaho scholars returned to quillwork in the 1980s and carried over into my time there.

From 1900 until the 1980s, the conditions for storage and conservation deteriorated or at least remained unimproved at most major museums. NAGPRA, of course, stimulated a revival of interest in Native American material culture and renovation of storage facilities. By the time I began museum research in 2004, new climate-controlled and up-to-date storage facilities had been implemented or planned for all the large facilities with Arapaho quillwork collections.

Within the wider pan-Indian neotraditional movement of the past few decades, though, interest in Arapaho culture has lagged behind others. Academic research and popular interest have tended to focus on groups and artistic traditions framed by either the popular imagination and or a pan-Indian construction of Plains history and culture. This is conspicuous in the current public museum displays of the National Museum of the American Indian. At the time of my visit in 2005, only two Arapaho items were visible, including two photographs and one video image, none of which was labeled as such, while quotes and artifacts of other Plains groups were everywhere. I felt so upset walking out that all I could think about was going to the nearest restaurant and eating a big feast of a meal. No item of Arapaho ritually made quillwork was present in the museum's exhibits, though I must add that the curatorial staff at the museum's research center was most helpful.

The Native American Graves Protection and Repatriation Act of 1990 helped revive interest in Native American material culture, but often in narrow or misplaced frames of concern. NAGPRA policy directed museums to supply tribes with inventories of cultural patrimony, funerary objects, and physical remains in their collections. The initiative drew many traditions out of the dark, hidden storage bins into public awareness for both Native and academic communities. During my field research in the 1990s, a group of Northern Arapaho elders and other spiritual leaders reviewed and visited various collections. Some sacred items were repatriated for ceremonial use, while others were placed in carefully restricted storage, but I know little about the details of that process and kept out of it for the most part because other experts seem to have it under control. Quillwork was not included in their definition of sacred objects and remains somewhat anomalous under the conditions NAGPRA maintains. The NAGPRA code defines "sacred objects" as "specific ceremonial objects which are needed by traditional Native American religious leaders for the practice of traditional Native American religions by their present day adherents" (NAGPRA 1990). This does not explicitly apply to quillwork or any other objects associated with extinct Arapaho ceremonies, such as the age-grade societies, women's Buffalo Lodge, or Ghost Dance. More applicable but still enigmatic is the conceivable inclusion of quillwork under the NAGPRA category of "cultural patrimony," meaning "an object having ongoing historical, traditional, or cultural importance central to the Native American group or culture itself, rather than property owned by an individual Native." It would be very difficult to argue that quillwork has had an "ongoing" relationship to either Arapaho tribe, yet as I discuss elsewhere in this book, its cultural importance is real but not in an uncomplicated sense.

In at least the Northern Arapaho community, the path to presenting knowledge about quillwork remains unclear and somewhat controversial. During my fieldwork since the late 1980s, local discussions have dwelled from time to time on the possibility of repatriating more items broadly considered sacred, including quillwork, for display in local exhibits. Tribal budget struggles and other cultural education priorities have worked against construction of such a museum up to the time of this writing. In all, since the 1990s quillwork artifacts held in museum collections have become potentially politicized objects in the current context of indigenous cultural property rights initiatives.

Since the 1970s, too, many Native communities have followed a path of neotraditional revitalization, with language renewal usually at the center of initiatives. In the Northern Arapaho tribe, schools and tribal organizations began in the early 1980s to develop applied anthropological projects in which one phase involved identifying and acquiring published and archival stocks of knowledge in efforts to revive language, culture, and history through local formal educational institutions. As mentioned at the outset of this book, one of the primary aims of the Heritage Center was to revitalize young people's and local artists' knowledge and use of Arapaho designs and objects. Through art curricula, classes, and public displays we aimed to bring the unique colors, forms, and patterns back into art for sale or local uses. A part of this effort brought to the fore concerns about how and in what form older artistic traditions should be used.

The history of the Arapaho discussion at Wind River about the relationship to anthropology and other forms of research probably began with the first encounter with fieldworkers. Opinions about the history of the relationship between anthropology and Arapaho people I encountered ranged from militant antagonism on one extreme to, on the other, respect for efforts and resulting evidence. Fed by these various political concerns, just-so stories and historical gossip circulate about the history of anthropological research. As in many communities, Arapaho people expect some reciprocity and "staying power" from researchers. They expect to see some commitment of long duration to the community from both the research and the researcher rather than floating without connections and flitting in and out of the community in the manner chartered by early researchers.

During my own research, anthropology entered an era of critical self-reflection about its participation in colonial expansion, within which most approaches reified a crude and generic us versus them dichotomy to alienate the historical specifics of the field encounter in each case, and many excluded voice and agency on the part of indigenous people, both in the historical context and in the contemporary critical academic discourse. Combined with the growing concerns surrounding NAGPRA, the new anthropological discourse I encountered in my presentations, discussions, or inquiries about quillwork often engendered a political uneasiness and interrogative mood. In every instance, I realized that I could not readily redress that discourse, so I let it pass by. I was confronted by the futility of providing the total context of the relationship between my research and the Northern Arapaho community in a few minutes to interlocutors with an a priori crude, generic dichotomy already moving as a "problem" in their minds.

During the mid-twentieth century, Euro-American popular interest in Arapaho quillwork also faded. Arapaho quillwork did not become one of the premier items for the Native American art market. Quillwork is rare in the public art market of the twenty-first century. Various museum research notes show that the value of quillwork has only in the past thirty years significantly increased beyond something comparable to Bradbury's payment for the first recorded purchase in 1810. Appraisals for the 1970s are in the range of a hundred to several hundred dollars for cradles. As all Native American art collectors and historians realize, the increased value has been a function of an expanding market for all antiquities, though inflation applies to some more than others. Objects once sold to collectors, tourists, or researchers for several dollars are now valued at thousands of dollars. Today, a few Arapaho quilled items enter the Native American antiquities market from time to time. They occasionally appear in galleries or pass through Sotheby's, Bonham's, and other major auction houses on their way to private collections, galleries, and now and then perhaps a museum. Even with historical value conversion of dollars, cradles are now valued over one hundred times more than what Kroeber and Dorsey paid for the same objects. On January 12, 2006, a quilled cradle sold at Christie's for an auction price of $7,200, though a finer example was being offered at the same time by the Morning Star Gallery in Santa Fe for $20,000. The auction value would thus be closer to the former and showroom retail value closer to the latter. Yet in comparison to other items, such as Plains ledger art and large items with beadwork, Arapaho quillwork is relatively modest in value. By comparison, for example, fully beaded Cheyenne cradles can fetch two to three times the price of Arapaho quilled cradles. To some extent, this is attributable to the fact that Arapaho women's quillwork does not fit into the popular image of or even academic concerns with Plains Indian culture and history.

To summarize, at some remote time in the past quillwork began as a sacred tradition central to Arapaho culture. Women made and gave away quillwork for the same purpose that lay behind all Arapaho ritual exchange: to generate a long and straight life for relatives and the tribe. Euro-Americans began to encounter quillwork in the early nineteenth century as objects to be bought as commodities in a market exchange, collected for scientific study or personal collections, and preserved for posterity. For Arapaho people, quillwork would have once been visible in every corner of everyday social life and present in every major and minor ceremony, but today it is no longer visible. The history of quillwork has followed a path from its origins in mythical time to a form woven into the ceremonial life of women and their relations to objects with competing meanings and values for people within and outside of the Arapaho world. Quillwork shifted from gifts of life made with ritual care to things associated with market value, symbolic meanings, accession numbers, ethnographic description, and eventually controversy and ambivalence in both Arapaho and academic culture. Throughout most of the twentieth century, quillwork faded from both Arapaho culture and academic interest. To anthropologists, quillwork faded out of vogue along with most of the vast Native American material culture collected in the discipline's early years.

Throughout the history of contact, the meaning of quillwork has changed for Arapaho people. It has moved from a core sacred tradition for generating life to a lost sacred tradition among others, such as the age-grade lodges, that must not be revived or renewed, because the succession of knowledge from generation to generation has been irreversibly broken. As such, it has become a taboo form about which there are various and competing views. During the period of cultural revitalization as an auxiliary to language renewal, more research has been undertaken, some Arapaho scholars have taken a strong interest, museums have upgraded their facilities, and a wealth of information has become available through any Internet connection in the world.

The contradictions of this history are obvious but should perhaps be repeated for emphasis. A ceremony with great historical depth in Plains Indian cultural history and one that aimed to promote long life did not itself survive the first decades of the reservation era. Ethnographers motivated to collect items of enduring interest to the human sciences had very fleeting interest in the objects themselves. However, despite the problems associated with salvage ethnography, knowledge about and examples of quillwork would likely not have survived without the efforts of Warden and Kroeber. Within the Plains Indian art market and art histories, many objects of less cultural relevance and shorter historical duration have acquired much greater value and interest than Arapaho women's quillwork art, an ancient and deep tradition. Once pervasive and central to cultural identity, by the mid-1900s quillwork forms had slipped out of Arapaho collective consciousness of the sacred, meaningful, and ancient.

Quillwork has moved in history from a practice and thing in motion with many connections, meanings, and functions in a real community to static objects and knowledge removed from that community. Once visible and moving in the Arapaho lived world, quillwork is now invisible and static. Quillwork has been decontextualized, but the local context that once defined it no longer exists and can never be reconstructed. It once generated—in its creation and symbolic exchange—values, knowledge, and meanings that wove social connections based on kinship and age distinctions. That connectivity has given way to disconnection through sequestration in museum storage spaces. This is not to say that the same religious spirit does not survive. Although permanently removed now from the core of religious life, the same life-oriented practices that once motivated quillwork still persist in Arapaho communities and women's lives, in particular. Ironically, although quillwork objects and knowledge were collected quickly to save them from human-caused culture loss for human interest of longer duration, they have since sat, relatively ignored by that interest, for many decades. Arapaho quillwork has not moved in the flows of exhibits, discourse, or publications about art, whether in the context of the Plains Indians, of Native America, of "primitive art," or of art in the broadest sense. The aesthetic value of Arapaho style robes caught the eye of Bradbury and Prince Maximilian, but decades later the anthropologically trained Kroeber did not seem to see the same value in a leanback cover. Only a few in anthropology, such as Boas and Lévi-Strauss (and companion scholars who took an interest in the 1990s), have seen the value since. In history, quillwork objects only briefly had and in some few cases today still have monetary value, but their circulation and value in markets has been relatively small. Once having a clear position in a religious process for generating life movement in a positive way, quillwork now has an unclear status, as an anomalous, ambiguous, and to some extent contested subject among competing ideologies and academic critical theories, some of which approach assigning negative or at least null value to it.

Conclusion

This is more than just a book about quillwork: it is also about Arapaho women, as seen through an understanding of quillwork's place in their lives and Arapaho spiritual traditions. Individual women made quillwork and passed the tradition on to successive generations, but it was always a process that involved a web of many connections with the natural environment, relatives, and sacred beings. The few names of quillworkers we know about are Firewood, Cedar-Woman, Backward, River-Woman, Sore-Legs, Thread-Woman, Flying-Woman, Ann Wolf, Singing Underwood, Night-Killer, Deer-Woman, Agnes Yellow Plume, Mrs. One-Eye Left Hand, and Mrs. White Bear. They followed a tradition established in myth by Woman-Above, Whirlwind Woman, and Splinter-Foot Girl, as well as several other unnamed protagonists.

This book is also about ways of seeing culture and creativity in motion. Quillwork was much more than an act of creation, the objects themselves, or text-like meanings. Women's lives and quillwork were always in motion and about movement to create many connections in the flow of life. Many kinds of motion were connected to quillwork in this book, including the movements and periodicities of sacred beings established in mythical time and embodied in quillwork designs; the various seasonal movements of Arapaho people to acquire the materials for quillwork in the natural world; the movement of a women's vows and projects, motivated through pity and respect, to ensure their relatives' life movement in a time of transition or crisis; the controlled actions (guided by the Seven Old Women) practiced in ceremonies for initiating projects, giving the creations away, discarding cradle covers, and passing on sacred bundles; the technical motion of women's hands in making quillwork, accompanied by focused stillness of the body and mind while sitting alone completing vows; circumscribed motion of others in the camp around tipis where quillwork was being done or sacred quill bag owners lived; the orchestrated habitus of young women as a prerequisite to initiation to quillwork; the movement of quilled objects exchanged between kin and families to create or transform social relations in the ongoing creation of persons and families; the embodied sensory experience for users and those around them as quilled things rested or moved about camp; the types of movement associated with the changing habitus over the life trajectory of both women and recipients intricately shaped by quillwork objects, designs, and practices; movement along various paths (by both the objects and knowledge about them) out of their original context into museums, texts, and collections, where they ceased to move in many ways; the shapes of movement and time used by both early and subsequent researchers (Arapaho and non-Arapaho alike) to understand quillwork; conceptual models prefigured by Western ideas and oppositions, particularly through anthropology, that are related to movement, history, and time in general; and, finally, the various types of physical and mental movement involved in the production of this book about quillwork. With the movement of their hands and their ceremonies, quillworkers connected shape with motion, space with time, myth with history, the deep past with the immediate present, their local world with a larger cosmos, their individual efforts with a web of kinship relations, and precise geometric shapes with the formless flux of experience. The aim here is to transcend approaches to art that circumscribe one kind of motion or time as primary, such as history, biography, productive process, narrative time, or cosmic time. It also tries to overcome the tendency to stop at some point in the creative process either before, during, or after the fact, such as with form, symbolic content, break into novelty, experienced reaction from a viewer's gaze, sociocultural function, material use-value, unidirectional agency, or teleological aesthetic ideal, to gain a fixed position from which to see the entirety of motion or movement as somehow caused, grounded, culminating, or directed within one locus. Quillwork was about all of these, but each must be positioned as a nexus relative to time and space in the process of creativity and encounters with it. Culture is always in and about motion of many kinds woven and weaving in time together in complex ways. Quillwork was and is an interweaving of technique, habitus, ritual movement, natural periodicities, phasing of the life trajectory, history, and cosmic time. Thus, the aim here is to expand understandings of human creativity as multiple. The driving concern is that neither the process nor the products can simply be abstracted from the total sociocultural system and historical context and then placed in a reductionistic or exclusionary conceptual frame of agency or creativity grounded in modern or postmodern ontology, space-time, contradictions, and modes of revisionism. All intercultural encounters are encounters of different kinds of motion, time, and flows.

Research, analysis, and writing likewise involve various kinds of movement and connectivity, which can either enable or restrict one's vision. My own movement has been different from that of earlier researchers. I have sat for a very long time in one culture and much longer within the evidence about Arapaho quillwork. My connections to both are also unique, though not necessarily "better" than those that other past, recent, or subsequent researchers have spun or will spin. I cannot have the connection that Warden had to Arapaho language and culture, for example, nor can I be a part of Arapaho lived culture today as much as some other folks can or that I would like. Nevertheless, after leaving Wind River over fifteen years ago, I never completely returned to an academic anthropologist's perspective. My interests are always and will probably always be Arapaho-centric. I study other things and cultures as a scholar, but when I study Arapaho things the movement of my thinking and eyes is different. Therefore, I cannot see quillwork entirely from any total outside view. I see with an odd, hybridized transcultural set of four eyes, one inside the Arapaho community and one inside academia, as well as one outside of each at the same time.

Ways of seeing motion always restrict how we see other kinds of motion. My own motion has been restricted such that many aspects of quillwork could not be included, comprehended, or as intricately described as others. My theoretical training and thinking have offered some proficiency in understanding interrelationships of time and space, as well as dimensions among each. To me, these connections are concrete because I not only think them but also see them happening—though to many readers, that view might seem quite abstract. By contrast, I realized that I could not see well and could only allude to the complete technical repertoire used by women in actually doing quillwork. While I pored over quillwork artifacts, I could not make adequate sense out of the stitching, bending, and lining out of quills. Someone who does beadwork or similar arts could probably look at these details and readily explain what women were doing, though, as often happens with such explanations, my eyes would probably glaze over and my mind would fill with haze. In addition, though I have some proficiency in the Arapaho language, I am sure that there are many other meaningful connections to be drawn about symbolism, etymology, and types of movement. A fluent speaker or a scholar devoted to specialized study of the language may find loose ends or even falsely tied ones in my connections, as well as be able to add many more from stories, words, and grammar related to quillwork.

Another thing that I cannot see clearly is how to move knowledge about quillwork and other past traditions back into Arapaho communities' efforts at reviving language and culture. Where does it fit in institutionalized educational programs and the ongoing resurgence of Arapaho religion? In all of these efforts, the place of lost sacred traditions, such as quillwork, is both paradoxical and unprecedented. I have had hours and hours of conversations about this general topic in the Northern Arapaho community. Quillwork is among many traditions for which knowledge is now available primarily through publications, archives, and museum collections. One challenge for anthropology and tribal initiatives is the systematic organization, interpretation, and dissemination of recent and past bodies of collected knowledge, which I argue is essential to the repatriation process and achieving greater self-determination. Hundreds of pages of notes, artifacts, and hours of audio and video recordings remain in storage both on and off the reservation, but too little is done to organize, interpret, and disseminate that knowledge. For all revitalization efforts, the struggle has been to find ways to get such knowledge of language, art, and history living and moving within school curricula, in how young people experience being Arapaho on a daily basis, and as part of everyday community life. Clearly, quillwork cannot be brought back as a living part of culture, because Arapaho tradition does not allow it, but given that restricted movement, the question remains as to how it can perhaps move in other ways. Equally salient from our experiences is that knowledge of such traditions cannot simply be transcribed into textual knowledge delivered solely through mainstream academic or even popular media.

In all, today there is an odd mix of contradictory ways of seeing and perhaps even more confounding ways of not seeing Arapaho quillwork. As with many efforts to understand Native American culture, women's agency in it, art itself, and human creativity, many more perspectives abound within community and academic contexts, as well as those that combine both, than when folks such as Kroeber, Warden, and Dorsey conducted their research. One thing I did not complete here was the task of explicitly addressing all of those views, though some connections are drawn throughout. To do so would have required a massive volume that diverted eyes from quillwork itself. In the Western authoritarian and critical movements alike toward knowledge, the purposes of some perspectives are to exclude, tacitly or explicitly, more knowledge than they include and often to divert attention to issues that have been concretely misplaced. Following an Arapaho oratorical tradition, I should also declare that I am sure that I have made some errors in this book, as in previous works, but I appeal that they be set aside to see the larger purposes that are in my heart and mind. The ultimate concern here is to move some eyes toward seeing quillwork through the lens of respect for the women whose creations and relations contributed to the life movement of Arapaho religion, history, and people for a very long time. Their quiet work was as much a part of cultural survival in hard times as were the efforts of more visible and public figures, about which quite a bit more has been written, discussed, and displayed.

APPENDIX

Modern Arapaho Orthography

The current accepted Arapaho alphabet is as follows:

b is a voiced bilabial stop, like the "b" in English, but unvoiced like a "p" sound at the end of words
c is a voiceless prepalatal affricative like the "ch" in English (e.g., "church") but voiced like a "j" sound at the beginning of words
e is a close-mid vowel like the "a" in the English word "cat" and sustained only in the long form of the sound, which is written */ee/*
h is a glottal fricative like the English "h" but always pronounced at the end of a syllable or word
i is a front-close vowel as in the English "bit" and in the long form written as */ii/*, which sounds like the long "e" sound in English (e.g., "meet")
k is a voiceless velar stop like "k" in English but voiced as a "g" sound at the beginning of words
n is an alveolar nasal as in English
o is a close–mid back vowel as in the English "got" and in the long form rendered as */oo/*, which sounds like the vowel sound in the pronunciation of "caught"
s is a voiceless alveolar fricative as in English
t is a voiceless alveolar stop much like the English "t" but voiced as a "d" sound at the beginning of words
u is a close-back vowel as in the English "put" and in the long form written as */uu/* and sounding like the long "u" sound in the English "cute"
w is a voiced bilabial semivowel, but pronounced and voiceless at the end of words
x is a velar fricative as in the German "ich"
y is a voiced mediopalatal semivowel as in English but voiceless finally
3 is a voiceless dental fricative as in the English "thin" or "three" (thus, the symbol) but never voiced as in English "than"
' is a glottal stop in which the glottis at the base of the throat is closed then opened

Diphthongs:

The vowel combination *ou* sounds like the long "o" sound as in the English "boat."
The *oe* diphthong sounds like the long "i" sound in the English "bike."
The *ei* combination is just as in the English "reins."

Notes

Introduction

1. Given the highly sensitive nature of this topic in the Northern Arapaho tribe, I do not use names or direct quotations on this issue.

2. The person to whom I refer here requested that I not use his or her name in publications.

Chapter 1. Cradles

1. Two examples of necklace bags made from Path Cradle quillwork are held in the NMAI collections: NMAI 105084 has a dark penultimate row, while NMAI 045068 has a red outer ring. Another example of the Red Path design, stored in the University of Nebraska State Museum, is a pouch made from cradle parts (UNSM A73.01.102).

2. Throughout my research of museum collections I counted the bands of quills used for various sections and forms with the expectation that there might be some consistency with recurring symbolic numbers of four, seven, ten, and multiples of ten, as discussed in chapter 3, but no such consistency can be verified even though there were some consistencies on individual items.

3. On example AMNH 50/958, there are ten red quills on one half section and ten white on the other with a black fiber divider of two quills in the center. Similarly, each ornament loop has seven sections divided by short black barriers of two to three quill widths. Two red sections on the ends are about seven quills in width, and the five white sections in the middle portion of the bend include three sections of about five quills in width and the central section hanging down with about ten quills.

4. Identical to the disk on NMAI 122152 is a detached cradle disk in the AMNH collections (AMNH 50/1047) (see Kroeber 1983: 69–70). A Red Path example from the Plains Indian Museum (PIM NA.111.4) has two rows of red but an extra ultimate white ring, and about eighty crossbars on the hood array. Another example, which sold at a Christie's auction in 2005 for $7,200.00 (Lot 155 01-12-06), has ten rings on the head disk, no white border ring, and one hundred crossbars (pers. comm., Vanessa Hernandez). The National Museum of Natural History holds two Red Path Cradles (NMNH 200742, 391982): one with a head disk of ten quilled rings; the other, eight rows followed by two beaded rows on the periphery. The first has approximately one hundred crossbars on the hood array, the second only about seventy. Another Red Path Cradle in the NMAI collections (NMAI 122152) has a round head disk, also with ten rings of quills forming two black-bordered red tipi triangles and two outer red rings at the margin. The banister work on the hood contains exactly one hundred crossbars.

5. A necklace made from Cornered Cradle parts at the NMAI (NMAI 205932) has ten quilled rings, including five rows for the tipi forms, four for the rectangular forms, and one

all-white ring for the outer ring border. The rectangles are about four to five centimeters long and two centimeters wide; they extend outward from the triangles like feet. The hood banister has one hundred original crossbars, though one appears to have fallen off. As on the Path, Red Path, and Spotted Cradle styles, all loops and bars are half red and half white with a black divider.

6. A cradle ornament at the Burke Museum (BMNH 2-3599) has ten rings on the head disk and five toes on each foot. A well-preserved example of the whole cradle at the Plains Indian Museum (PIM NA.111.47) has ten rows on the head ornament and 110 crossbars on the hood banister. Another displayed by the Morning Star Gallery has the same design but twelve rings on the head ornament disk and 90 crossbars. A head disk at the National Museum of Natural History (NMNH 200604) has nine rows including four for the tipi form section, four for the feet and claw forms, and a white border. A breast ornament made from cradle ornaments at the American Museum of Natural History (AMNH 50/2-4640) has nine rings and somewhat different feet with only four claws, and both the top and the lower rows in black. The hood banister form originally had over 80 crossbars, but several are apparently missing.

7. A Lodge-style disk (though identified as a shirt ornament) is also on display at the Field Museum (FMNH 61358). It, too, originally had nine rings, but the center section is missing and the whole design is bounded by a white beaded background ring with twelve flat blue triangle designs, usually symbolizing mountains elsewhere in beadwork. The disk may have indeed been used as a shirt ornament at some point, with the outer beading ring added later, after it had been used. The disk may have once been a cradle head disk and was then reused for a shirt design or breast ornament. The black figures on this disk were made of black plant fiber. On a pouch at the California Academy of Sciences (CAS 0900-0052) is a nearly identical disk with a missing center and similar beaded border but with twenty-four blue mountain triangle forms. Another example identified as Dakota is shown with a baby enclosed and hanging from a horse in a historical photograph taken by Mitchell, McGowan, and Company, probably at Fort Robinson or elsewhere at Red Cloud Agency, South Dakota, in 1874 (SPC Stereo Plains Dakota 00211500, Smithsonian Institution, National Anthropological Archives). Northern Arapaho men served as scouts there under General Crook around that time, so it is likely Arapaho in origin. The cradle is also distinctly the Lodge style Warden identifies and appears to be almost identical, though with a larger head disk, to the only existing complete example of its type from the Denver Art Museum.

8. On the surviving example, the head ornament has a yellow cross and is bounded by a black border framing a red background within each bar. The overall background of the disk is white. There are eleven rings of quills. Each cross form is five quill rows wide and about twice that length at the outer base.

9. Only two examples of the head disk remain. One appears on an adapted necklace pendant at the National Museum of Natural History (NMNH 20065); the other was reused as one side of a pouch stored at the American Museum of Natural History (AMNH 50/1-1327). Both have two mirrored red tipis forming the familiar hourglass shape along the vertical axis, each with two small yellow rectangles inside each tipi section on the former example and only one longer yellow form on each triangle of the latter. The former has solid black rays bordering the tipi triangle sides; the latter has narrow triangle segments of white bounded by black. Against a white background, each has black rays or ribs extending away from the tipi triangles into the white background on alternating rings. Each black arc extends about one-third of the distance over the white field. The center rosette and final ring are white on both examples. The AMNH pouch form is bordered by a ring of white beadwork with dark blue mountain triangle forms around the outer edge, continuous around the periphery. As on other pouch or breast ornament necklaces made from cradle ornaments, this beaded edge was probably added later, though beaded boundaries do appear on other quillwork disks.

10. In the larger left and right segments, the head disk has eight arcs of alternating white plain quilled rings and black fiber rings with white for the center rosette and black in the last outer ring, though a white beaded row was perhaps added for a ninth ring that extends around the entire circumference. All but the outer arcs of the red triangular tip sections have faded; therefore, no certain determination that there were yellow squares within those fields can be made. The four hood pendants have been attached in pairs on each lateral side of the pouch and there are ten head pendants at the bottom. One of the two top bars on a cradle is just above the ten pendants at the bottom of the arrangement; the other is at the top. Approximately twenty-eight hood banister crossbars were attached in the spaces between the other pendants. The quillwork style on the crossbars follows the half white/half red with black divider pattern on all the predominantly red/white cradle styles described above. Likewise, the loop pendants and paired strips have the typical five-segment pattern of two outer red sections and three white ones including two short sections and one long central section.

11. Numerous examples of this type are in existing collections, including a complete cradle (NMAI 132257), several isolated cradle ornament elements, and parts recombined for pouches and necklace forms (NMAI 205933; AMNH 50/1-1338; FMNH 61290). The NMAI example has a head pendant with twelve quilled rings, a solid yellow central rosette, and a continuous yellow outer ring. It was acquired by William Wildschut, ethnologist and museum collector on the plains, from the Wind River Reservation in Wyoming in 1924. It has the full complement of ten head pendants, two strips, four hood pendants, seven rib-leg pairs on the body, and exactly one hundred crossbars on the hood array. The frame is made of red willow and the cover of canvas. The crossbars are quilled in a half red and half yellow section with a middle section of two black borders surrounding a short central green section.

12. Item NMAI 205933 is a necklace made from the disk, hood array, and ten head ornaments of a cradle. All features and patterns are the same except that the central disk has thirteen rings including an extra central yellow ring, an array of only ninety-one bars, and black instead of yellow loop dewclaws. AMNH 50/1-1338 is a pouch made from a Green and Yellow Cradle disk and nine head ornaments. Exactly like the necklace above, the disk originally had thirteen rings, but the central rosette has been replaced by a beaded circle with white background, blue cross, and four red squares at the four directions. The Field Museum displays a detached disk pendant identical to the last two discussed, though the caption identifies it as a shirt pendant.

13. The ten-loop set at the peak, crossbars, hood loop-dewclaw pendant pairs, and rib straps on the cradle held at the Riverside Metropolitan Museum all have a pattern of red and white in the larger outer sections with a small section of green in the center and black borders. There are approximately 110 crossbars on the hood array. The black sections throughout are apparently of fiber and have faded to brown. The cover itself is made from flour-sack cloth (Jones and Whitmore-Ostlund 1980).

14. A beaded disk of this Yellow Cradle style is at the Peabody Museum (PB 45600002), though that may be a large tipi ornament. It has eleven rows of beadwork and no central yellow section or outer teeth consistent with the Yellow Lodge disk, though. One example of a full cradle is held at the Field Museum (FMNH 61470). The head disk has ten rings of quillwork forming the common central vertical tipi symmetry and a yellow background on the wings with a black-white-black divider section. The pendants follow the same pattern of yellow and red large outer sections with a small white central section set off by black borders. There are one hundred crossbars on the hood array, ten peak pendants, the common two strips with them, seven rib pairs, and four paired loop-dewclaw pendants. Besides these typical ornaments, on each side of the cradle are four triple-barred pendants with three bells each. The bars follow the same yellow-black-white-black-red pattern of quillwork and are much like tipi ornaments of the same triple design.

15. An example from the Field Museum (FMNH 58003) has fourteen rows of quillwork on the head ornament, including two for a dark blue border. On all other quilled ornaments and straps, a short dark blue section divides the longer yellow and shorter white sections. Another cradle from the American Museum of Natural History (AMNH 50/1050) has twelve rows and no dark border but has a strip of yellow and white quillwork on each short end of the rectangular head ornament. Both examples have white or yellow wool tufts bounding the two lateral sides of the cross. On the body portion, the ribs are quill-wrapped with white and yellow and decorated with three loop pendants as on tipi ornaments. The four pairs of ornaments arranged continuously around the rim of the hood are yellow on one example (AMNH 50/1050) and white on another (FMNH 58003). Warden's drawings indicate that the ornaments are yellow-white-yellow in equal sections (Warden-Dorsey 1903–1906: Box 2, Folder 19:6–7). Each ornament has a tuft of white on each end. The central pendant strip has a longer middle white section than the outer two, thus forming the same rectangular cross pattern on the head disk.

16. There are two known examples: one at the Field Museum (FMNH 58120) and another at the American Museum of Natural History (AMNH 50/1079). Both originated in Wyoming with Northern Arapaho quillwork artists. The rectangular head pendant on the latter is sixteen quill rows wide, including four all-red lines on each side of the cross, four rows for the central long white section of the cross, and four rows each for the two outer, shorter white sections. The head ornament on a similar cradle from the Field Museum has no beaded border and only fourteen rows of quills, with only one row of solid red quills on the outer background sections. Neither example's head ornament has the tufts as on the Yellow Oblong style. Both cradles have almost identical ornamentation, though the cradle at the AMNH has 107 crossbars on the hood array and the Field Museum cradle only 100. Each crossbar has a large red section toward the outside, a large white section toward the inside, and a double-line black divider with white inner section in the center. On both are the common ten hoof-loop ornaments and double bars on the hood array and seven pairs of rib straps on the body. Unlike the Yellow Oblong style, both have the typical four dual looped ornaments with dewclaws on the hood, which on other cradle styles represent the Four Old Men. On both Red Oblong cradles, the long end of each of the three cross sections has a short section set off by a black boundary. The rectangle is bordered by a yellow beaded boundary with twelve green three-block formations Kroeber defines elsewhere as "rock" designs.

17. A cradle at the National Museum of Natural History conforms to Warden's description of this type (NMNH 165774). The hood has seventeen quilled rows, while each side of the body has thirteen. Warden notes in his drawings that the head and body sections should each have twenty lines. Each of the hood lines on the existing example has a central large red section and two outer yellow sections. Each of the five sections is divided by a short white section bounded by black. Each end of the row also has a short black section. Red tufts coincide with the boundaries of the central red section and the outer boundaries of the hood lines. As on other lined styles, the sides have only two sections of the dominant color yellow and red tufts on the borders of central red sections and the outer edges of each line. Also like other similar styles, there are four loop ornaments on each side of the body section, three coinciding with the three ties for the front and a fourth at the bottom between what would be the baby's legs. The two triangular ornaments on the peak each have three thongs of buckskin with beaded cross strands between them. The point of each triangle closest to the cradle begins with ten rows of yellow beads, followed by two black, two white, two black, and four red rows at the outer base of the form. Each buckskin thong has a bell attached at the bottom. The hood has a beaded rim that runs parallel to the quilled lines, and along it are five tiny medicine bundles and three bells associated with three of the bundles. Thus, two bundles seem to be missing bells.

Chapter 2. Tipi Ornaments, Robes, Leanback Covers, and Other Quilled Objects

1. A beaded set of Black Lodge disk ornaments that Kroeber collected in 1899 in Oklahoma resides in the American Museum of Natural History collection (AMNH 50/368A–E). This set is missing the pendants usually attached to disks. A beaded central disk example is held at the University of Nebraska State Museum (UNSM A06253).

2. Several groups of this type are at the American Museum of Natural History, but not all items appear to go together as a tipi set: (1) AMNH 50/306A–Y consists of three side disks with seven rings each, one side rosette of five rings with hair pendants, and twenty front pendants, all made from fiber or corn husk; (2) AMNH 50/360BCE includes three beaded side pendants with five rows of beads and no pendants attached (the large disk numbered 50/360A is not an example of Yellow Lodge style and appears to have been misidentified by Kroeber); (3) AMNH 50/667A–E is a large beaded disk with one large and one very narrow black spoke, thirty teeth for the outside ring, and four small disks; and (4) AMNH 50/580AB is a large disk with forty teeth and small disk attached. The Burke Museum in Seattle (BMNHC 2-4056) has a large beaded Yellow Lodge disk with ten rings, including the outer ring of thirty-five teeth. The National Museum of the American Indian (NMAI 167208) holds a large beaded disk with ten rings, thirty teeth on the outer ring, and two buffalo-hair pendants.

3. There are two other examples of tipi ornaments identified as Arapaho in museums, but these do not conform to the types Warden and Kroeber describe. The Field Museum holds a set of disks (FMNH 67927) in beadwork with designs identical to the Yellow Lodge style but with green rather than white spokes and an outer ring of yellow rather than red. The National Museum of the American Indian holds a single beaded top ornament (NMAI 167202) with a similar design but with blue spokes. These are both likely to be Cheyenne designs borrowed or mislabeled when acquired in Oklahoma among the Southern Arapahos and Southern Cheyennes.

4. The name of this and other robes is animate in gender.

5. Another adult pair of moccasins from the AMNH (1/5708AB) has a similar form but with ten solid quilled lines, along with a similar border with white background. Kroeber could provide no interpretation of the symbolism. The forms in blue, red, and yellow along the border elsewhere in Arapaho art symbolize mountains or rocks. Another similar example of the basic type, held at the National Museum of the American Indian (NMAI 132253), has six solid red quilled lines on the instep, two of which extend around to the back, and, for the border, a sky blue background in beading with alternating yellow and white mountain triangular designs. A similar pair at the National Museum of Natural History (NMNH 351007) has seven red lines with a central small yellow square surrounded by a darker red section in each line, thus forming the common trapezoidal form. The border is a white beaded background with alternating red and green right triangles.

Chapter 4. Quillwork in Mythical Traditions

1. While not citing the source in his published work, Kroeber's field notes indicate that he acquired this statement from a person named Fire, who may have been Firewood, the same quillworker who contributed the bulk of evidence and interpretative material to Cleaver Warden's research.

References

Alberti, Samuel J. M. M. 2005. Objects and the Museum. *Isis* 96 (4): 559–71.

Anderson, Caroline J. 1980. American Indian Cradle Boards. In *Field Museum of Natural History Bulletin 51*, pp. 16–21. Chicago: Field Museum of Natural History.

Anderson, Jeffrey D. 1997. Introduction to *Traditions of the Arapaho,* by George Dorsey and Alfred L. Kroeber, v–xxx. Reprint, Lincoln: University of Nebraska Press.

———. 1998. Ethnolinguistic Dimensions of Northern Arapaho Language Shift. *Anthropological Linguistics* 40 (1): 1–64.

———. 2000. The Motion-Shape of Whirlwind Woman in Arapaho Women's Quillwork. *European Review of Native American Studies* 14 (1): 11–21.

———. 2001a. *The Four Hills of Life: Northern Arapaho Knowledge and Life Movement.* Anthropology of North American Indians series. Lincoln: University of Nebraska Press.

———. 2001b. Northern Arapaho Conversion of a Christian Text: The *Our Father. Ethnohistory* 48 (4): 689–712.

———. 2003. *One Hundred Years of Old Man Sage: An Arapaho Life Story.* Anthropology of North American Indians series. Lincoln: University of Nebraska Press.

———. 2005. Ghost Dance Songs. In *Algonquian Spirit: Contemporary Translations of Algonquian Literatures,* edited by Brian Swann, 448–62. Lincoln: University of Nebraska Press.

———. 2006. The Poetics of Tropes and Dreams in Arapaho Ghost Dance Songs. In *New Perspectives on Native North America: Cultures, Histories, Representations,* edited by Sergei A. Kan and Pauline Turner Strong, 122–61. Lincoln: University of Nebraska Press.

———. 2011. The History of Time in the Northern Arapaho Tribe. *Ethnohistory* 58 (2): 229–62.

Appadurai, Arjun. 1986. *The Social Life of Things: Commodities in Cultural Perspective.* Cambridge: Cambridge University Press.

Bass, Althea. 1966. *The Arapaho Way.* New York: Potter.

Bateson, Gregory. 1972. *Steps to an Ecology of Mind.* New York: Ballantine.

Benedict, James B. 1992. Footprints in the Snow: High-Altitude Cultural Ecology of the Colorado Front Range, U.S.A. *Arctic and Alpine Research* 24 (1): 1–16.

Benjamin, Walter. (1936) 1986. The Work of Art in the Age of Mechanical Reproduction. In *Illuminations*, edited by Hannah Arendt, translated by Harry Zohn, 217–52. New York: Schocken Books.

Berger, John. 1972. *Ways of Seeing.* London: British Broadcasting Corporation.

Berlin, Brent, and Paul Kay. 1969. *Basic Color Terms: Their Universality and Evolution.* Berkeley: University of California Press.

Berlo, Janet C. 1993. Dreaming of Double Woman: The Ambivalent Role of the Female Artist in North American Indian Myth. *American Indian Quarterly* 17 (1): 31–43.

Boas, Franz. (1927) 1955. *Primitive Art.* Reprint, New York: Dover.

Bol, Marsha. 1996. Collecting Symbolism among the Arapaho: George A. Dorsey and C. Warden, Indian. In *The Great Southwest of the Fred Harvey Company and the Santa Fe Railroad,* edited by Marta Weigle and Barbara A. Babcock, 110–24. Phoenix: Heard Museum.

———. 2001. Identity Recovered: Portrait of a Northern Arapaho Quillworker. In *Painters, Patrons, and Identity: Essays in Native American Art to Honor J. J. Brody,* edited by Joyce Szabo, 33–47. Albuquerque: University of New Mexico Press.

Bol, Marsha, and Nellie Z. Star Boy Menard. 2000. "I Saw All That": A Lakota Girl's Puberty Ceremony. *American Indian Culture and Research Journal* 24:25–42.

Bourdieu, Pierre. 1977. *Outline of a Theory of Practice.* Cambridge: Cambridge University Press.

Bradbury, John. 1904. *Bradbury's Travels in the Interior of America, 1809–1811.* Vol. 5 of *Early Western Travels, 1748–1846,* edited by Reuben Gold Thwaites. Cleveland: A. H. Clark Company.

Carnegie Museum of Natural History. n.d. *Arapaho Material Notes.* Pittsburgh, Penn.

Clifford, J., and G. E. Marcus, eds. 1986. *Writing Culture: The Poetics and Politics of Ethnography.* Berkeley: University of California Press.

Coleman, Winfield W. 1980. The Cheyenne Women's Sewing Society. In *Plains Indian Design Symbology and Decoration,* edited by Gene Bull and George P. Horse Capture, 50–69. Cody, Wyo.: Buffalo Bill Historical Center.

Crispin, Tom. 1935. The Four Old Men. *Indians at Work* 2 (20): 12–13. Washington, D.C.: Office of Indian Affairs.

Current Anthropology. 1962. Anthropology Horizons: Report on a Symposium Organized and Chaired by Professor A. L. Kroeber. *Current Anthropology* 3 (1): 79–97.

Deloria, Vine, Jr. 1991. Research, Redskins, and Reality. *American Indian Quarterly* 15 (4): 457–68.

Dempsey, Hugh A. 1963. Religious Significance of Blackfoot Quillwork. *Plains Anthropologist* 8 (19): 52–53.

Dorsey, George A. 1903. *The Arapaho Sun Dance: The Ceremony of the Offerings-Lodge.* Field Columbian Museum, Publication 75, Anthropological Series, vol. 4. Chicago: Field Columbian Museum.

———. 1907. The Anthropological Exhibits at the American Museum of Natural History. *Science,* n.s., 25 (641): 584–89.

———. n.d. Arapaho Material. Carnegie Museum of Natural History Archives. Pittsburgh, Penn.

Dorsey, George A., and Alfred L. Kroeber. 1903. *Traditions of the Arapaho.* Field Columbian Museum, Publication 81, Anthropological Series, vol. 5. Chicago: Field Columbian Museum.

Douglas, Frederic H. 1941. A Northern Arapaho Quilled Cradle. In *Material Culture Notes: Reports from the Ethnographic Laboratory,* 53–59. Denver: Denver Art Museum.

Dundes, Alan. 1964. *The Morphology of North American Indian Folktales.* Helsinki: Suomalainn Tiedeakatemia Academia Scientiarum Fennica.

Eggan, Fred. 1937. The Cheyenne and Arapaho Kinship System. In *Social Anthropology of North American Tribes: Essays in Social Organization, Law, and Religion,* edited by Fred Eggan, 35–95. Chicago: University of Chicago Press.

Fabian, Johannes. 1983. *Time and the Other: How Anthropology Makes Its Object.* New York: Columbia University Press.

Feder, Norman. 1980. Plains Pictographic Painting and Quilled Rosettes: A Clue to Tribal Identification. *American Indian Art Magazine* 5 (2): 54–62.

Fowler, Loretta Kay. 1982. *Arapahoe Politics, 1851–1878: Symbols in Crises of Authority.* Lincoln: University of Nebraska Press.

Geertz, Clifford. 1983. *Local Knowledge: Further Essays in Interpretive Anthropology.* New York: Basic Books.

Gell, Alfred. 1998. *Art and Agency: An Anthropological Theory.* Oxford, U.K.: Clarendon Press.

Gilmore, Robert. 1990. The Northern Arapaho Cradle. *American Indian Art Magazine* 16:64–71.

Goss, Robert V. 2003. *Serving the Faithful in Yellowstone: Henry Klamer and the General Store in the Upper Geyser Basin.* N.p.: self-published.

Greene, Candace S. 1992. Soft Cradles of the Central Plains. *Plains Anthropologist* 37 (139): 95–113.

———. 2001. Art until 1900. In *Handbook of North American Indians,* vol. 13, *Plains,* edited by Raymond J. DeMallie, 1039–54. Washington, D.C.: Smithsonian Institution Press.

Grinnell, George B. 1924. *The Cheyenne Indians: Their History and Ways of Life,* vols. 1 and 2. New Haven, Conn.: Yale University Press.

Hail, Barbara. 2010. "To Honor Her Kindred": Women's Arts Centered in the Tipi. In *Tipi: Heritage of the Great Plains,* edited by Nancy B. Rosoff and Susan Kennedy Zeller, 119–40. Brooklyn, N.Y.: Brooklyn Museum.

Hallowell, A. Irving. (1960) 1976. Ojibwa Ontology, Behavior, and World View. In *Contributions to Anthropology: Selected Papers of A. Irving Hallowell,* with introduction by Raymond D. Fogelson, 357–90. Chicago: University of Chicago Press.

Hassrick, Royal. 1964. *The Sioux: Life and Customs of a Warrior Society.* Norman: University of Oklahoma Press.

Hilger, Sister M. Inez. 1936–40. Field Notes. National Anthropological Archives, Smithsonian Institution. Washington, D.C.

———. 1952. *Arapaho Child Life and Its Cultural Background.* Bureau of American Ethnology, Bulletin 148. Washington, D.C.: Smithsonian Institution.

Historical Currency Converter. http://futureboy.us/fsp/dollar.fsp.

Hugh-Jones, Christine. 1979. *From Milk River: Spatial and Temporal Process in Northwest Amazonia.* Cambridge: Cambridge University Press.

Hunt, David C., Marsha V. Gallagher, William H. Goetzmann, and William J. Orr. 1984. *Karl Bodmer's America.* Lincoln: Joslyn Art Museum and University of Nebraska Press.

Jablow, Joseph. 1950. *The Cheyenne in Plains Indian Trade Relations.* Monographs of the American Ethnological Society 19. N.p.: American Ethnological Society.

Jakobson, Roman. 1960. Closing Statements: Linguistics and Poetics. In *Style in Language,* edited by Thomas A. Sebeok, 350–77. Cambridge, Mass.: MIT Press.

Jones, Rex L., and Catherine Whitmore-Ostlund. 1980. Cradles of Life. *American Indian Art Magazine* 5 (4): 36–41.

Knight, Chris. 1997. The Wives of the Sun and Moon. *Journal of the Royal Anthropological Institute* 3 (1): 133–53.

Kroeber, Alfred L. 1901. Decorative Symbolism of the Arapaho. *American Anthropologist* 3 (1): 308-336.

———. 1916. *Arapaho Dialects.* University of California Publications in American Archaeology and Ethnology 12, no. 3, pp. 71–138. Berkeley: University of California Press.

———. 1916–20. Field Notes. Smithsonian Institution, National Anthropological Archives, Manuscript 2560. Washington, D.C.

———. 1939. *Cultural and Natural Areas of Native North America.* Berkeley: University of California Press.

———. 1983. *The Arapaho.* Foreword by Fred Eggan. Reprint, Lincoln: University of Nebraska Press. Parts 1, 2, and 3 originally published in 1902, 1904, and 1907, respectively.

Kroeber-Boas Correspondence. 1899. American Museum of Natural History Archives. New York.

Lakoff, George, and Mark Johnson. 1980. *Metaphors We Live By.* Chicago: University of Chicago Press.

Langer, Susanne K. 1953. *Feeling and Form: A Theory of Art.* New York: Charles Scribner and Sons.

Lassiter, Luke Eric. 2005. Collaborative Ethnography and Public Anthropology. *Current Anthropology* 46 (1): 83–106.

Lévi-Strauss, Claude. 1973. Structuralism and Ecology. *Social Science Information* 12 (1): 7–23.

———. 1978. *The Origin of Table Manners.* Vol. 3 of *Introduction to the Science of Mythology.* Translated by J. Weightman and D. Weightman. New York: Harper and Row.

Liep, John. 2001. Introduction to *Locating Cultural Creativity,* edited by John Liep, 1–15. London: Pluto.

Lowie, Robert H. 1916. *Plains Indian Age-Societies and Comparative Summary.* Anthropological Papers of the American Museum of Natural History, vol. 11, no. 13, pp. 877–1031. New York: American Museum of Natural History.

Lyford, Carrie A. n.d. *Quill and Beadwork of the Western Sioux.* Washington, D.C.: Education Division, U.S. Office of Indian Affairs.

Marcus, G. E., and M. M. J. Fisher. 1986. *Anthropology as Cultural Critique: An Experimental Moment in the Human Sciences.* Chicago: University of Chicago Press.

Marcus, George E., and Fred R. Myers. 1995. The Traffic in Art and Culture: An Introduction. In *The Traffic in Art and Culture,* edited by George E. Marcus and Fred R. Myers, 1–55. Berkeley: University of California Press.

Marriott, Alice. 1982. The Trade Guild of the Southern Cheyenne Women. In *Native North American Art History: Selected Readings*, edited by Zena P. Mathews and Aldona Jonaitis, 247–55. Palo Alto, Calif.: Peek Publications.

Mauss, Marcel, and Nathan Schlanger. 2006. *Techniques, Technology and Civilisation*. New York: Durkheim Press/Berghahn Books.

Maximilian, Prince of Wied. 1904. *Maximilian, Prince of Wied's Travels in the Interior of North America, 1832–1834*. Vols. 22–25 of *Early Western Travels, 1748–1846*, edited by Reuben Gold Thwaites. Cleveland: A. H. Clark Company.

Merleau-Ponty, Maurice. 1962. *Phenomenology of Perception*. London: Routledge.

———. 1964. *The Primacy of Perception and Other Essays on Phenomenological Psychology, the Philosophy of Art, History, and Politics*. Evanston, Ill.: Northwestern University Press.

Michelson, Truman. 1910. Field Notes. Smithsonian Institution National Anthropological Archives. Washington, D.C.

———. 1912. *Preliminary Report on the Linguistic Classification of Algonquian Tribes*. Bureau of American Ethnology Twenty-eighth Annual Report (1906–07). Washington, D.C.: Government Printing Office.

———. 1933. Narrative of an Arapaho Woman. *American Anthropologist* 35:596–610.

Mooney, James. 1896. *The Ghost-Dance Religion and Sioux Outbreak of 1890*. In *Fourteenth Annual Report of the Bureau of Ethnology, 1892–93*, part 2, pp. 641–1110. Washington, D.C.: Government Printing Office.

———. 1907. Arapaho. In *Handbook of American Indians North of Mexico*, edited by Frederick Webb Hodge, 72–74. Bureau of American Ethnology Bulletin 30, part 1. Washington, D.C.: Smithsonian Institution.

Munn, Nancy. (1973) 1986a. *Walbiri Iconography*. Chicago: University of Chicago Press.

———. 1986b. *The Fame of Gawa: A Symbolic Study of Value Transformation in a Massim (Papua New Guinea) Society*. Cambridge: Cambridge University Press.

———. 1992. The Cultural Anthropology of Time: A Critical Essay. *Annual Review of Anthropology* 21:93–123.

NAGPRA (Native American Graves Protection and Repatriation Act). 1990. National Park Service, U.S. Department of the Interior. http://www.nps.gov/nagpra/mandates/25usc3001etseq.htm.

Orchard, William C. 1971. *The Techniques of Porcupine-Quill Decoration among the North American Indians*. The Museum of the American Indian Heye Foundation, vol. 4, no. 1. New York: Museum of the American Indian.

Powell, Peter J. 1977. Beauty for New Life: An Introduction to Cheyenne and Lakota Sacred Art. In *The Native American Heritage: A Survey of North American Indian Art*, by Evan M. Maurer. Chicago: Art Institute of Chicago.

Reichard, Gladys A. 1921. Literary Types and Dissemination of Myths. *Journal of American Folklore* 34 (133): 269–307.

Report of Agent in Wyoming Territory. 1883. *Annual Report of the Commissioner of Indian Affairs to the Secretary of the Interior*. Washington, D.C.: Government Printing Office.

Report of Agent in Wyoming Territory. 1885. *Annual Report of the Commissioner of Indian Affairs to the Secretary of the Interior*. Washington, D.C.: Government Printing Office.

Report of Agent in Wyoming. 1897. *Annual Report of the Commissioner of Indian Affairs to the Secretary of the Interior.* Washington, D.C.: Government Printing Office.

Rich, George W. 1971. Rethinking the "Star Husbands." *Journal of American Folklore* 84 (334): 436–41.

Roth, H. Ling. 1923. American Quillwork: A Possible Clue to Its Origin. *Man* 23:113–16.

Salzmann, Zdenek. 1983. *Dictionary of Contemporary Arapaho Usage.* Arapaho Language and Culture Instructional Materials Series, no. 4. Wind River Indian Reservation, Wyo.: Northern Arapaho Tribe.

———. 1988. *The Arapaho Indians: A Research Guide and Bibliography.* Westport, Conn.: Greenwood Press.

Santina, Adrianne. 2004. Recreating the World: Tipi Ornaments by Arapaho and Cheyenne Women. *Women's Studies* 33 (7): 933–60.

Sapir, Edward. (1927) 1949a. Anthropology and Sociology. In *Selected Writings of Edward Sapir: Language, Culture, and Personality,* edited by David G. Mandelbaum, 332–45. Berkeley: University of California Press.

———. (1924) 1949b . The Grammarian and His Language. In *Selected Writings of Edward Sapir: Language, Culture, and Personality,* edited by David G. Mandelbaum, 150–59. Berkeley: University of California Press.

Sawyer, Keith R. 1998. Introduction to *Creativity in Performance,* edited by R. Keith Sawyer, 1–5. Westport, Conn.: Greenwood Publishing Group.

Schneider, Mary Jane. 1983. Women's Work: An Examination of Women's Roles in Plains Indian Arts and Crafts. In *The Hidden Half: Studies of Plains Indian Women,* edited by Patricia Albers and Beatrice Medicine, 101–21. Washington, D.C.: University Press of America.

Scott, Hugh Lenox. 1907. The Early History and the Names of the Arapaho. *American Anthropologist* 9:545–60.

Spier, Leslie. 1921. The Sun Dance of the Plains. *American Museum of Natural History Anthropological Papers,* vol. 16, part 7, pp. 451–527. New York: American Museum of Natural History.

Spoonhunter, Bob. 1985. *Arapaho Memories.* Ethete: Wyoming Indian High School.

Starkloff, Carl F. 1974. *The People of the Center: American Indian Religion and Christianity.* New York: Seabury Press.

Stoller, Marianne L. 1957. *A Sacred Bundle of the Arapaho Indians.* Annals of the Carnegie Museum 35, pp. 11–35. Pittsburgh: Carnegie Museum.

Swagerty, William. 2001. History of the United States Plains until 1850. In *Handbook of North American Indians,*_vol. 13, *Plains,* edited by Raymond J. DeMallie, 256–80. Washington, D.C.: Smithsonian Institution Press.

Swanson, Guy E. 1976. Orpheus and Star Husband: Meaning and the Structure of Myths. *Ethnology* 15 (2): 115–33.

Taylor, Colin. 1962. Early Plains Indian Quill Techniques in European Museum Collections. *Plains Anthropologist* 7 (15): 58–69.

Thompson, Stith. 1964. The Star Husband Tale. In *The Morphological Study of North American Indian Folklore,* edited by Alan Dundes, 414–73. Englewood Cliffs, N.J.: Prentice Hall.

Toll, Oliver W. 1914. Report on Visit of Arapaho Indians to Estes Park. Manuscript from the Collections of the Colorado Historical Society. Colorado Historical Society. Denver.

Trenholm, Virginia Cole. 1970. *The Arapahoes, Our People.* The Civilization of the American Indian Series, vol. 105. Norman: University of Oklahoma Press.

U.S. Bureau of the Census. 1975. *Historical Statistics of the United States, Colonial Times to 1970,* part 2. Bicentennial Edition. Washington, D.C.: Government Printing Office.

Warden, Cleaver, and George A. Dorsey. 1903–1906. Notes and Manuscripts on Religion and Material Culture, 1903, 1905, 1906, n.d. Field Museum of Natural History Archives, A1. Chicago. Cited throughout as Warden-Dorsey 1903–1906.

Weiner, Annette B. 1976. *Women of Value, Men of Renown: New Perspectives in Trobriand Exchange.* Austin: University of Texas Press.

Wiseman, Boris. 2007. *Lévi-Strauss: Anthropology and Aesthetics.* Cambridge: Cambridge University Press.

Wissler, Clark. 1921. Introduction to *American Museum of Natural History Anthropological Papers,* vol. 16, pp. iv–xi. New York: American Museum of Natural History.

Wolff, Eldon G. 1945. Porcupine Quill Embroidery. *Museum Record* (Milwaukee), v. 2, p. 7.

Young, Frank W. 1970. A Fifth Analysis of the Star Husband Tale. *Ethnology* 9 (4): 389–413.

———. 1978. Folktales and Social Structure: A Comparison of Three Analyses of the Star-Husband Tale. *Journal of American Folklore* 91 (360): 691–99.

Index

References to illustrations are in italic type.

www.ingramcontent.com/pod-product-compliance
Ingram Content Group UK Ltd.
Pitfield, Milton Keynes, MK11 3LW, UK
UKHW051132260726
13967UKWH00010B/3001

9 780806 155838